LINCOLN CHRISTIAN COLLEGE

W9-BVH-052

NEW PERSPECTIVES ON GRAMMAR TEACHING IN SECOND LANGUAGE CLASSROOMS

ESL AND APPLIED LINGUISTICS PROFESSIONAL SERIES

Eli Hinkel, Series Editor

Hinkel/Fotos, Eds.   New Perspectives on Grammar Teaching in Second Language Classrooms

Hinkel   Second Language Writers Text: Linguistic and Rhetorical Features

Birch   English L2 Reading: Getting to the Bottom

NEW PERSPECTIVES ON GRAMMAR TEACHING IN SECOND LANGUAGE CLASSROOMS

Edited by
Eli Hinkel
Seattle University
and
Sandra Fotos
Senshu University

Lawrence Erlbaum Associates, Publishers
2002   Mahwah, New Jersey   London

President/CEO:	Lawrence Erlbaum
Executive Vice-President, Marketing:	Joseph Petrowski
Senior Vice-President, Book Production:	Art Lizza
Director, Editorial:	Lane Akers
Director, Sales and Marketing	Robert Sidor
Director, Customer Relations:	Nancy Seitz
Senior Acquisitions Editor:	Naomi Silverman
Textbook Marketing Manager:	Marisol Kozlovski
Assistant Editor:	Lori Hawver
Cover Design:	Kathryn Houghtaling Lacey
Textbook Production Manager:	Paul Smolenski
Full-Service & Composition:	Black Dot Group/An AGT Company
Text and Cover Printer:	Hamilton Printing Company

This book was typeset in 10/12 pt. Baskerville, Bold, and Italic.
The heads were typeset in Baskerville, Baskerville Bold, and Baskerville Bold Italic.

Copyright © 2002 by Lawrence Erlbaum Associates, Inc.
  All rights reserved. No part of the book may be reproduced in
  any form, by photostat, microform, retrieval system, or any other
  means, without the prior written permission of the publisher.

Lawrence Erlbaum Associates, Inc., Publishers
10 Industrial Avenue
Mahwah, New Jersey 07430

Library of Congress Cataloging-in-Publication Data

New perspectives on grammar teaching in second language classrooms / Eli Hinkel and
  Sandra Fotos (eds.).
      p.   cm. (ESL and applied linguistics professional series)
  Includes bibliographical references and index.
      Contents: Introduction From theory to practice : a teacher s view The place of
grammar instruction in the second/foreign language curriculum / Rod Ellis Accuracy
and fluency revisited / Jack C. Richards Ten criteria for a spoken grammar / Michael
McCarthy and Ronald Carter Grammar and communication : new directions in theory
and practice / Martha Pennington The grammar of choice / Diane Larsen-Freeman
Why it makes sense to teach grammar in context and through discourse / Marianne
Celce-Murcia Structure-based interactive tasks for the EFL grammar learner / Sandra
Fotos Methodological options in grammar teaching materials / Rod Ellis Teaching
grammar in writing classes : tenses and cohesion / Eli Hinkel Relative clause reduction
in technical research articles / Peter Master Why English passive is difficult to teach
(and learn) / Eli Hinkel.
      ISBN 0-8058-3955-0 (alk. paper)
      1. Language and languages Study and teaching. 2. Grammar, Comparative and
general Study and teaching. I. Hinkel, Eli. II. Fotos, Sandra. III. Series.
P53.412.N48 2001
4189.0071 dc21   2001023175

Books published by Lawrence Erlbaum Associates are printed on acid-free paper,
and their bindings are chosen for strength and durability.

Printed in the United States of America
10   9   8   7   6   5   4

Contents

Preface

The chapters in this collection present a variety of approaches to teaching grammar within different curricular and methodological frameworks. Recognizing that second/foreign language instruction runs the gamut from the purely communicative methods often found in the English as a second language (ESL) situation to the teacher-led grammar instruction and translation activities that often characterize the English as a foreign language (EFL) classroom, this volume emphasizes flexibility and adaptability in selection of an approach determined by the teaching situation, the type of learners, and their particular language requirements.

THE ORGANIZATION OF THE BOOK

The book is divided into three sections, and an introduction is included with each. Grammar instruction can take many forms and be carried out with various pedagogical goals in mind. It can benefit diverse types of learners by increasing their overall proficiency and improving their language skills. Keeping in mind the extraordinarily diverse and numerous settings in which ESL and EFL are taught, the collection of chapters in this volume presents the why's and the how-to's of grammar teaching. Part I focuses on the ways to include grammar in second and foreign language curricula and points out the reasons that make grammar teaching necessary in ESL/EFL

pedagogy. Ellis reviews the arguments for grammar teaching aimed at producing awareness of structures, followed by Richards' discussion of the
strengths of a communicative, task-based approach. McCarthy and Carter
treat spoken grammar from the perspective of corpus-based language
research, and the section concludes with Pennington's discussion of four
theoretical approaches to grammar pedagogy and their applications.

Part II gives a variety of research-driven approaches to grammar teaching pedagogy, leading off with Larsen-Freeman's flexible approach to
teaching grammar, emphasizing that communication always involves a
choice of forms to represent meaning and sociopragmatic functions of language. In the following chapter, Celce-Murcia advocates discourse-based
grammar instruction that offers accessible and practical methodology for
grammar teaching. The section moves to Fotos' description of structure-
based communicative tasks providing instruction on grammar points within a meaning-focused context and continues with Ellis' methodological
analysis of instructional options used in current grammar textbooks.
Hinkel's chapter describes an approach to developing classroom teaching
materials through discovery tasks and authentic language use, based on
examples for teaching verb tenses in context.

Part III presents the teaching of particular grammatical structures,
based on empirical research, and shows how applied linguistics research
can inform grammar teaching. Master's chapter analyzes the use of
reduced relative clauses in academic and technical writing, with specific
teaching suggestions based on the research results. In the final chapter,
Hinkel presents her research findings dealing with the lexical and syntactic
considerations of the English passive voice and provides activities and recommendations for teaching.

This collection of chapters tries to balance theory with pedagogy, recognizing that teachers need to formulate what is suitable for them within
their particular teaching situations. This book can be a starting point for
readers, allowing them to develop their own blend of theory, pedagogy,
explicit instruction, and meaning-focused use of grammar structures.

NEW PERSPECTIVES ON GRAMMAR TEACHING IN SECOND LANGUAGE CLASSROOMS

From Theory to Practice: A Teacher's View

Eli Hinkel
Seattle University, Washington

Sandra Fotos
Senshu University, Tokyo, Japan

To appreciate the need for flexibility in grammar teaching/learning, this introduction first examines the changes over time regarding what constitutes effective grammar pedagogy. There may be no single best approach to grammar teaching that would apply in all situations to the diverse types of learners a teacher can encounter. However, teachers' familiarity with different approaches to grammar instruction and language learning can allow them to apply to their particular situation the most effective blend of features that each has to offer. In addition, familiarity with a variety of views and approaches can lead to recognition that many approaches share common features and appreciation of an eclectic view of teaching grammar.

TRADITIONAL GRAMMAR INSTRUCTION

As many grammarians have noted (e.g., Herron, 1976; Howatt, 1984; Rutherford, 1987), for more than 2,000 years, studying a second language primarily consisted of grammatical analysis and translation of written forms. Developed for analysis of Greek and Latin, this method divided the target language into eight parts of speech: nouns, verbs, participles, articles, pronouns, prepositions, adverbs, and conjunctions. Learning the language required study of the eight categories in written text and the development of rules for their use in translation.

However, when 18th-century grammarians moved beyond the Greek and Roman classics and began the study of English, again using the eight categories to generate grammar rules, it became clear that the parts of speech could not be used as effectively to analyze a language in which word order and syntax produced grammatical function (Herron, 1976) and where rules often had multiple exceptions. Nonetheless, this traditional approach remained the basis of instructional pedagogy in the United States and England until recently (Howatt, 1984), and is still being used in a number of countries as the primary method of English instruction. This is particularly true for many English as a foreign language (EFL) classrooms, where English is learned mainly through translation into the native language and memorization of grammar rules and vocabulary.

STRUCTURAL GRAMMAR AND THE AUDIO-LINGUAL AND DIRECT APPROACHES

When linguists compared and described world languages at the end of the 19th century and the beginning of the 20th century, it was again found that using the eight parts of speech as an organizational framework was not appropriate. Furthermore, since many of these languages had no written form, analysis necessarily shifted to description of the sound system. Languages thus came to be analyzed through three subsystems (Larsen-Freeman & Long, 1991): the sound system (phonology); the discrete units of meaning produced by sound combinations (morphology); and the system of combining units of meaning for communication (syntax), an approach called structural or descriptive linguistics. When this structural view of language was combined with the stimulus-response principles of behaviorist psychology, the audio-lingual and direct approaches to second language learning emerged.

Audio-lingualism and related direct approaches arose during and after the Second World War, when development of spoken fluency in second languages was required. These approaches were also a reaction to the grammar-translation methodology, which produced learners who could not use the language communicatively even though they had considerable knowledge of grammar rules. Nonetheless, the spoken language was still presented in highly structured sequences of forms, usually beginning with *to be* and proceeding through more complex forms in a linear manner, often accompanied by a formal grammar explanation. Sequencing of the syllabus depended on contrastive analysis, a structural comparison of the learner's native language and the target language so that areas of potential difficulty could be identified and emphasized. Pedagogy in this approach was based on drills and repetitions for accurate production of the target language.

FUNCTIONAL APPROACHES

In the 1960s, British linguists developed a system of categories based on the communicative needs of the learner (Johnson & Marrow, 1981), and proposed a syllabus based on communicative functions. Grammar content was organized on the basis of the forms required for particular communicative or situational activities such as "asking questions" or "at a restaurant." At first glance, this appeared to be the opposite of a structural syllabus, but, because certain structures are often associated with specific functions, there was actually a structural basis to functional grammar instruction (Tomlin, 1994).

Such structure-based syllabuses have been termed "synthetic" (Long & Crookes, 1992) because they present rules and drills for specific grammatical or functional aspects of a language in a linear sequence from "easy" to "difficult" and stress immediate production of correct forms. Examination of many English as a second language (ESL)/EFL textbooks today reveals that they are often functionally/situationally based, with a dialogue introducing target structures and vocabulary, a formal explanation of the grammar points covered, practice exercises ranging from controlled to free production of the grammar structures and vocabulary, and perhaps a meaning-focused task or reading that elicits use of the structure during performance. Commenting on the durability of this approach, Skehan (1998, p. 94) labels it the three *P*s: presentation, practice, and production, where the first stage involves presentation of a single grammar point, the second requires learner practice within a controlled framework, and the final stage is learner production of the form more spontaneously.

UNIVERSAL GRAMMAR AND THE ROLE OF SYNTAX

Although there has been no "Universal Grammar" approach, the dominance of structural linguistics, with its focus on surface forms, was largely overturned in 1957 by the publication of Chomsky's monograph *Syntactic Structures*. Rejecting the structuralist idea of language as habit, Chomsky viewed language as a generative process existing innately in the human brain and based on syntax, which consisted of a surface structure, or the apparent form of an utterance, and a deep structure, the mental concept underlying a particular semantic interpretation. It was therefore possible to identify syntactic universals for all languages such as agent (subject) and object, and Universal Grammar was hypothesized to underlie all languages. A key distinction was competence, that is, what the learner knows about the language, and performance, that is, how a learner uses the language (Cook, 1994).

COGNITIVE APPROACHES

With the development of Chomskian theories of Universal Grammar and syntax in the 1950s and 1960s, explicit grammar instruction received renewed emphasis. Grammar teaching and classroom curricula were designed to build on what learners already knew, giving them opportunities to construct new meanings and emphasizing deductive learning. This cognitive view of language learning held that grammar was too complex to be learned naturally and that language requires mental processing for learners to be able to attain linguistic competence. The cognitive method of L2 (second language) teaching was based on cognitive approaches to human psychology and language acquisition and relied on transformational and generative grammar theories. At the time, the cognitive view of language acquisition held that language includes an infinite number of structures that speakers could create and understand, and that L2 pedagogy needs to include the teaching of grammar as a foundational framework for all L2 skills. L2 methodology adopted in the 1970s and early 1980s centered on traditional formal grammar instruction and had the added goal of developing learners' analytical linguistic skills (McLaughlin & Zemblidge, 1992).

COMMUNICATIVE LANGUAGE TEACHING AND HUMANISTIC APPROACHES

However, in the 1970s, particularly in California, a new type of pedagogy arose in response to the greatly increased number of ESL learners, who outnumbered native English speakers in some school districts. Many of these learners knew grammar rules but could not use the target language communicatively, and others urgently needed immediate survival competency in English. The related humanist approaches were also developed in the late 1970s and 1980s as communicative activities designed to give learners positive feelings toward the instructional process so that language acquisition was facilitated. Used primarily with basic learners, these communicative/humanistic approaches gave no formal grammar instruction but rather presented quantities of meaning-focused input containing target forms and vocabulary. The assumption was that the learners would acquire the forms and vocabulary naturally, during the process of comprehending and responding to the input, similar to a way a child learns the first language.

Krashen's Monitor Model of the 1970s and 1980s had a great deal of influence on the rise of communicative pedagogy. His hypothesis of language acquisition pivoted on learner linguistic competence achieved by means of natural language acquisition in the process of real communication when learners are exposed to many facets of language use, such as listening, speaking, and reading. Krashen's Input Hypothesis stipulated that the learning of L2 depends on the presence of "comprehensible input" in the form of meaningful activities, listening and speaking, and reading for enjoyment. Thus, the communicative method of L2 teaching does not feature explicit grammar teaching or correcting learner errors.

Although the communicative methods reflecting Krashen's model of L2 acquisition suggested that learners would arrive at intuitive "correctness" (Krashen & Terrell, 1983, p. 58) of their language, given exposure to and experience with L2, and that explicit grammar instruction was not needed, L2 researchers, methodologists, and practitioners have commented that grammatical competence is essential for communication (Brown, 1994; Larsen-Freeman, 1991) but cannot be attained solely through exposure to meaningful input.

Another important limitation of a purely communicative approach is that certain types of language knowledge and skills are difficult to attain in the process of naturalistic learning, for example, academic and professional speaking and writing. It has been suggested that advanced proficiency and accuracy in spoken and written production are essential for effective functioning in academic, professional, and some vocational communications, so attaining high levels of language competence and performance may require instructed learning (Ellis, 1996).

FOCUS ON FORM

To address these limitations of purely communicative methodology, a new approach to grammar instruction combines formal instruction and communicative language use. Called "focus on form," it is based on the distinction between explicit instruction on grammar forms (with an *s*) and meaning-focused use of form (no *s*) in such a way that the learner must notice, then process the target grammar structure in purely communicative input. This concept holds that traditional structural syllabuses that teach specific sequences of grammar forms do not produce communicative competence (Long, 1991), only formal knowledge of grammar rules unless the learners themselves have reached the stage of interlanguage development at which they are psycholinguistically ready to acquire the instructed forms (Pienemann, 1984).

Communicative syllabuses are suggested to be equally inadequate because of their neglect of grammar instruction, tending to produce fossilization and classroom pidgins (Skehan, 1996), and lower levels of accuracy than would be the case under formal instruction. This consideration has received support from a review of research comparing instructed with uninstructed language learning, finding significant advantages for instruction in terms of the learners' rate of learning and level of achievement (Long, 1988). Considerable research followed on methods for integrating grammar instruction with communicative language learning in such a way that learners are able to recognize the properties of target structures in context and develop accuracy in their use (Doughty & Williams, 1998; Fotos & Ellis, 1991).

NOTICING AND CONSCIOUSNESS RAISING

Many teachers and researchers currently regard grammar instruction as "consciousness raising" (Schmidt, 1990, 1993; Sharwood Smith, 1981, 1993; Skehan, 1998) in the sense that awareness of a particular feature is developed by instruction even if the learners cannot use the feature at once. Such awareness is produced not only by instruction on specific forms but may also result from "input enhancement," that is, operations performed on meaning-focused input in such a way that the target features stand out to the learner (Sharwood Smith, 1993). Other researchers, such as Fotos and Ellis (1991), note that instructed grammar learning of L2 grammar can also serve as communicative input, based on which learners can internalize grammar rules. This is seen as especially important for the EFL situation, in which communicative exposure to the target language is usually lacking. They also point out that knowledge of grammatical structures developed through formal instruction can make these structures more relevant and applicable for learners and, thus, easier to internalize.

However, although the role of input and interaction has been the focus of considerable research, current findings (Gass, Mackey, & Pica, 1998, p. 305) suggest that input and interaction alone cannot determine the learner acquisition process but rather "set the scene for potential learning." The learner's internal factors, particularly the noticing and continued awareness of structures mentioned above, are of more significance in predicting successful acquisition.

The psycholinguistic foundations for this view involve the distinction between two types of grammatical knowledge: explicit and/or declarative knowledge, which is conscious knowledge about grammatical rules and forms developed through instruction; and implicit or procedural knowledge, which is the ability to speak a language unconsciously developed through acts of meaning-focused communication.

Whereas in the past these two knowledge systems were often treated as separate, it has recently been suggested that they are connected and that one possible interface is learner awareness or consciousness of particular grammatical features developed through formal instruction (Schmidt,

1990). Once a learner's consciousness of a target feature has been raised through formal instruction or through continued communicative exposure, the learner often tends to notice the feature in subsequent input (Ellis, 1996; Schmidt, 1990, 1993). Such noticing or continued awareness of the feature is suggested to be important because it appears to initiate the restructuring of the learner's implicit or unconscious system of linguistic knowledge (Ellis, 1996; Schmidt, 1990, 1993; Sharwood Smith, 1993). When a language point is noticed frequently, learners develop awareness of it and unconsciously compare it with their existing system of linguistic knowledge, unconsciously constructing new hypotheses to accommodate the differences between the noticed information and their L2 competence. Then they test these new hypotheses—again unconsciously—by attending to language input and also by getting feedback on their output using the new form (Swain, 1985). In this way, implicit knowledge has been created.[1]

According to this model, activities that raise learners' awareness of grammar forms—whether through explicit instruction or through communicative exposure that encourages learners to become aware of the forms—can assist learners to acquire these forms.

INTERACTION FOR GRAMMAR LEARNING

Within a purely communicative methodology, output has not been seen as important as input because language is thought to be acquired by comprehending input. However, in real communication one needs to understand and be understood; therefore, comprehensible output is also essential for successful communication to take place. To a great extent, L2 output (or production) depends on the learner's linguistic and other communicative skills, and L2 use entails an ability not just to comprehend, but also to produce comprehensible output congruent with target language norms (Ellis, 1997). From this perspective, learner implicit knowledge of L2 grammar is important. However, language systems are enormously complex and entail a large number of features that need to be attended to, for example, semantic, lexical, syntactic, pragmatic, phonetic, and sociocultural (Celce-Murcia, 1991). For example, to determine what types of learning situations are suitable for different learners of different languages to attain L2

---

[1]Although educators usually consider automatization to consist of recalling grammar rules and accurately producing instructed forms, it was noted as early as 1984 (Gregg, 1984) that production of explicit knowledge as formulaic language that has been memorized and automatized through use cannot be distinguished from production derived from implicit knowledge.

proficiency, Spolsky (1989) constructed a list of 74 conditions that lead to successful learning of a L2. For beginning learners, the extent of linguistic knowledge acquired naturally may be sufficient. However, to achieve intermediate and advanced linguistic and sociolinguistic skills, learners need to produce language that can increase their interactional exposure to the L2. L2 production also allows learners the additional opportunity to refine their linguistic knowledge by means of hypothesis testing. Based on their experience, many classroom teachers believe that participating in interactions and activities that lead to increased output contributes to learner internalization of L2 knowledge.

DISCOURSE–BASED APPROACHES
TO GRAMMAR INSTRUCTION

As mentioned, the concerns of ESL/EFL teachers, methodologists, and other experts on L2 teaching and learning about the effectiveness of the communicative methodology for diverse types of learners has resulted in new approaches to teaching L2 grammar that combine the positive aspects of natural learning and authentic use with those of explicit grammar instruction. In addition to focus on form discussed above, another direction of research deals with authentic language uses and structures and their meanings in discourse and text. The applications of corpus research findings to L2 grammar teaching appear to be particularly fruitful, and today we know a great deal more about the structure of authentic language as used by its speakers than we did even 10 or 15 years ago.

Research of linguistic features and grammar in actual spoken and written communication has been carried out in such areas as spoken and written discourse analysis, spoken and written language corpora (Biber, 1988), and studies of naturally occurring data, as well as experimental studies of elicited data. In addition, many investigations have addressed instructional approaches and techniques for grammar teaching to determine what classroom pedagogy and techniques can best serve the needs of learners at various levels of proficiency.

Discourse analysis examines contextual uses of language structures and investigates what speakers do to express meaning in various interactional settings. In addition to examinations of spoken discourse, studies of written discourse have also shed light on how meaning is conveyed in many types of written texts and genre. Analysis of written and spoken discourse seems to provide a practical avenue for grammar teaching and learning (McCarthy, 1991). Another benefit of using discourse in the classroom is that learners can start to notice how language contexts affect grammar and meaning and how speakers vary their linguistic structures depending on the sociolinguistic features of interaction.

Similarly, examinations of spoken and written language corpora seek to gain insight into linguistic regularities found in large-scope data sets. Corpora of spoken language allow researchers to analyze the features of English in narratives, service encounters, on-the-job situations, negotiations, and giving opinions in situations with family, colleagues, or debates (Carter & McCarthy, 1997). The corpora of written English include such genre as newspaper reports, editorials, and articles on religion and hobbies; official and government documents; the academic prose in chemistry, biology, sociology, and engineering; fiction; mysteries; science fiction; and biographies; as well as personal, business, and professional letters. By far the most comprehensive reference grammar of spoken and written English was developed by Biber, Johansson, Leech, Conrad, and Finegan (1999) to determine systematic patterns in language use, based on the findings of corpus analysis of conversations, fiction, newspapers, and academic prose. In addition to the descriptions of grammatical constructions traditionally found in reference grammars, Biber et al's. study also deals with considerations of register, lexis, and discourse variations to show how English grammar functions in real spoken and written texts.

Many of these analyses can inform L2 grammar teaching and be used in communicative activities. For example, if instruction in the meanings and appropriate use of clauses can be beneficial for a particular group of learners, teachers and material writers can determine what types of clauses are actually used in what types of spoken and written English. The advantage that corpus analysis accords teachers, curriculum developers, and textbook writers is that the aspects of grammar encountered in real spoken and written English can become instructional foci for learners.

Experimental studies of naturally occurring and elicited language dealing with L2 grammar have been devoted to the use of language by different types of learners and in various environments, for example, what happens in L2 grammatical development when speakers of different L1s (first language) learn L2, how learners of different ages acquire L2, and what learner background factors affect L2 learning and acquisition. For example, investigations based on natural or elicited data have dealt with the order of learning and acquisition of specific grammatical structures, such as tenses, morphemes, clauses, and noun systems. The wealth of applied linguistics findings creates an environment in which teachers and methodologists can endeavor to establish the effectiveness of their techniques and materials.

THE CASE FOR GRAMMAR TEACHING

Grammar learning and acquisition can enhance learner proficiency and accuracy and facilitate the internalization of its syntactic system, thus supplementing the development of fluency (Ellis, 1996). Designing tasks and curricula that build on what learners already know represents one of the strengths of explicit grammar teaching within the format of communicative and interactional activities. Richards (1994, 1998) describes a number of effective communicative activities centered around classroom interaction, and he indicates that the quality of the interaction between the teacher and the learner and between the learner and the task has a great deal of impact on the extent of learning. He also explains that it is not the adherence to a particular teaching method but teachers' involvement with the grammar-focused activities and their ability to personalize teaching and to make activities engaging that often promotes successful learning.

Although grammar teaching has been a thorny issue among teachers, teacher educators, methodologists, and other ESL/EFL professionals, it has continued to be one of the mainstays in English language training worldwide. All major publishers of ESL and EFL texts include grammar textbooks in their lists. Some particularly popular volumes have become best-sellers, despite their traditional approach to L2 grammar teaching. Furthermore, because the explicit teaching of grammar has been and remains at the core of the grammar-translation methodology adopted in many countries, students who arrive to obtain their language training in Great Britain, the United States, Australia, and other English-speaking countries often demand grammar instruction. As Brown (1994, p. 349) comments, "[f]or adults, the question is not so much whether to teach or not teach grammar, but rather, what are the optimal conditions for overt teaching of grammar."

To this end, the chapters in this book are based on thorough research, sound methodology, the findings of analyses of real language use and communication, and application of these findings to teaching and learning. They represent a wide range of approaches to L2 grammar teaching, seek to address practical instructional issues, and assist teachers in finding ways to benefit learners. Their strengths are in the novelty of contextualized and realistic grammar instruction, rooted in how language is used in real life.

REFERENCES

Biber, D. (1988). *Variation across speech and writing*. Cambridge, UK: Cambridge University Press.
Biber, D., Johansson, S., Leech, G., Conrad, S., & Finegan, E. (1999). *Longman grammar of spoken and written English*. London: Longman.

Brown, H. D. (1994). *Teaching by principles: An interactive approach to language pedagogy.* Englewood Cliffs, NJ: Prentice Hall.

Carter, R., & McCarthy, M. (1997). *Exploring spoken English.* Cambridge, UK: Cambridge University Press.

Celce-Murcia, M. (1991). Grammar pedagogy in second and foreign language teaching. *TESOL Quarterly, 25,* 459–480.

Chomsky, N. (1957). *Syntactic structures.* The Hague: Moulton.

Cook, V. (1994). Universal Grammar and the learning and teaching of second languages. In T. Odlin (Ed.), *Perspectives on pedagogical grammar* (pp. 25–48). Cambridge, UK: Cambridge University Press.

Doughty, C., & Williams, J. (1998). *Focus on form in classroom second language acquisition.* Cambridge, UK: Cambridge University Press.

Ellis, R. (1996). *The study of second language acquisition.* Oxford: Oxford University Press.

Ellis, R. (1997). *SLA research and language teaching.* Oxford: Oxford University Press.

Fotos, S., & Ellis, R. (1991). Communication about grammar: A task-based approach. *TESOL Quarterly, 25,* 605–628.

Gass, S., Mackey, A., & Pica, T. (1998). The role of input and interaction in second language acquisition. *Modern Language Journal, 82,* 299–307.

Gregg, K. (1984). Krashen's model and Occam's razor. *Applied Linguistics, 5,* 79–100.

Herron, C. (1976). An investigation of the effectiveness of using an Advance Organizer in the foreign language classroom. *Modern Language Journal, 78,* 190–198.

Howatt, A. (1984). *A history of English language teaching.* Oxford: Oxford University Press.

Johnson, K., & Marrow, E. (1981). *Communication in the classroom.* Hong Kong: Longman.

Krashen, S., & Terrell, T. (1983). *The natural approach: Language acquisition in the classroom.* New York: Pergamon.

Larsen-Freeman, D. (1991). Teaching grammar. In M. Celce-Murcia (Ed.), *Teaching English as a second or foreign language* (2nd ed., pp. 279–295). Boston: Heinle and Heinle.

Larsen-Freeman, D., & Long, M. (1991). *An introduction to second language acquisition research.* New York: Longman.

Long, M. (1988). Instructed interlanguage development. In L. Beebe (Ed.), *Issues in second language acquisition: Multiple perspectives* (pp. 115–141). New York: Newbury House.

Long, M. (1991). Focus on form: A design feature in language teaching methodology. In K. de Bot, D. Coste, R. Ginsberg, & C. Kramsch (Eds.), *Foreign language research in cross-cultural perspective* (pp. 39–52). Amsterdam: John Benjamins.

Long, M., & Crookes, G. (1992). Three approaches to task-based syllabus design. *TESOL Quarterly, 26,* 27–56.

McCarthy, M. (1991). *Discourse analysis for language teachers.* Cambridge, UK: Cambridge University Press.

McLaughlin, B., & Zemblidge, J. (1992). Second language learning. In W. Grabe & R. Kaplan (Eds.), *Introduction to applied linguistics* (pp. 61–78). Reading, MA: Addison-Wesley.

Pienemann, M. (1984). Psychological constraints on the teachability of languages. *Studies in Second Language Acquisition, 6,* 186–214.

Richards, J. (1994). *Reflective teaching in second language classrooms.* Cambridge, UK: Cambridge University Press.

Richards, J. (1998). *Beyond training.* Cambridge, UK: Cambridge University Press.

Rutherford, W. (1987). *Second language grammar learning and teaching.* New York: Longman.

Schmidt, R. (1990). The role of consciousness in second language learning. *Applied Linguistics, 11,* 129–158.

Schmidt, R. (1993). Awareness and second language acquisition. *Annual Review of Applied Linguistics, 13,* 206–226.

Sharwood Smith, M. (1981). Consciousness raising and the second language learner. *Applied Linguistics, 2,* 159–168.

Sharwood Smith, M. (1993). Input enhancement in instructed SLA: Theoretical bases. *Studies in Second Language Acquisition, 15,* 165–179.

Skehan, P. (1996). A framework for the implementation of task-based instruction. *Applied Linguistics, 17,* 38–62.

Skehan, P. (1998). *A cognitive approach to language learning.* Oxford: Oxford University Press.

Spolsky, B. (1989). *Conditions for second language learning.* Oxford: Oxford University Press.

Swain, M. (1985). Communicative competence: Some roles of comprehensible input and comprehensible output in its development. In S. Gass & C. Madden (Eds.), *Input and second language acquisition* (pp. 235–253). Rowley, MA: Newbury House.

Tomlin, R. (1994). Functional grammars, pedagogical grammars and communicative language teaching. In T. Odlin (Ed.), *Perspectives on pedagogical grammar* (pp. 140–178). Cambridge, UK: Cambridge University Press.

Grammar in Language Teaching

The four chapters included in Part I of this book focus on the place of grammar teaching in curricula and classroom methodologies. These chapters identify flexible ways in which the teaching of grammar can be incorporated in second and foreign language instruction in practically any English as a second language (ESL)/English as a foreign language (EFL) curricula, including the teaching of language skills with specific goals. Taken together, the chapters provide an overview of a great deal of current research that informs second/foreign language teaching and promotes learning and acquisition of grammar. The authors present these research findings, supplemented with their studies and experience, to help practicing classroom teachers benefit from the current advancements in applied linguistics, task-work, corpus analyses, and treatments of language as a system of communication. The authors of the chapters included in Part I approach grammar teaching as one of the cornerstones in enabling learners to communicate meaningfully and accurately and, thus, advance their communicative skills and second language fluency. They see the teaching of grammar as part and parcel of language teaching and helping learners to develop the skills essential for their success in diverse environments where English is used.

In "The Place of Grammar Instruction in the Second/Foreign Language Curriculum," Rod Ellis points to much recent research on ESL/EFL learning and acquisition and notes that without grammar instruction, learners frequently fail to achieve advanced levels of grammatical competence. He further finds that it is possible (and, in fact, necessary) to include a grammar component in the language teaching curriculum together with the instruction centered around communicative tasks. He emphasizes that research has shown that grammar instruction can improve the quality of second and foreign language learning. In his view, the crucial issues that underlie the design of ESL/EFL curricula are not whether grammar should be taught, but at what stage in L2 development grammar needs to be taught to maximize its benefits for the learner. Another important issue that Ellis addresses in his chapter is the ways in which grammar instruction should be included in second and foreign language teaching curricula. He argues that beginning students whose language base is comparatively small may not be ready for explicit grammar instruction and that exposure to structural work can begin once learners have had an opportunity to increase their lexical repertoire and language base. Ellis' model for grammar teaching at subsequent levels relies on curricula that can be designed to address learner problems with grammar directly by focusing on the areas that have been identified as particularly difficult to acquire. Ellis emphasizes that the primary goal of explicit and focused grammar instruction is to heighten learners' awareness of grammatical features and systems, and most importantly, to promote learner "noticing" of grammar regularities. He points out that the traditional ways of teaching grammar, in which rules are presented and drilled, have not been successful, but grammar instruction to enhance noticing by means of discovery tasks can lead to acquisition and automatization.

In "Accuracy and Fluency Revisited," Jack Richards examines the effectiveness of grammar-learning when students are engaged in communicative tasks. He points out that although learners' exposure to language increases when they work with certain types of tasks, task work needs to be focused and carefully designed in order to lead to the acquisition of grammar. In addition, he explains that in task work, noticing linguistic forms and the environments in which they occur often leads to learners' increased abilities to identify the grammatical systems of the second and foreign language. Richards also points out that task work can allow learners to experiment and restructure their hypotheses about the target language and stresses that the grammar gap in task work needs to be proactively addressed. Richards emphasizes that accuracy in second/foreign language should be encouraged and that the cognitive complexity of task work needs to increase as learners' skills continue to develop. In his view, language instruction needs to include focused tasks to facilitate learners' noticing grammatical forms and to promote accuracy in communicative teaching.

The uses of various grammatical structures in spoken language are at the center of Michael McCarthy's and Ronald Carter's chapter, "Ten Criteria for a Spoken Grammar." Based on their analysis of a large corpus of spoken data, the authors present a model for including grammar teaching in a curriculum designed to develop learner speaking skills essential for communicating in real life. McCarthy and Carter identify the key differences between the traditional teaching of spoken English and the features of their corpus. They specify that communicative approaches to the teaching of second language have to include a grammar component. Because the use of spoken English is prevalent worldwide and has become the lingua franca in many domains of human activity, it is important that learners attain spoken fluency in ways congruent with real language use. For example, they note that the teaching of specific grammatical features, such as clauses, tense, and voice, should shift from traditional (and somewhat bookish) techniques to a way that helps learners become better communicators. McCarthy's and Carter's 10 criteria that are common in spoken English represent a foundation for designing grammar speaking curricula in ESL and EFL alike.

As a general summary of advancements in grammar research for pedagogical purposes, Martha Pennington synthesizes the current treatments of grammar in linguistics and discourse. In "Grammar and Communication: New Directions in Theory and Practice," she discusses the organizing principles of language as a communication system and explains how advances in the study of grammar can make research findings applicable to language teaching. Pennington reviews the Minimalist approach to syntax (Noam Chomsky), Incremental Grammar developed by David Brazil, Action Grammar originated by Herbert H. Clark, and Relevance Theory proposed by Dan Sperber and Deirdre Wilson. In Pennington's view, these can and should inform second/foreign language teaching to provide learners the best advantages of current research. Pennington argues that, compared to traditional grammar, each of these approaches offers a more realistic and practical view of language and can lead to creating pedagogical grammars centered on communication. She proposes four principles that can serve as a foundation for effective pedagogical grammars: collocational, compositional, contexted, and contrastive. In Pennington's view, the four Cs represent the key characteristics that set the innovative treatments of language apart from the traditional rule-bound approaches.

The Place of Grammar Instruction in the Second/Foreign Language Curriculum

Rod Ellis
University of Auckland, New Zealand

The place of grammar instruction in the second/foreign language curriculum has been strongly debated in the past 30 years. In teaching methods reliant on a structural syllabus (e.g., grammar translation, audiolingualism, Total Physical Response, situational language teaching), grammar held pride of place. However, with the advent of communicative language teaching (see, e.g., Allwright, 1979) and "natural" methods (e.g., Krashen & Terrell, 1983), this place has been challenged and in some cases, a "zero position" has been advocated (e.g., Krashen, 1982) on the grounds that teaching grammar does not correlate with acquiring grammar. More recently, various arguments have been advanced for incorporating a "focus on form"[1] into the language curriculum (e.g., Doughty & Williams, 1998), motivated by research findings that suggest that "natural" language learning does not lead to high levels of grammatical and sociolinguistic competence (e.g., Swain, 1985). The purpose of this chapter is to consider a number of reasons why grammar should be included in a second language (L2) curriculum. The chapter also addresses how a grammar component might

---

[1]Long (1988) distinguishes between a "focus on forms" and a "focus on form." The former refers to traditional approaches to grammar teaching based on a structure-of-the-day approach. The latter refers to drawing learners' attention to linguistic forms (and the meanings they realize) in the context of activities in which the learner's primary focus of attention is on meaning.

be incorporated into a communicative curriculum. Finally, it outlines an approach to the teaching of grammar that is compatible with the curricular framework being proposed.

THE CASE FOR TEACHING GRAMMAR

A case for teaching grammar can be mounted from different perspectives: (1) acquisition theory, (2) the learner, and (3) language pedagogy. Taken together, arguments based on these perspectives provide a compelling argument in favor of teaching grammar.

Acquisition Theory

It is now widely acknowledged that L2 learners, particularly adults, fail to achieve high levels of grammatical competence even if they have ample opportunity to learn the language naturally. Hammerly (1991) indicates that many naturalistic learners, even after years of exposure to the L2, often fail to proceed beyond the second level on the American Council on the Teaching of Foreign Languages (ACTFL) scale of language proficiency. Kowal and Swain (1997) and Swain (1985) point out that learners in Canadian immersion programs (i.e., programs in which the target language serves as the medium of instruction for teaching subject content) achieve high levels of discourse and strategic competence but frequently fail to acquire even basic grammatical distinctions, such as *passé composé* and *imparfait* in French.

There are many possible reasons for learners' failure to achieve high levels of grammatical competence, including the following:

1. Age: Once learners have passed a "critical period" (about 15 years of age in the case of grammar) the acquisition of full grammatical competence is no longer possible.
2. Communicative sufficiency: Learners may be able to satisfy their communicative needs without acquiring target language norms.
3. Limited opportunities for pushed output: Research (e.g., Allen, Swain, Harley, & Cummins, 1990) has demonstrated that the linguistic environment to which learners are exposed in the classroom may indeed be limited in quite significant ways.
4. Lack of negative feedback: It has been suggested that some grammatical structures cannot be acquired from positive input, which is all that is typically available to learners learning an L2 "naturally" (see White, 1987).

If (1) is the reason, not much can be done to alleviate the problem pedagogically, as teachers are clearly powerless to alter the age of their learners. However, there is growing doubt concerning the validity of the critical period hypothesis where grammar is concerned; it is becoming clear that there are large numbers of learners who, given sufficient time and motivation, are successful in acquiring target language norms even if they start learning the L2 after the age of 15. If (2) and (3) are the reasons, two possible solutions suggest themselves. One is improving the quality of the interactional opportunities learners experience, for example, by ensuring that learners' communicative needs are enhanced by requiring them to produce "pushed output." One way of achieving this is by devising a curriculum of communicative tasks that are linguistically demanding (e.g., call for learners to activate their rule-based as opposed to lexical competence—see Skehan, 1998). The other solution is to focus learners' attention on grammatical form (and, of course, the meanings they realize) through some kind of grammar teaching. Point (4) also indicates the need for grammar teaching, as this serves as one of the more obvious ways in which learners can obtain the negative feedback needed to acquire "difficult" structures.

Given that the possible reasons for learners' failing to achieve target language norms vary in the kind of solution they point to, it is obviously important to establish whether the "teach grammar" solution is, in fact, effective. Earlier (see Fotos & Ellis, 1991), I summarized the main findings of what is now a substantial body of empirical research that has investigated the effects of form-focused instruction on interlanguage development. This summary, I would claim, remains valid today. It states:

1. Formal instruction helps to promote more rapid L2 acquisition and also contributes to higher levels of ultimate achievement (Long, 1988).

2. There are psycholinguistic constraints which govern whether attempts to teach learners specific grammatical rules result in their acquisition. Formal instruction may succeed if the learners have reached a stage in the developmental sequence that enables them to process the target structure (Pienemann, 1984). Conversely, it will not succeed if learners have not reached the requisite developmental stage.[2]

3. Production practice is not sufficient to overcome these constraints. There is now clear evidence to suggest that having learners produce sentences that model the target structure is not sufficient to guarantee its acquisition as implicit knowledge. Studies by Schumann (1978), R. Ellis (1984), and Kadia (1988), among others, suggest that formal instruction directed at developmental or difficult grammatical structures has little

---

[2]A recent article by Spada and Lightbown (1999) does cast some doubt on the claim that developmental sequences are inviolable. This study found that learners who were at an early stage in the acquisition of question forms were able to learn question forms at an advanced stage as a result of formal instruction, suggesting they were not constrained by the kind of psycholinguistic constraints on acquisition proposed by Pienemann. Spada and Lightbown suggest that the effectiveness of instruction may depend less on the learners' stage of development than on the type of instruction.

effect on performance in spontaneous language use. (The term *developmental* refers here to structures that are acquired in stages and involve the learner passing through a series of transitional phases before mastering the target structure. Examples of developmental structures are negatives and interrogatives.)

4. It is possible, however, that formal instruction directed at relatively simple grammatical rules (such as plural or copula *be*) will be successful in developing implicit knowledge, as such forms do not require the mastery of complex processing operations (Pica, 1983; Pienemann, 1984).

5. Formal instruction is effective in developing explicit knowledge of grammatical features. There is substantial evidence to suggest that formal instruction is successful if the learning outcomes are measured by means of an instrument that allows for controlled, planned, language use (e.g., an imitation test, a sentence-joining task, or a grammaticality judgment task). It is in this kind of language use that learners are able to draw on their explicit knowledge. Studies by Kadia (1988); Lightbown, Spada, and Wallace (1980); Schumann (1978); and Zobl (1985) all support such a conclusion.

6. Formal instruction may work best in promoting acquisition when it is linked with opportunities for natural communication (Spada, 1986).

In short, although there are constraints that govern both when and what type of grammar teaching is likely to work, there is clear evidence that, providing these constraints are taken into account, teaching grammar can have a beneficial effect on learners' interlanguage development. This conclusion is now widely accepted by Second Language Acquisition (SLA) researchers (see Doughty and Williams, 1998).

The Learner's Perspective

An equally strong reason for including grammar in the L2 curriculum is that many learners expect it. Adult learners typically view "grammar" as the central component of language and, irrespective of the type of instruction they experience, are likely to make strenuous efforts to understand the grammatical features they notice. In an analysis of the diaries written by ab initio learners of German in an intensive foreign language course at a university in London (Ellis, R., unpublished manuscript), I was struck by the depth of the learners' concern to make sense of the grammar of German. Their diaries are full of references to grammar—of their struggle to understand particular rules and their sense of achievement when a rule finally "clicked." It should be noted, too, that "grammar" for these learners consisted of explicit rules that they could understand; it was not the kind of implicit grammar that comprises interlanguage.

Of course, not all learners will orientate so strongly to studying grammar. Some, younger learners for example, may be more inclined to view language functionally—as a tool for communicating—and may be less able to benefit from grammar instruction. Nevertheless, it is my contention that many successful learners are not only prepared to focus on form but actively seek to do so (see Reiss, 1985). For such learners, a "communicative" syllabus that eschews a focus on grammar may be missing the mark.

A Pedagogical Perspective

One of the arguments that was advanced against the kind of notional/functional syllabus that appeared in the late 1970s and early 1980s was that "notions" and "functions" do not provide a basis for the systematic coverage of the language to be taught (see Brumfit, 1981). Examples of notions are *possibility* and *past time*, whereas examples of functions are *requests* and *apologies*. The problem with such constructs is that they are not generative in the way grammar is. A similar criticism can be leveled at the current fashion for task-based or thematically based syllabuses. There can be no guarantee that the teaching activities that are based on such syllabuses provide a full and systematic coverage of the grammar of the L2. To some extent, tasks can be devised so that they require learners to use specific grammatical features, but, at least where production tasks are concerned, there are limits on the extent to which these features are essential in performing the tasks (see the comments later in this chapter) as learners are adept at avoiding the use of structures that they find difficult. Arguably, the only way to ensure a systematic coverage of the grammar of the L2, then, is by means of a structural syllabus. Such a syllabus provides teachers and learners with a clear sense of progression—something that I think is missing from both notional and task-based syllabuses. However, this does not mean the abandonment of meaning-based syllabuses and a straight return to the structural syllabus. Rather, I see a need for both. This involves a curriculum that incorporates both types of syllabus. We will now turn to the question of how grammar can be incorporated into a language curriculum.

THE PLACE OF GRAMMAR IN THE CURRICULUM

Deciding the place of grammar in the language curriculum involves seeking answers to the following questions:

1. At what stage of learners' general L2 development should grammar be taught?

2. With what intensity should grammar be taught?
3. Can the teaching of grammar be integrated into meaning-focused instruction?

The first question concerns the general timing of the grammar instruction. The second deals with whether grammar instruction should be intense or spread over a period of time. The third concerns the crucial matter of the relationship between the grammar and the communicative components of a syllabus.

The Timing of Grammar Instruction

An assumption of traditional approaches to grammar is that it should be taught from the very beginning stages of a language course. This assumption derives from behaviorist learning theory, according to which learning consists of habit formation. Learners must be taught correct habits from the start to avoid the unnecessary labor of having to unlearn wrong habits in order to learn the correct ones later. As Brooks (1960) put it, "Error, like sin, is to be avoided at all cost." Such a view is not supported by current theories of L2 acquisition. Interlanguage development is seen as a process of hypothesis-testing and errors as a means of carrying this out (Corder, 1967). Learners follow their own built-in syllabus. Thus, it is now widely accepted that errors are both a natural and inevitable consequence of the processes of acquisition. In other words, there is no longer a theoretical basis for teaching grammar to prevent errors.

There are, in fact, some fairly obvious reasons for not teaching grammar to beginners. First, as the immersion studies have shown (see Johnson & Swain, 1997), learners do not need grammar instruction to acquire considerable grammatical competence. Learners with plentiful opportunities to interact in the L2 are likely to acquire basic word order rules and salient inflections without assistance. For example, L2 learners who have never received instruction are able to acquire the rules for ordering elements in the English noun phrase; they do not put the adjective after the noun, even when this is the ordering in their L1 (Hughes, 1979). They are also able to acquire the English auxiliary system and, over time, use this in a target-like manner in interrogatives and negatives. Probably, they will also acquire at least some complex structures such as simple relative clauses in which the relative pronoun functions as subject (as in "Mary married the man *who* lived next door"). Of course, not all learners will acquire these grammatical features; some learners, like Schumann's Alberto (Schumann, 1978), will fossilize early. But many learners will go quite a long way without any attempt to teach them grammar. In other words, up to a point, the acquisition of a grammar takes place naturally and inevitably, providing learners experience appropriate opportunities for hearing and using the L2.

A second, more powerful reason for not teaching grammar to beginners is that the early stage of L2 acquisition (like the early stage of L1 acquisition) is naturally agrammatical. Language learners begin by learning items—words or formulaic chunks. They communicate by concatenating these, stringing them together into sequences that convey meaning contextually, as shown in these examples from Ellis (1984):

Me no (= I don't have any crayons)

Me milkman (= I want to be the milkman)

Dinner time you out (= It is dinner time so you have to go out)

Me no school (= I am not coming to school on Monday)

Such utterances are ubiquitous in the spontaneous, communicative speech of beginner L2 learners, both child and adult. It is only later that learners begin to grammaticalize their speech. According to N. Ellis (1996), they do this by extracting rules from the items they have learned—bootstrapping their way to grammar. It would seem, then, that the early stages of language acquisition are lexical rather than grammatical (see also Klein & Perdue, 1992; Lewis, 1993).

If grammar teaching is to accord with how learners learn, then, it should not be directed at beginners. Rather, it should await the time when learners have developed a sufficiently varied lexis to provide a basis for the process of rule extraction. In crude terms, this is likely to be at the intermediate-plus stages of development. There is a case, therefore, for reversing the traditional sequence of instruction, focusing initially on the development of vocabulary and the activation of the strategies for using lexis in context to make meaning and only later seeking to draw learners' attention to the rule-governed nature of language.

The Intensity of Grammar Instruction

Independent of when grammar should be taught is the question of how intense the instruction should be once it starts. Is it better, for example, to spend substantial periods of time focusing on a relatively few (albeit problematic) grammatical structures, or is it better to deal less intensively with a broad range of structures?

There are now a number of studies that demonstrate that when problematic grammatical structures are taught intensively learners acquire them. Harley (1989), for example, describes an instructional treatment for dealing with the distinction between *passé composé* and *imparfait* that lasted eight weeks! Thankfully, this resulted in marked gains in the accuracy of these verb forms that were sustained over time. One wonders, however, how feasible such intense treatments are in the context of the complete language curriculum. If such lengthy periods of time are devoted to a single grammatical structure there will be little time left to focus on the numerous other grammatical problems the learners experience.

Underlying this question of the intensity of the instruction is another question. What is the goal of grammar instruction? Is it to lead learners to full control of the targeted structures? Or is it to make them aware of the structures and, perhaps, of the gap between their own interlanguage rule and the target language rule? Grammar instruction, again influenced by behaviorist learning theory, has assumed that the goal of grammar instruction is complete accuracy. It is this assumption that appears to motivate the call for intense doses of instruction of the kind Harley provided. However, a more cognitive view of L2 learning suggests that acquisition begins with awareness, and that once this has been triggered learners will achieve full control through their own resources in due time. Such a view supports a less intense, broader-based grammar curriculum.

The Relationship Between Code-Focused and Message-Focused Instruction

Traditional language teaching was code-focused, although there were probably always some opportunities for message-focused activity, even in the most audiolingual of courses. With the advent of communicative language teaching, however, more importance, quite rightly, has been given to message-focused language activity, not just because this is seen as needed to develop communicative skills in an L2, but also because it caters to the natural acquisition of grammar and other aspects of the code (see, e.g., Prabhu, 1987). Perhaps the key issue facing designers of language curricula is how to relate the code-focused and the message-focused components. There are two basic options.

The first is the *integrated option*. Integration can be achieved in two ways:

1. Communicative tasks that have been designed to focus attention on specific properties of the code. I have referred to these elsewhere as "focused communicative tasks." Such an approach represents a proactive approach toward integration; it takes place at the level of the curriculum content.

2. Teachers' feedback on learners' attempts to perform communicative tasks. Such feedback can focus on specific errors that learners make. This approach is reactive in nature; it takes place, not at the level of content, but methodologically. The feedback can be instant (i.e.,

can occur as an immediate response to a learner error) or it can be delayed (i.e., take place after the communicative task has been completed).[3]

There are enormous problems in designing focused communicative tasks (see Loschky & Bley-Vroman, 1993) that preclude using them as a means of achieving curricular integration. As I have already noted, learners are adept at sidestepping the grammatical focus while performing a communicative task, unless of course they are told what the focus is; in which case, it can be argued that the task ceases to be communicative and becomes a situational grammar exercise. Integration is more likely to be achieved reactively rather than proactively, although there are some obvious problems here, not least concerning the nature of the feedback; should it be explicit, which potentially endangers the communicative nature of the task, or implicit, when it might not be noticed? Currently, however, strong arguments have been advanced for what Long (1991) has called "a focus on form" (i.e., reactive feedback while learners' primary attention is on message). The claim is that drawing learners' attention to form in the context of ongoing communicative endeavor is compatible with the type of input processing that is needed for interlanguage development.

The second approach for relating the two elements of a language curriculum is the *parallel option*. Here no attempt is made to integrate a focus on code and message; instead, these are entirely separate components. In such a syllabus, the main component would consist of communicative tasks, designed to engage learners in the receptive and productive processes involved in using language to convey messages. A second, smaller component would consist of a list of grammatical structures to be systematically taught. There would be no attempt to create any links between the two components. The time allocated to the two components would vary according to the learners' general level of proficiency. Thus, at the elementary level there would be only communicative tasks (receptive rather than productive in the first instance). At the intermediate stage, once learners had established a lexical basis for the acquisition of grammar, the focus on code (which could include pronunciation and discourse as well as grammar) would kick in, growing progressively larger as time passed, until it occupied close to half of the total time available with advanced learners. This proportional curriculum model (Yalden, 1983) is shown in Fig. 2.1.

---

[3]Little is currently known about the relative efficacy of immediate and delayed negative feedback on learners' acquisition of grammatical features. Most studies of negative feedback have focused on the type of feedback (e.g., whether it is implicit or explicit) rather than the timing. This is clearly an area that needs to be investigated.

Elementary	Intermediate	Advanced
Communicative tasks		
Code-focused tasks		

FIG. 2.1   The relationship between the communicative and code components of a syllabus.

This proposal flies in the face of what is generally considered to be good practice in language pedagogy—namely, that the curriculum should be carefully constructed to ensure an integration of skills, with tasks carefully sequenced to ensure a systematic and graded progression. However, such syllabuses, although superficially sensible, ignore the essential fact that skill integration is not something that is achieved externally by the curriculum designer (or teacher) but must be achieved internally by the learners themselves, in accordance with their built-in syllabuses and their particular learning goals. Curriculum designers have hung themselves quite needlessly on the gallows of the integrated syllabus.

There are strong arguments to support the view that the goal of the code-oriented component of the syllabus should be awareness rather than performance; that is, the syllabus should be directed at developing learners' conscious understanding of how particular code features work, not at ensuring that learners are able to perform them accurately and fluently. In more technical terms, this entails a syllabus directed at explicit rather than implicit knowledge of the L2. As I have argued elsewhere (see Ellis, R., 1991a, 1993, 1997), it is unrealistic to try to intervene directly in interlanguage development by teaching implicit knowledge, as this constitutes a highly complex process, involving intake and gradual restructuring, which we still understand quite poorly and which is not amenable to one-shot (or even to several-shot) pedagogic ministrations. In contrast, explicit knowledge can be taught relatively easily in the same way that history dates or mathematical formulae can be taught[4]. Of course, explicit knowledge constitutes a lesser goal than implicit knowledge, as effective communication activity requires the latter type of knowledge. This limitation, however, is less severe if it can be shown that explicit knowledge plays an important facilitating role in helping learners acquire implicit knowledge by encouraging "noticing" and "noticing the gap" (Schmidt & Frota, 1986). If learn-

---

[4]This assumes that many L2 learners are capable of learning a wide range of explicit rules. Such an assumption is controversial, however. Krashen (1982) claims that learners are only capable of learning simple rules (e.g., third-person -s). However, there is research evidence to suggest that Krashen seriously underestimates learners' capacity for explicit knowledge (see, e.g., Green & Hecht, 1992).

ers know about a grammatical feature they are more likely to heed it when they come across it in the input and also to attend to how it differs from the current interlanguage rule that underlies their own performance in the L2. In other words, the goal of a grammar syllabus becomes not that of teaching learners to use grammar but of helping them to understand how grammar works. In this respect, but not others, this position is closer to that of the cognitive code method than to behaviorism.

A crucial issue is the content of the code-oriented component of the syllabus. Clearly, this will have to go beyond grammar, to include pronunciation (perhaps) and discourse features. Here, however, I will consider only the question of grammar content. Clearly, this content should be derived from our understanding of the learning problems that learners experience; that is, the content should be remedial in nature, focusing on areas of grammar where learners are known to make errors. There are, in fact, many such areas that are common to all learners. The so-called developmental errors reflect learning problems that are universal. Examples are as follows:

- omission of plural -*s*
- omission of third person -*s*
- overuse of the article *the* (and corresponding underuse of *a*)
- the double comparative (e.g., "more faster")
- resumptive pronouns in relative clauses (e.g., "The man who my sister had married *him* . . .")
- process verbs (e.g., "The size was increased greatly.")

Our knowledge of such problem areas of grammar provides a solid base for the development of a general grammar syllabus, applicable to all language learners. Of course, syllabuses designed for specific groups of learners will need to take account of the fact that there are also some errors directly traceable to first language influence. Probably, though, the transfer errors are less numerous than the developmental errors (see Ellis, R., 1994).[5]

Curriculum designers also need to consider how this grammatical content can be graded. There is a growing and somewhat confused literature dealing with this issue. Although there is general agreement that grading

---

[5]Many errors, of course, are the result of both developmental and transfer processes. Thus, whereas all L2 learners seem to have problems distinguishing the use of *the* and *a* learners whose L1 does not include an article system (e.g., Japanese or Korean learners) are likely to experience the problems for longer, often failing to completely overcome them, even though they achieve a very advanced level of overall proficiency.

should proceed in accordance with difficulty, there is much less agreement regarding what this actually involves. This results, in part, from the failure to recognize that what is difficult with regard to implicit knowledge may not be difficult in terms of explicit knowledge. For example, teaching learners to understand the rule for third-person -*s* (explicit knowledge) is relatively easy, but teaching them to use this feature accurately and fluently (implicit knowledge) is problematic. Thus, third-person -*s* can be thought of as an easy explicit feature but a difficult implicit feature. The question that needs to be addressed, then, is what criteria influence the level of difficulty learners are likely to experience in acquiring grammatical features as explicit knowledge? Table 2.1 suggests some of the criteria. At this juncture, it is not possible to apply these criteria in a systematic fashion, although it might be argued that these are the very criteria that have been traditionally applied in the development of structural syllabuses. Thus, designers of grammatical structures can call on this tradition with some confidence.

TABLE 2.1
Criteria for determining the difficulty of grammatical structures as explicit knowledge approach for teaching grammar

Criteria	Definition	Example
1. Formal complexity	The extent to which the structure involves just a single or many elements.	Plural -*s* is formally simple; relative clauses involve many elements.
2. Functional complexity	The extent to which the meanings realized by a structure are transparent or opaque.	Plural -*s* is is transparent; articles are opaque.
3. Reliability	The extent to which the rule has exceptions.	Third-person -*s* is very reliable; the rule for periphrastic genitives is much less reliable.
4. Scope	The extent to which the rule has a broad or narrow coverage.	The Present Simple Tense has broad scope; the Future Perfect Tense has narrow scope.
5. Metalanguage	The extent to which the rule can be provided simply with minimum metalanguage.	Plural -*s* is simple; reflexive pronouns are more difficult; subject verb inversion is even more difficult.
6. L1/L2 contrast	A feature that corresponds to an L1 feature is easier than a feature that does not.	For French learners of English, the position of adverbs in sentences is difficult.

Finally, it should be noted that the two principal curricula options—integrated and parallel—are not, in fact, mutually exclusive. It would be perfectly possible to complement a parallel syllabus that includes a nonintegrated grammar component with Long's "focus on form" through reactive feedback to errors that learners make when performing tasks from the communicative component of the syllabus. There are considerable strengths in such a proposal as a focus on form. It may be one way in which teachers can encourage learners to make use of their explicit knowledge to "notice" features in the input. This raises the intriguing possibility of forging a link between the focus on form and the teaching of explicit knowledge (i.e., by teachers directing feedback on features that have recently been explicitly taught). It is doubtful, however, if such a link can ever be anything other than opportunistic. In general, the focus of teachers' feedback in the communicative strand of the curriculum will not match the focus in the grammar component. Nor do I see this as something for which to strive for the reasons I have already given.

AN APPROACH FOR TEACHING GRAMMAR

The approach for teaching grammar that will now be outlined is premised on the assumption that the focus of the instruction should be *awareness* rather than *performance*. There are, in fact, two senses of *awareness*. First, learners can be made *aware* of the formal properties of the language as they experience these in input; that is, they can be made to consciously "notice" them. Second, learners can be made *aware* in the sense of forming some kind of explicit representation of a target form (i.e., developing explicit knowledge). Figure 2.2 shows these two senses of awareness. The particular approach to teaching grammar that I will now describe involves attempts to induce both kinds of awareness.

	Awareness (1)	Awareness (2)	
		explicit knowledge	
input			output
	intake (noticed forms)	implicit knowledge	

FIG. 2.2 Two types of awareness in L2 acquisition.

The materials (Ellis & Gaies, 1998) consist of a series of units, each directed at a single grammatical problem. The approach is remedial, with the error targeted in a unit indicated in an "error box." By asking "Do my students make this error?" the teacher is able to determine whether to teach the unit.

A unit consists of five kinds of activities:

1. Listening to comprehend: Here students listen to a continuous text that has been contrived to contain several examples of the target structure. On this occasion, however, they are required to focus on the message-content of the text.

2. Listening to notice: In this activity the students listen to the text a second time (and if necessary a third or fourth time) to identify the target structure. To assist the process of noticing the structure, they are asked to complete a gapped version of the text. It should be noted, however, that this fill-in-the-gap activity differs from traditional grammar exercises in that students do not have to rely on their competence to complete the text; they can obtain the missing words by listening carefully. "Listening to Notice" is intended to raise the first type of awareness in the students. Oral rather than written texts have been chosen to induce real-time input processing.

3. Understanding the grammar point: This activity is directed at helping learners develop explicit knowledge of the grammar point (i.e., awareness). They are helped to analyze the "data" provided by the text, which they have now completed, and to "discover" the rule. A discovery approach to teaching explicit knowledge is favored on the grounds that it is more motivating and that it also serves a learner-training function. By completing such tasks, learners can develop the skills needed to analyze language data for themselves and so build their own explicit grammars of English. However, there is a grammar reference section (at the back of the book) to which students can refer to check the accuracy of the explicit rule they have formed.

4. Checking: The students are given a further text (this time, written) containing errors. They are asked to identify the errors and correct them. This kind of grammaticality judgment task is chosen because it lends itself to the use of explicit knowledge (see Ellis, R., 1991b). It also fosters the skill of monitoring, which, as Krashen (1982) has pointed out, draws on explicit knowledge.

5. Trying it: Finally, there is an opportunity for students to try out their understanding of the target structure in a short production activity. The emphasis here is not so much on practicing the structure as on proceduralizing students' declarative knowledge, a step DeKeyser (1998)

considers to be necessarily intermediate between the teaching of explicit knowledge and its full automatization as implicit knowledge.[6]

These materials are not designed to develop implicit knowledge. Indeed, this can hardly be achieved in a single hour, the typical length of time needed to complete a unit. They are directed at developing students' awareness of grammar. As such, the materials do not constitute a complete curriculum but rather the kind of grammar component I have described in the previous section. They will need to be complemented with task-based materials of a communicative nature.

CONCLUSION

This chapter has sought to make a case for teaching grammar. However, the case is a circumscribed one, and it is perhaps useful to conclude by saying what is not being proposed as well as what is.

It is NOT being proposed that:

- We revert back completely to a structural syllabus.
- We teach beginners grammar.
- We attempt to teach learners to use grammatical features accurately and fluently through intensive practice exercises.
- We teach grammar communicatively (e.g., by embedding a grammar focus into communicative tasks).

It is being proposed that:

- We include a grammar component in the language curriculum, to be used alongside a communicative task-based component.
- We teach grammar only to learners who have already developed a substantial lexical base and are able to engage in message-focused tasks, albeit with language that is grammatically inaccurate.

---

[6]DeKeyser's claim that explicit knowledge can be converted into implicit knowledge by means of automatizating practice can be challenged for the reasons explained earlier in this chapter. However, his idea of "proceduralizing declarative knowledge" seems a useful one. Thus, the materials stop at this stage and make no attempt to supply the kind and amount of practice that DeKeyser acknowledges is needed for automatization.

- We teach grammar separately, making no attempt to integrate it with the task-based component (except, perhaps, methodologically through feedback).
- We focus on areas of grammar known to cause problems to learners.
- We aim to teach grammar as awareness, focusing on helping learners develop explicit knowledge.

These proposals are theoretically based and, as such, provide a solid foundation for the teaching of grammar. However, it needs to be acknowledged that there is more than one theory of L2 acquisition and that somewhat different proposals based on alternative theories are possible (see DeKeyser, 1998, for example). This is likely to ensure that the place of grammar in the curriculum and the nature of grammar teaching will be hotly debated in the years ahead.

REFERENCES

Allen, P., Swain, M., Harley, B., & Cummins, J. (1990). Aspects of classroom treatment: Toward a more comprehensive view of second language education. In B. Harley, P. Allen, J. Cummins, & M. Swain (Eds.), *The development of second language proficiency* (pp. 57–81). Cambridge, UK: Cambridge University Press.

Allwright, R. (1979). Language learning through communication practice. In C. Brumfit & K. Johnson (Eds.), *The communicative approach to language teaching.* Oxford: Oxford University Press.

Brooks, B. (1960). *Language and language learning.* New York: Harcourt Brace and World.

Brumfit, C. (1981). Notional syllabuses revisited: A response. *Applied Linguistics, 2,* 90–92.

Corder, S. P. (1967). The significance of learners' errors. *IRAL, 5,* 149–159.

DeKeyser, R. (1998). Beyond focus on form: Cognitive perspectives on learning and practicing second language grammar. In C. Doughty & J. Williams (Eds.), *Focus on form in classroom second language acquisition* (pp. 42–63). Cambridge, UK: Cambridge University Press.

Doughty, C., and Williams, J. (Eds). (1998). *Focus on form in classroom second language acquisition.* Cambridge, UK: Cambridge University Press.

Ellis, N. (1996). Sequencing in SLA: Phonological memory, chunking and points of order. *Studies in Second Language Acquisition, 18,* 91–126.

Ellis, R. (1984). Classroom second language development. Oxford: Pergamon.

Ellis, R. (1991a). *Second language acquisition and second language pedagogy.* Clevedon, UK: Multilingual Matters.

Ellis, R. (1991b). Grammaticality judgments and second language acquisition. *Studies in Second Language Acquisition, 13,* 161–186.

Ellis, R. (1993). The structural syllabus and second language acquisition. *TESOL Quarterly, 27,* 91–113.

Ellis, R. (1994). *The study of second language acquisition.* Oxford: Oxford University Press.

Ellis, R. (1997). *SLA research and language pedagogy.* Oxford: Oxford University Press.

Ellis, R. *A metaphorical analysis of learner beliefs.* Unpublished manuscript. University of Auckland, NZ.

Ellis, R., & S. Gaies. (1998). *Impact grammar.* Hong Kong: Longman Addison Wesley.

Fotos, S., & Ellis, R. (1991). Communicating about grammar: A task-based approach. *TESOL Quarterly, 25*, 605–628.

Gass, S., & Madden, C. (Eds.). (1985). *Input in second language acquisition.* Rowley, MA.: Newbury House.

Green, P., & Hecht, K. (1992). Implicit and explicit grammar: An empirical study. *Applied Linguistics, 13*, 168–184.

Hammerly, H. (1991). *Fluency and accuracy.* Clevedon, UK: Multilingual Matters.

Harley, B. (1989). Functional grammar in French immersion: A classroom experiment. *Applied Linguistics, 10*, 331–359.

Hughes, A. (1979). Aspects of a Spanish adult's acquisition of English. *Interlanguage Studies Bulletin, 4*, 49–65.

Johnson, R. K., & Swain, M. (Eds.). (1997). *Immersion education: International perspectives.* Cambridge, UK: Cambridge University Press.

Kadia, K. (1988). The effect of formal instruction on monitored and sponatenous interlanguage performance. *TESOL Quarterly, 22*, 509–15.

Klein, W., & Perdue, C. (1982). *Utterance structure: Developing grammars again.* Amsterdam: John Benjamins.

Kowal, M., & Swain, M. (1997). From semantic to syntactic processing: How can we promote it in the immersion classroom. In R. K. Johnson, & M. Swain (Eds.). *Immersion education: International perspectives* (pp. 284–310). Cambridge, UK: Cambridge University Press.

Krashen, S. (1982). *Principles and practice in second language acquisition.* Oxford: Pergamon.

Krashen, S., & Terrell, T. (1983). *The natural approach.* Oxford: Pergamon.

Lewis, M. (1993). *The lexical approach.* Hove, UK: Language Teaching Publications.

Lightbown, P., Spada, N., & Wallace, R. (1980). Some effects of instruction on child and adolescent ESL learners. In R. Scarcella & S. Krashen (Eds.), *Research in second language acquisition* (pp. 74–98). Rowley, MA: Newbury House.

Long, M. (1988). Instructed second language acquisition. In L. Beebe (Ed.), *Issues in second language acquisition: Multiple perspectives* (pp. 113–142). New York: Newbury House.

Long, M. (1991). Focus on form: A design feature in language teaching methodology. In K. de Bot, D. Coste, R. Ginsberg, & C. Kramsch (Eds.), *Foreign language research in cross-cultural perspectives* (pp. 39–52). Amsterdam: John Benjamins.

Loschky, L., & Bley-Vroman, R. (1993). Grammar and task-based methodology. In G. Crookes & S. Gass (Eds.), *Tasks and language learning: Integrating theory and practice* (pp. 123–167). Clevedon, UK: Multilingual Matters.

Pica, T. (1983). Adult acquisition of English a second language under different conditions of exposure. *Language Learning, 33*, 465–497.

Pienemann, M. (1984). Psychological constraints on the teachability of languages. *Studies in Second Language Acquisition, 6*, 186–214.

Prabhu, N. (1987). *Second language pedagogy.* Oxford: Oxford University Press.

Reiss, M. (1985). The good language learner: Another look. *Canadian Modern Language Review, 41*, 511–523.

Schmidt, R., & Frota, S. (1986). Developing basic conversational ability in a second language: A case study of an adult learner. In R. Day (Ed.). *Talking to learn: Conversation in a second language* (pp. 237–326). Rowley, MA.: Newbury House.

Schumann, J. (1978). *The pidginization processes: A model for second language acquisition.* Rowley, MA.: Newbury House.

Skehan, P. (1988). *A cognitive approach of language learning.* Oxford: Oxford University Press.

Spada, N. (1986). The interaction between types of content and type of instruction: Some effects on the L2 proficiency of adult learners. *Studies in Second Language Acquisition, 8*, 181–199.

Spada, N., & Lightbown, P. (1999). Instruction, first language influence and developmental readiness in second language acquisition. *Modern Language Journal, 18,* 1–22.

Swain, M. (1985). Communicative competence: Some roles of comprehensible input and comprehensible output in its development. In S. Gass & C. Madden (Eds.), *Input in second language acquisition* (pp. 235–255). Rowley, MA: Newbury House.

White, L. (1987). Against comprehensible input: The input hypothesis and the development of second language competence. *Applied Linguistics, 8,* 95–110.

Yalden, J. (1983). *The communicative syllabus: Evolution, design and implementation.* Oxford: Pergamon.

Zobl, H. (1985). Grammars in search of input and intake. In S. Gass & C. Madden (Eds.), *Input in second language acquisition* (pp. 329–344). Rowley, MA: Newbury House.

Accuracy and Fluency Revisited

Jack C. Richards
SEAMEO Regional Language Centre, Singapore

The status of grammar-focused teaching (or as it is currently referred to, *form-focused instruction,* see Doughty & Williams, 1998) has undergone a major reassessment in the past 25 years. The advent of communicative language teaching ostensibly saw the demise of grammar-based instruction: Grammatical syllabi were superseded by communicative ones based on functions or tasks, grammar-based methodologies such as the Presentation-Practice-Production (P-P-P) lesson format underlying the situational approach gave way to function and skill-based teaching, and accuracy activities such as drills and grammar practice were replaced by fluency activities based on interactive small group work. This led to the emergence of a *fluency-first pedagogy* (Brumfit, 1979) in which priority is given to providing opportunities for information sharing and negotiation of meaning in the classroom, and where students' grammar needs are determined on the basis of their performance on fluency tasks rather predetermined by a grammatical syllabus. The present chapter examines the issue of the level of language often used by learners during fluency work and reviews approaches to addressing this problem within a communicative methodology.

Article reproduced from *Prospect 14,* with permission from the National Centre for English Language Teaching and Research (NCELTR), Australia. © Macquarie University.

FROM GRAMMAR-FOCUSED
TO TASK-FOCUSED INSTRUCTION

The movement away from grammar-focused instruction has been supported by the findings of second language acquisition research. Skehan (1996a, p. 19) observes, "The underlying theory for a P-P-P approach has now been discredited. The belief that a precise focus on a particular form leads to learning and automatization (that learners will learn what is taught in the order in which it is taught) no longer carries much credibility in linguistics or psychology."

A core component of fluency-based pedagogy is task work. Nunan (1989, p. 10) offers this definition: "the communicative task [is] a piece of classroom work which involves learners in comprehending, manipulating, producing or interacting in the target language while their attention is principally focussed on meaning rather than form. The task should also have a sense of completeness, being able to stand alone as a communicative act in its own right."

While carrying out communicative tasks, learners are said to receive comprehensible input and modified output, processes believed central to second language acquisition and that ultimately lead to the development of both linguistic and communicative competence (Pica et al., 1989). The belief that successful language learning depends on immersing students in tasks that require them to negotiate meaning and engage in naturalistic and meaningful communication is at the heart of much current thinking about language teaching and has lead to a proliferation of teaching materials built around this concept, such as discussion-based materials, communication games, simulations, role-plays, and other group or pair-work activities. Skehan (1996 p. 17) comments optimistically, "the research strand of SLA now underpins neatly the range of classroom activities imaginatively devised by practitioners of CLT."

The differences between traditional grammar-focused activities and communicative task work can be summarized as as in Table 3–1 (Brumfit, 1979; Ellis, 1994; Lubelska & Mathews, 1997; Skehan, 1996a; Tarone, 1983).

In advocating the use of task work in language teaching the assumption is that their use will help learners develop not only communicative skills but also an acceptable standard of linguistic performance. Task work is not intended to promote development of a nonstandard form of English but is seen as part of the process by which linguistic and communicative competence are developed. Skehan (1996a) distinguishes between strong and weak forms of a task-based approach. A strong form sees tasks as the basic unit of teaching and drives the acquisition process. A weak form sees tasks as a vital part of language instruction but is embedded in a more complex pedagogical context. Tasks are necessary, but may be preceded by focused

TABLE 3.1
Summary of Grammar- and Task-Focused Activities

Grammar-Focused Activities

Reflect typical classroom use of language
Focus on the formation of correct examples of language
Produce language for display (i.e., as evidence of learning)
Call on explicit knowledge
Elicit a careful (monitored) speech style
Reflect controlled performance
Practice language out of context
Practice small samples of language
Do not require real authentic communication

Task-Focused Activities

Reflect natural language use
Call on implicit knowledge
Elicit a vernacular speech style
Reflect automatic performance
Require the use of improvising, paraphrasing, repair, and reorganization
Produce language that is not always predictable
Allow students to select the language they use
Require real communication

instruction, and after use, may be followed by focused instruction that is contingent on task performance (Skehan, 1996a, p. 39).

But how is an acceptable level of linguistic performance achieved during task work? The strong form of task-based teaching suggests that form will largely look after itself with incidental support from the teacher. Grammar has a mediating role, rather than serving as an end in itself (Thornbury, 1998, p. 112), something that is said to empower both teachers and learners. "The teacher and the learner have a remarkable degree of flexibility, for they are presented with a set of general learning objectives and problem-solving tasks, and not a list of specific linguistic items" (Kumaravadivelu, 1993, p. 99). As students carry out communicative tasks they engage in the process of negotiation of meaning, employing strategies such as comprehension checks, confirmation checks, and clarification requests. These strategies lead to a gradual modification of learners' language output, which over time takes on more and more target-like features.

SECOND THOUGHTS ABOUT TASK WORK

Despite the claims made for task work and the positive effects of fluency activities on classroom motivation, interest level, and use of authentic language, a number of concerns remain. One relates to claims made for mod-

ification of the learner's linguistic output through the process of negotiation of meaning. In a careful reexamination of negotiation of meaning,
Foster (1998) studied intermediate English as a foreign language (EFL)
students completing information-gap tasks in dyads and small groups. She
found little evidence for negotiated interaction and modified utterances
and concludes that "contrary to much SLA theorising, negotiating for
meaning is not a strategy that language learners are predisposed to employ
when they encounter gaps in their understanding" (p. 1) (see also
Musumeci, 1996, for similar findings).

Another concern is the effect of extensive task-work activities on the
development of linguistic competence. What is often observed in language
classrooms during fluency work is communication marked by low levels of
linguistic accuracy. Higgs and Clifford (1982), for example, reporting
experience with foreign language teaching programs at the Defence Language Institute, observed:

> In programs that have as curricular goals an early emphasis on unstructured
> communication activities—minimising, or excluding entirely, considerations
> of grammatical accuracy—it is possible in a fairly short time . . . to provide stu-
> dents with a relatively large vocabulary and a high degree of fluency. . . .
> These same data suggest that the premature immersion of a student into an
> unstructured or "free" conversational setting before certain fundamental lin-
> guistic structures are more or less in place is not done without cost. There
> appears to be a real danger of leading students too rapidly into the "creative
> aspects of language use", in that if successful communication is encouraged
> and rewarded for its own sake, the effect seems to be one of rewarding at the
> same time the incorrect communication strategies seized upon in attempting
> to deal with the communication strategies presented. (p. 78)

This is the issue of the grammar gap in task work referred to in the title of
this chapter. The grammar-gap problem has also been identified by Swain
and her colleagues (1988) in Toronto, who have studied the acquisition of
French by English-speaking students in French immersion classes. It was
found that in spite of the input-rich communicatively oriented classrooms
the students participated in, the students did not develop native-like proficiency in French. Although they are fairly well able to get their meanings
across in French, even at intermediate and higher grade levels, they often do
so with nontarget-like morphology, syntax, and discourse patterns. (pp. 5–6).

An example of the quality of language used by students during task work
is seen in the following example, observed during a role-play task in an EFL
secondary school English lesson (Lubelski & Mathews, 1997). One student
is playing the role of a doctor and the other a patient, and they are dis-
cussing a health problem.

Speaker 1: I'm thirty-four . . . thirty-five.

Speaker 2: Thirty . . . five?

Speaker 1: Five.

Speaker 2: Problem?

Speaker 1: I have . . . a pain in my throat.

Speaker 2: [In Spanish: What do you have?]

Speaker 1: A pain.

Speaker 2: [In Spanish. What's that?]

Speaker 1: [In Spanish: A pain.] A pain.

Speaker 2: Ah, pain.

Speaker 1: Yes, and it makes problem to me when I . . . swallow.

Speaker 2: When do you have . . . ?

Speaker 1: Since yesterday morning.

Speaker 2: [In Spanish: No, I mean, where do you have the pain?] It has a pain in . . . ?

Speaker 1: In my throat.

Speaker 2: Ah. Let it . . . getting, er . . . worse. It can be, er . . . very serious problem and you are, you will, go to New York to operate, so . . . operation, er . . . the seventh, the 27th, er May. And treatment, you can't eat, er, big meal.

Speaker 1: Big meal, I er, . . . I don't know? Fish?

Speaker 2: Fish you have to eat, er fish, for example.

This example illustrates the point made by Higgs and Clifford (1982, p. 61) that in task work "communicative competence is [often used as] a term for communication *in spite of* language, rather than communication *through* language." Skehan suggests that the level of communication often observed during task work results from students relying on a lexicalized system of communication that is heavily dependent on vocabulary and memorized chunks of language as well as both verbal and nonverbal communication strategies to get meanings across. Accurate use of grammar or phonology is not necessary in such cases. In the example above, for example, one student avoids asking (or does not know how to ask), "What is your problem?" and simply says, "Problem?" Instead of saying, "How long have you had the problem" the students asks, "When do you have . . . ?" Instead of negotiating for the intended question the second student jumps straight in with the expected answer: "Since yesterday morning." There is no recognition of the inappropriateness of "*it makes problem to me when I . . . swallow.*" Skehan (1996a, p. 21) comments:

This [task-based] approach places a premium on communication strategies linked to lexicalized communication. These strategies provide an effective incentive for learners to make best use of the language they already have. But they do not encourage a focus on form. They do not provide an incentive for structural change towards an interlanguage system with greater complexity. The advantages of such an approach are greater fluency and the capacity to solve communication problems. But these advantages may be bought at too high a price if it compromises continued language growth and interlanguage development. Such learners, in other words, may rely on prefabricated chunks to solve their communication problems. But such solutions do not lead them to longer-term progress, even though they do lead to resourcefulness in solving problems.

This poses the central dilemma of communicative language teaching, namely, how can a communicative orientation to teaching be reconciled with the need to ensure learners achieve acceptable levels of grammatical accuracy? The answer to this question depends on an understanding of the processes of second language learning.

GRAMMAR IN RELATION TO SECOND LANGUAGE ACQUISITION PROCESSES

Drawing on VanPatten (1993), Ellis (1994), Skehan (1996a) and others, five stages of the learning process will be distinguished here in order to arrive at a rationale for grammar-focused instruction in teaching and teaching materials: input, intake, acquisition, access, output.

A Model of Second Language Learning and Use

I	II	III	IV	V
Input ——	Intake ——	Acquisition ——	Access ——	Output

I. Input

Input refers to language sources that are used to initiate the language learning process. Textbooks and commercial materials, teacher-made materials, and teacher-initiated classroom discourse all serve as input sources in language classes. Traditionally, teaching materials were planned around or included an explicit linguistic syllabus on the assumption that this determined the learner's acquisition of the target language. Some theorists see no need for any such syllabus, arguing that a syllabus must be meaning-based and that grammar needs can be dealt with incidentally. Krashen (1985) represents this extreme position, arguing that exposure to comprehensible target language input is in itself sufficient to trigger acquisition. Others would accept the inclusion of some form of a linguistic syllabus, not on the grounds that it represents an acquisition sequence but that it provides a way of simplifying the input. Grammatical simplification is seen as essential in providing input at an appropriate level of difficulty.

At the input stage in language learning an attempt may be made to focus learners' attention on particular linguistic features of the input (sometimes known as "input enhancement") by such means as:

Simplification of input: the language corpus the learners are exposed to (both via textbooks and the teacher's discourse) may contain a restricted set of tenses and structures.

Frequency of exposure: a target form may occur frequently within a source text (such as when a text is written to bring in several occurrences of the past tense or the past continuous).

Explicit instruction: a target form may be presented formally together with information about how it is used, followed by practice.

Implicit instruction: students' attention may be drawn to a target form, and they may have to induce the rule or system underlying its use.

Consciousness raising: activities are provided to make learners aware of certain linguistic features in the input, without necessarily requiring them to produce the features.

From a current perspective (unlike earlier perspectives in which some of these processes were assumed to result in learning) none of these approaches to providing a grammatical focus at the input stage are in themselves assumed to bring about learning; however, they are intended to facilitate the next stage in the learning process, intake.

II. Intake

VanPatten (1993, p. 436) defines intake as "that subset of the input that is comprehended and attended to in some way. It contains the linguistic 'data' that are made available for acquisition." Some portion of the input is assumed to remain in long-term memory and form the data on which the processes of language acquisition are engaged. Factors thought to affect how items pass from input to intake include the following:

Complexity: items should be at an appropriate level of difficulty.
Saliency: items must be noticed or attended to in some way.
Frequency: items must be experienced with sufficient frequency.
Need: the item must fulfill a communicative need.

Generally speaking, we can assume frequency of occurrence in the language learning corpus (the input) to effect intake, but not always. The reason that some grammatical items such as articles, third-person *s*, and certain tense and auxiliary forms are acquired late (or never acquired) may be related to the fact that such forms have low saliency (they are not noticed) or low communicative need (they have no effect on communication), despite their high frequency of occurrence.

III. Acquisition

This refers to the processes by which the learner incorporates new learning item into his or her developing system or interlanguage. SLA researchers have stressed the need for more powerful theories of acquisition than the simplistic "imprinting through practice" theories of the P-P-P approach, and a number of different learning theories are currently available (Ellis, 1994). SLA research has demonstrated that learning is not a mirror image of teaching. Learners do not pass from a state of not knowing a particular target structure to a state of knowing and using it accurately. A number of processes appear to be involved:

> **Noticing:** learners need to recognize differences between forms they are using and target-like forms. A learner will not be motivated to try out a new linguistic structure if he or she is not aware of the differences between his or her current interlanguage system and the target language system (Schmidt, 1990). Schmidt and Frota (1986) found that the new forms a learner incorporated into speech were generally those that had been noticed in the speech people addressed to the learner. Forms that were present but not noticed were not used. However, not all acquisition is prompted by conscious awareness of linguistic features. Unconscious discovery of rules appears also to be involved.
>
> **Discovering rules:** according to the theory of Universal Grammar (UG), learning also involves identification of the grammatical variables that operate in the target language and account for the specific linguistic characteristics of that language, such as the rules underlying target language word order, clause patterns, nominal groups, phrase structures, and so forth. Currently some researchers believe learners have an innate understanding of grammatical variables. UG theory suggests that "learners are learning aspects of grammar that we are not teaching them" and that "they have unconscious knowledge of grammar systems which we, as teachers, are often unaware of" (Shortall, 1996, p. 38). DeKeyser adds a further clarification of this position (1998):

> If a structure is part of UG, and UG is accessible to the second language learner, then all that is needed is sufficient input to trigger acquisition, unless L2 is a subset of L1. In the latter case, negative evidence is required. . . . If a structure is not part of UG or cannot be acquired without negative evidence [information about what is not possible in the language] then a rather strong variant of focus on form, including rule teaching and error correction, will be required. (p. 43)

Accommodation and restructuring: VanPatten (1993, p. 437) describes these processes as:

> those that mediate the incorporation of intake into the developing system. Since the internalisation of intake is not a mere accumulation of discrete bits of data, data have to "fit in" in some way and sometimes the accommodation of a particular set of data causes changes in the rest of the system. In some cases, the data may not fit in at all and are not accommodated by the system. They simply do not make it into the long-term store.

Skehan (1996a, p. 19) sees restructuring as involving "a willingness and capacity, on the part of the learner, to reorganise their own underlying and developing language system, to frame and try out new hypotheses and then to act upon the feedback which is received from such experimentation." Restructuring is currently viewed as central to the process of interlanguage development, accounting for the way in which learners' grammatical systems show evidence of ongoing revision and expansion rather than progression in a simple linear order.

Experimentation: much of the learner's output in the target language can be described as the result of experimentation as the learner forms hypotheses about the target language and tests them out. The learner draws on whatever has been acquired and uses it in a tentative and uncertain way, constructing what the learner hopes will be target-like utterances. This is seen in much of the discourse produced by the learners in the role-play task cited above. Researchers stress that the trying out of new language forms is essential to the acquisition process and that acquisition is most likely to occur in contexts "where the learner needs to produce output which the current interlanguage system cannot handle . . . [and so] . . . pushes the limits of the interlanguage system to handle that output" (Tarone & Liu, 1995, pp. 120, 121, cited in Swain, 1998, p. 11).

IV. Access

Access refers to the learner's ability to draw on his or her interlanguage system during communication. The context in which the learner is using the language as well as its purpose (in casual conversation, in a formal or public setting, to tell a story, or give instructions) may affect the extent to which the learner is successful in calling up aspects of the acquired system: ". . . [A]ccess involves making use of the developing system to create output" (Skehan (1966a, p. 47). Skehan refers to this process as "fluency," which concerns "the learner's capacity to mobilise an interlanguage system to communicate meanings in real time." Access may be "totally, partially, or not at all successful, depending on task demand, previous experience (practice) and other factors" (VanPatten, 1993, p. 436). In other words, it may be much easier in some circumstances for the learners to use aspects of the acquired system than in others.

V. Output

Finally, output refers to the observed results of the learners' efforts. Although some theorists have proposed that output (active use of the language resulting in the production of language) is not essential to acquisition—that is, input is sufficient (e.g., Krashen, 1985). Others (e.g., Swain) have proposed that output is essential to acquisition. However, output is more likely to facilitate acquisition when the learners are "pushed," that is, required to reshape their utterances and to use the target language more coherently and accurately. This is confirmed by examples of second language users who speak a language relatively fluently but using a very restricted lexicon and syntax and who show no evidence of improvement in accuracy over time (e.g., taxi drivers and vendors in EFL settings), since the restricted purposes for which they use the language do not push them to expand or restructure their linguistic resources (Allen, Swain, Harley, & Cummins, 1990; Schmidt, 1983).

ADDRESSING GRAMMAR WITHIN TASK WORK

As the model of second language learning above illustrates, a focus on grammar can be addressed at several different stages of the teaching/learning process, that is, at the stages of Input, Intake, Acquisition, Access, or Output. Skehan proposes the following principles as the basis of a methodology that includes a focus on form as part of an overall communicative approach to teaching:

- Exposure to language at an appropriate level of difficulty
- Engagement in meaning-focused interaction in the language
- Opportunities for learners to notice or attend to linguistic form while using the language
- Opportunities to expand the language resources learners use (both lexical and syntactic) over time

The remaining section of this chapter examines how this can be attempted during the design or implementation phases of classroom tasks.

There are potentially three points at which a focus on grammar can be provided in task work—prior to the task, during the task, and after the task. These will be illustrated with general examples and also with reference to the design of a typical fluency activity—a role-play task. The role-play example is from Richards and Hull (1986), which contains a set of role-play activities that are structured to provide language support at the three intervention points described here.

Addressing Accuracy Prior to the Task

Pretask activities have two goals: (1) to provide language support that can be used in completing a task and (2) to clarify the nature of the task so that students can give less attention to procedural aspects of the task and hence monitor the linguistic accuracy of their performance while carrying out a task. Skehan notes (1996b, p. 53), "Pre-task activities can aim to teach, or mobilise, or make salient language which will be relevant to task performance." This can be accomplished in the following ways.

1. By preteaching certain linguistic forms that can be used while completing a task. For example, prior to a role-play task that practices "calling an apartment owner to discuss renting an apartment" in Richards and Hull (1986), students first read ads for apartments and learn key vocabulary they will use in a role play. They also listen to and practice a dialog in which a prospective tenant calls an apartment owner for information. The dialog serves both to display different questioning strategies as well as model the kind of task the students will perform. Other pretask activities used in the role-plays include brainstorming activities, vocabulary classification tasks, and prediction tasks, all of which serve to generate both language awareness and develop schemata relevant to a task.

2. By reducing the cognitive complexity of the task. If a task is difficult to carry out, learners' attention may be diverted to the structure and management of the task, leaving little opportunity for them to monitor the language they use on the task. One way of reducing the cognitive complexity of a task is to provide students with a chance for prior rehearsal. This is intended to "ease the processing load that learners will encounter when actually doing a task" (Skehan 1996b, p. 4). This could be achieved by watching a video or listening to a cassette of learners doing a task similar to the target task, or could consist of a simplified version of a task similar to the one the learners will carry out. Dialog work prior to carrying out the role-play noted above also serves a similar function.

3. By giving time to plan the task. Time allocated to planning prior to carrying out a task can likewise provide learners with schema, vocabulary,

and language forms that they can call on while completing the task. Planning activities include vocabulary-generating activities such as word classification and organization, information generating activities such as brainstorming, or strategy activities in which learners consider a range of strategies to consider in solving a problem, discuss their pros and cons, and then select one they will apply to the task. In Richards and Hull (1986) some of the planning activities include generating a set of questions that could be asked during an interview, prior to role-playing an interview. Ellis (1987) found that the availability of planning time affects the accuracy with which the learners' use some target language forms but only if planning time is used to focus on form (rather than, say, organization of information).

Addressing Accuracy During the Task

A focus on form can be facilitated during the completion of a task by choosing how the task is to be carried out. The way a task is implemented can determine whether it is carried out fluently and with an acceptable level of linguistic performance, or disfluently with excessive dependence on communication strategies, employment of lexical rather than grammaticalized discourse, and with overuse of ellipsis and nonlinguistic resources. Task implementation factors include the following:

Participation: whether the task is completed individually or with other learners

Procedures: the number of procedures involved in completing the task

Resources: the materials and other resources provided for the learners to use while completing the task

Order: the sequencing of a task in relation to previous tasks

Product: the outcome or outcomes students produce, such as a written product or an oral one

The effect of participation arrangement on task performance has been noted by Brown et al., 1984 (cited in Skehan, 1996a, p. 26): "The greater the number of participants there are in a task the greater the pressure on those transacting a task, and the greater the likelihood that fluency will predominate as a goal over accuracy and complexity/restructuring."

Foster found that dyads rather than groups "coupled with the obligation to exchange information, was the 'best' for language production, negotiations and modified output" (1988, p. 18).

Resources students work from can also affect task performance. The use of pictures in a storytelling task might provide an accessible framework or schema for the story, clarifying such elements as setting, characters, events, outcomes, and so on, giving the learners more opportunity to focus their planning or performance on other dimensions of the task. Or in conducting a survey task, the design or the resources students use could have a crucial impact on the appropriatness of the language used in carrying out the task. If the survey form or questionnaire the students use provides models of the types of questions they should ask, it may result in a better level of language use during questioning and make other aspects of the task easier to manage, since less planning will need to be devoted to formulating appropriate questions. In the role plays discussed earlier (Richards & Hull, 1986), considerable refinement was needed of the cue sheets students used in carrying out their role plays before a format was found that gave partial language support and guided but did not dominate students' improvisations during each activity.

Procedures used in completing a task can also be used to influence language output. A task that is divided into several shorter subtasks may be more manageable than one without such a structure allowing students to deal with one section of the task at a time. For example, the procedures used in the role-play activities above consisted of

1. preparatory activity designed to provide schema, vocabulary, and language
2. dialog listening task, to model shorter version of target task
3. dialog practice task, to provide further clarification of task
4. first practice, using role-play cues
5. follow-up listening
6. second role-play practice

The order of a task in relation to other tasks may influence use of target structures. For example, if students are to carry out a task that requires the use of sequence markers, a prior activity that explains sequence markers and models how they are used may result in more frequent use of sequence markers during the performance of the target task (see Swain, 1985, 1988).

The product focus of a task will also influence the extent to which students have an opportunity to attend to linguistic form. A task may be completed orally, it may be recorded, or may have to be written. In each case different opportunities for language awareness are involved. Swain (1988) describes how tasks with a written product provide an opportunity for students to focus on form.

> Students, working together in pairs, are each given a different set of numbered pictures that tell a story. Together the pair of students must jointly construct the story line. After they have worked out what the story is, they write it

down. In doing so, students encounter linguistic problems they need to solve to continue with the task. These problems include how best to say what they want to say; problems of lexical choice; which morphological endings to use; the best syntactic structures to use; and problems about the language need to sequence the story correctly. These problems arise as the students try to "make meaning," that is, as they construct and write out the story, as they understand it. And as they encounter these linguistic problems, they focus on linguistic form—the form that is needed to express the meaning in the way they want to convey it. (p. 3)

Learners can also record their performance of a task and then listen to it and identify aspects of their performance that require modification.

By Addressing Accuracy After the Task

Grammatical appropriateness can also be addressed after a task has been completed (see Willis, 1996). Activities of this type include the following:

Public performance: after completing a task in small groups, students now carry out the task in front of the class or another group. This can have the effect of prompting them to perform the task at a more complex linguistic level. Aspects of their performance that were not initially in focus during in-group performance can become conscious, as there is an increased capacity for self-monitoring during a public performance of a task.

Repeat performance: the same activity might be repeated with some elements modified, such as the amount of time available. Nation (1990), for example, reports improvements in fluency, control of content, and to a lesser extent, accuracy when learners repeated an oral task under time constraints, and argues that this is a way of bringing about long-term improvement in both fluency and, to some extent, accuracy.

Other performance: students might hear more advanced learners (or even native speakers) completing the same task, and focus on some of the linguistic and communicative resources employed in the process (e.g., Richards, 1985).

CONCLUSION

While providing an appealing alternative to grammar-based teaching, the use of communicative language tasks plus ad hoc intervention by the teacher to provide corrective feedback on errors that arise during task completion may not be sufficient to achieve acceptable levels of grammatical accuracy in second language learning. Hence the need to consider how a greater focus on grammatical form can be achieved during the process of designing and using tasks. Skehan (1996a) sees this as involving "a constant cycle of analysis and synthesis: . . . achieved by manipulating the focus of attention of the learners . . . and there should be a balanced development towards the three goals of restructuring, accuracy, and fluency." In this chapter I have attempted to provide a brief overview of how this can be attempted through advocating what Skehan terms a weak form of a task-based approach. However, a number of substantive issues remain.

To begin with, we need a clear understanding of the goals of grammar-focused intervention, since as we have seen, a number of different processes are involved in SLA as well as various stages in the learning and teaching process. DeKeyser (1998, p. 62) points out that teaching may attempt to address different stages in the learning process: "instilling knowledge about rules, turning this knowledge into something that is qualitatively different through practice, or automatizing such knowledge further in the sense that it can be done faster with fewer errors and less mental effort." In addition, we need a better understanding of which target language structures are most amenable to any of the forms of intervention described above, and which are not. Some things can be worked out implicitly whereas others may benefit from explicit instruction. For example, learning how to use the past tense appropriately during narrative tasks presumably involves different kinds of problems from mastery of the article system. And although it has been assumed that focus on grammar should always be an integral part of a communicative task and not a discrete activity isolated from meaningful communication, this claim requires much further study, since it will depend on which stage in the acquisition process is being targeted. Because of the importance of linguistic form in second language communication and the amount of attention currently being given to the role of form-focused instruction in language teaching, we can expect these issues to continue to be at the forefront of applied linguistic theory and research for the foreseeable future.

REFERENCES

Allen, P., Swain, M., Harley, B., & Cummins, J. (1990). Aspects of classroom treatment: Towards a more comprehensive view of second language education. In B. Harley, P. Allen, J. Cummins, & M. Swain (Eds.), *The development of second language proficiency* (pp. 57–81). Cambridge, UK: Cambridge University Press.

Brumfit, C. (1979). Communicative language teaching: An educational perspective. In C. J. Brumfit & K. Johnson (Eds.), *The communicative approach to language teaching* (pp. 183–191). Oxford: Oxford University Press.

DeKeyser, R. (1998). Beyond focus on form: Cognitive perspectives on learning and practising second language grammar. In C. Doughty & J. Williams (Eds.), *Focus on form in classroom second language acquisition* (pp. 42–64). New York: Cambridge University Press.

Doughty, C., & Williams, J. (Eds.). (1998). *Focus on form in classroom second language acquisition.* New York: Cambridge University Press.

Ellis, R. (1987). Interlanguage variability in narrative discourse: Style shifting in the use of the past tense. *Studies in Second Language Acquisition, 9,* 1–20.

Ellis, R. (1994). *The study of second language acquisition.* Oxford: Oxford University Press.

Foster, P. (1998). A classroom perspective on the negotiation of meaning. *Applied Linguistics, 19,* 1–23.

Higgs, T., & Clifford, R. (1982). The push towards communication. In T. Higgs (Ed.), *Curriculum, competence, and the foreign language teacher.* Skokie, IL: National Textbook.

Kumaravadivelu, B. (1993). Maximizing learning potential in the communicative classroom. *ELT Journal, 47,* 12–21.

Krashen, S. (1985). *The input hypothesis.* Harlow, UK: Longman.

Lubelski, D., & Mathews, M. (1997). *Looking at language classrooms: Trainer's guide.* Cambridge, UK: Cambridge University Press.

Musumeci, D. (1996). Teacher-learner negotiation in content-based instruction: Communication or cross purposes? *Applied Linguistics, 17,* 286–325.

Nation, P. (1990). Improving speaking fluency. *System, 17,* 377–384.

Nunan, D. (1989). *Designing tasks for the communicative classroom.* Cambridge, UK: Cambridge University Press.

Pica, T., Holliday, Lewis, N., & Morganthaler, L. (1989). Comprehensible output as an outcome of linguistic demands on the learner. *Studies in Second Language Acquisition, 11,* 63–90.

Richards, J. C. (1985). Conversational competence through role-play activities. *RELC Journal, 16,* 82–100.

Richards, J. C., & Hull, J. (1986). *As I was saying.* Reading, MA: Addison Wesley.

Schmidt, R. (1983). Interaction, acculturation and the acquisition of communicative competence. In N. Wolfson & E. Judd (Eds.), *Sociolinguistics and second language acquisition.* Rowley, MA: Newbury House.

Schmidt, R., & Frota, S. (1986). Developing basic conversational ability in a second language. In R. Day (Ed.), *Talking to Learn* (pp. 237–326). Rowley, MA: Newbury House.

Schmidt, R. (1990). The role of consciousness in second language learning. *Applied Linguistics, 11,* 129–58.

Shortall, T. (1996). What learners know and what they need to learn. In J. Willis & D. Willis (Eds.), *Challenge and change in language teaching* (pp. 31–42). Oxford: Heinemann.

Skehan, P. (1996a). Second language acquisition research and task-based instruction. In J. Willis & D. Willis (Eds.), Challenge and change in language teaching (pp. 17–30). Oxford: Heinemann.

Skehan, P. (1996b). A framework for the implementation of task-based instruction. *Applied Linguistics, 17,* 38–61.

Swain, M. (1985). Communicative competence: Some roles of comprehensible input and comprehensible output in its development. In S. Gass & C. Madden (Eds.), *Input in second language acquisition* (pp. 235–253). Rowley, MA: Newbury House.

Swain, M. (1988). Manipulating and complementing content teaching to maximize second language learning. *TESL Canada Journal, 6,* 68–83.

Swain, M. (1998, April). Integrating language and content teaching through collaborative tasks. Paper presented at the RELC Conference, Singapore.

Tarone, E. (1983). On the variability of interlanguage systems. *Applied Linguistics, 4,* 143–63.

Thornbury, S. (1998). Comments on "Direct approaches in L2 instruction." *TESOL Quarterly, 32,* 109–116.

VanPatten, W. (1993). Grammar-teaching for the acquisition-rich classroom. *Foreign Language Annals, 26,* 435–450.

Willis, J., & Willis, D. (Eds.), (1996). *Challenge and change in language teaching.* Oxford: Heinemann.

4

Ten Criteria for a Spoken Grammar[1]

Michael McCarthy and Ronald Carter
University of Nottingham, UK

INTRODUCTION

In recent articles and books, we have reported some of the findings of our research into the grammatical characteristics of the five-million-word CAN-CODE (Cambridge and Nottingham Corpus of Discourse in English) spoken corpus (Carter & McCarthy, 1995a, 1995b, 1997; Carter, Hughes, & McCarthy, 1998; Hughs & McCarthy, 1998; McCarthy, 1998). Although these works have tended to focus on specific aspects of spoken grammars, a common thread unites them: the belief that spoken grammars have uniquely special qualities that distinguish them from written ones, wherever we look in our corpus, at whatever level of grammatical category. In our work, too, we have expressed the view that language pedagogy that claims to support the teaching and learning of speaking skills does itself a disservice if it ignores what we know about the spoken language. Whatever else may be the result of imaginative methodologies for eliciting spoken language in the second-language classroom, there can be little hope for a natural spoken output on the part of language learners if the input is stubbornly rooted in models that owe their origin and shape to the written language. Even much corpus-based grammatical insight (for example, the otherwise excellent

---

[1]The editors would like to thank Cambridge University Press for permission to cite examples from their corpus.

early products of the University of Birmingham COBUILD corpus project) has been heavily biased toward evidence gleaned from written sources. Therefore, we believe it is timely to consider some of the insights a spoken corpus can offer, and to attempt to relate them more globally to the overall problem of designing a pedagogical spoken grammar. We do this in the form of 10 principles that might inform any spoken grammar project, and which, we feel, give us a distinct purchase on this relatively recent area of pedagogical interest.[2] Each of the 10 principles will be exemplified with extracts from the CANCODE spoken corpus. CANCODE was established at the Department of English Studies, University of Nottingham, United Kingdom, and is funded by Cambridge University Press, with whom the sole copyright resides. The corpus consists of five million words of transcribed conversations. The corpus tape recordings were made in a variety of settings including private homes, shops, offices and other public places, and educational institutions (though informal settings) across the islands of Britain and Ireland, with a wide demographic spread. For further details of the corpus and its construction, see McCarthy (1998).

ESTABLISHING CORE UNITS OF A SPOKEN GRAMMAR

Even a cursory glance at a conversational transcript immediately raises the problem of the frequent occurrence of units that do not conform to the notion of well-formed "sentences" with main and subordinate clauses (see Lerner, 1991). Conversational turns often consist just of phrases, or of incomplete clauses, or of clauses with subordinate clause characteristics but that are apparently not attached to any main clause, and so forth. Hockett (1986) pertinently notes that linguists have tended to ignore such phenomena, but "speakers and hearers do not ignore them—they carry a sizeable share of the communicative load." Example 1 shows some of the kinds of units frequently encountered in a spoken corpus. Problematic areas for a traditional grammar, here and in following examples, are printed in italic type:

Example 1

Speakers are sitting at the dinner table talking about a car accident that happened to the father of one of the speakers.

---

[2]Although we claim that widespread interest in spoken grammars is recent, we do not wish to dismiss the pioneering work of grammarians such as Palmer and Blandford (1969), who were way ahead of their time in seeing what was important for a grammar of spoken language (for examples and a brief discussion, see McCarthy, 1998, pp. 17–18). Early spoken grammars, however, did not have the benefit of large-scale computerized corpora, and it is this we refer to in our use of the words "relatively recent."

Speaker 1: I'll just take that off. *Take that off.*

Speaker 2: *All looks great.*

Speaker 3: [laughs]

Speaker 2: Mm.

Speaker 3: Mm.

Speaker 2: I think your dad was amazed wasn't he at the damage.

Speaker 4: Mm.

Speaker 2: It's not so much the parts. It's the labour charges for

Speaker 4: *Oh that. For a car.*

Speaker 2: Have you got hold of it?

Speaker 1: Yeah.

Speaker 2: *It was a bit erm.*

Speaker 1: Mm.

Speaker 3: Mm.

Speaker 2: *A bit.*

Speaker 3: That's right.

Speaker 2: I mean they said they'd have to take his car in for two days. And he says All it is is s= straightening a panel. *And they're like,* Oh no. It's all new panel. You can't do this.

Speaker 3: *Any erm problem.*

Speaker 2: *As soon as they hear insurance claim.* Oh. Let's get it right.

Speaker 3: Yeah. Yeah. *Anything to do with+*

Speaker 1: *Yow.*

Speaker 3: *+ coach work is er+*

Speaker 1: Right.

Speaker 3: *+ fatal isn't it.*

Speaker 1: *Now.*

Here we may observe the following phenomena:

1. Indeterminate structures (is the second *Take that off* an ellipted form of *I'll just take that off*? Is it an imperative? Is *All looks great* well formed? What is the status of *And they're like?*)
2. Phrasal utterances, communicatively complete in themselves, but not sentences (*Oh that. For a car. Any problem.*)
3. Aborted or incomplete structures (*It was a bit erm . . . A bit.*)
4. "Subordinate" clauses not obviously connected to any particular main clause (*As soon as they hear insurance claim.*)

5. Interrupted structures with other speaker contributions intervening (*Anything to do with . . . coach work is er . . . fatal isn't it.*)
6. Words of unclear grammatical class (*Yow. Now.*)

An even more complex question arises with *joint-production* grammatical units; that is to say, when a grammatical unit is complete only when a second participant adds his or her contribution, as in Example 2.

Example 2

[Customer and a waiter in a restaurant:]

Customer: Yeah. *Let's just have er*
Waiter: *Some rice?*
Customer: Yeah.

These phenomena, normal in everyday talk, raise questions about the nature of basic units and classes in a spoken grammar, and the solution would seem to be to raise the status of the word, phrase, and clause to that of (potentially) independent units; to recognize the potential for joint production of units; and to downplay the status of the sentence as the main target unit for communication. But the fact that well-formed sentences exist side by side with a variety of other types of units raises further questions, too, which include: What status does the traditional notion of SVO clause structure for a language like English have in conversational data? Are the "ellipted" utterances of conversation really just a reduced and partial form of the "real" grammar? Or are the well-formed sentences of written texts elaborated versions of the sparse and economical basic spoken structures, elaborated because they have less contextual support in writing and therefore necessarily must increase the amount of redundancy? There are by no means simple answers to these questions, but one's stance toward them can have major implications for what is considered correct or acceptable in a pedagogical grammar. If we accept the integrity of nonstandard units in a spoken grammar, then in general terms a spoken grammar is likely to be more liberal in what it accepts as "adequately formed," which itself may be preferable to the term "well formed," with its connotations of native-speaker intuition. Native speakers, when asked to judge the grammaticality of decontextualized sentences, are more than likely to attempt a minimal contextualization (something akin to a written sentence), and their judgments may have no greater validity than that (i.e., that the sentence is grammatical or ungrammatical by written standards). Corpus evidence is different from intuitive judgments: It is not "in there" (internal, in the grammarian's or informant's head); rather it is "out there" (external, recorded as used, and preferably supported by widespread occurrences across a number of speakers). External evidence points us toward a socially embedded grammar, one with criteria for acceptability based on adequate communicability in real contexts, among real participants. It is evidence that cannot simply be dismissed as "ungrammatical."

PHRASAL COMPLEXITY

Pedagogical grammars generally describe the full structural complexity of any given unit (e.g., see Swan, 1995, p. 8 on the potential sequences of adjectives before noun heads), but significant differences may exist in the distribution of potential elements in actual discourse. The noun phrase is a good case in point. Although, in English, there is considerable potential for accumulating adjectives and noun modifiers before the head noun, this rarely in fact happens in everyday conversational data. If we take the noun *house* in headword position, for example, we find 1,379 occurrences of it in a 2.5-million-word sample of the CANCODE corpus. In these examples, where attributive adjectives occur, there is an overwhelming preference for simple determiner + one adjective + noun configurations, such as the following.

Examples 3 and 4

3. **Speaker 1:**   Yeah it's *a big house,* six bedrooms
4. **Speaker 1:**   It's *a large house,* lovely, just right

The longest adjectival structure that occurs with *house* is: *Detached four-bedroomed house.* It will be noted, furthermore, in Examples 3 and 4, that further specification of the house is given in posthead appositional items (*six bedrooms* and *just right*). In a mixed written corpus sample of the same number of words, it is not difficult to find more complex adjectival configurations.

Examples 5 and 6

5. Living in *a big, dirty communal house* eating rubbish . . . (*The Guardian,* October 13, 1991, p. 16)
6. The *cozy lace-curtained* house . . . (*The Observer,* March 22, 1992, p. 22)

The point about these examples is not what can be said, but what is routinely said. Any speaker clearly may exercise the option to create a structurally complex noun phrase in ordinary conversation, but he or she will probably be heard as at best rather formal and at worst pedantic and bookish. However, a pedagogical issue of some importance arises here: If we label structures as *said* or *not said*, we run the risk of returning to the bad old days of behaviorism, describing behavior rather than the system of language that users employ. A partial solution lies in how we define *grammar*. A useful distinction can be made between deterministic grammar and probabilistic grammar. Deterministic grammar addresses structural prescription (e.g., that the past-tense morpheme in English is *-ed* rather than *-ing*, or that *the* precedes the noun rather than follows it). Determinism has served language teaching for centuries. Probabilistic grammar, on the other hand, considers what forms are most likely to be used in particular contexts, and the probabilities may be strong or weak. Itkonen (1980, p. 338) makes a distinction between "correct sentences" and "factually uttered sentences," and that is the direction we are also pursuing here. Probabilistic grammars by definition need real data to support their statements of probability, as well as analytical evaluation to get at the form–function relationships in particular contexts, from which usable probabilistic statements can then be constructed. Probabilistic grammar as a concept has been around for some time: Halliday (1961, p. 259) saw the basic nature of language as probabilistic and not as "always this and never that." He has in recent years refocused on this problem, with the help of corpus evidence. His concern is principally with how often the items in binary grammatical systems (e.g., present versus nonpresent) actually occur in relation to each other in real data. He concludes that the statistics of occurrence are "an essential property of the system—as essential as the terms of the opposition itself" (Halliday, 1991, p. 31). Halliday would acknowledge that a probabilistic statement such as "single-adjective noun phrases are *x* times more frequent in corpus A than in corpus B" does not necessarily have great predictive power, but he argues that it is important for interpreting the choice of form. Halliday (1992) supports our present position in arguing for the importance of examining different probabilities of occurrence in different registers, since it is unlikely that items in binary systemic opposition will be equiprobable in a corpus of any particular register. Halliday's disciples within the systemic–functional school of linguistics have further investigated unequal probabilities of occurrence of grammatical forms: For example, Nesbitt and Plum (1988) take a similar quantitative line in their research into the distribution of clause complexes. In our own published research (Carter & McCarthy, 1999), we have used grammatical probabilities to describe the occurrence of the English *get*-passive verb phrase (e.g., *He got killed*, in contrast to *He was killed*), which occurred 139 times in a

1.5 million word sample of CANCODE spoken data. In our sample, 124 of the 139 examples referred in some way or another to what have been called "adversative" contexts (Chappell, 1980), that is, a state of affairs that is seen by the conversational participants as unfortunate, undesirable, or problematic. This is a strong probability, but does not preclude the occurrence of utterances such as *I got picked for the county*, which is newsworthy, but not "unfortunate" in its context (a tennis player describing the climb to success). Such "glad-tidings" examples, however, account for less than 5% of the relevant data. Equally interesting was the fact that 130 of the 139 *get*-passive examples had no agent explicitly stated, which is another case of a structural potential simply not being realized, in 93% of the recorded occurrences. We would argue that such probabilistic statements are in fact extremely useful in a pedagogical grammar; indeed, it is hard to envisage a proper description of the *get*-passive that would be pedagogically useful without including information for the learner about its overwhelming probability of occurrence in informal spoken contexts, with "unfortunate" events, and the unlikelihood of the occurrence of a typical passive *by*-agent phrase.

Thus, the issue of phrasal and other types of complexity and their different distribution in data may be subject to the principles of a probabilistic grammar, with the reminder that probabilities are not determinations, and that creative freedom and potential variation are always possible, in special circumstances, in order to avoid the grammar becoming overly behaviouristic.

TENSE, VOICE, ASPECT, AND INTERPERSONAL AND TEXTUAL MEANING

Linguists have long recognized the different distributions of tense- and aspect-forms in different kinds of data. A good example of this is Waugh (1991), who looked at the distribution of the French *passé simple* (or preterite) form, which seems to be restricted to certain types of written text. One of the key factors, she asserts, is the concept of *detachment*: novels, stories, historical works, tales, legends, newspaper and magazine articles, and so forth (where the *passé simple* is most used) "are addressed to whom it may concern" (p. 243), in other words, an unnamed and only vaguely conceptualized recipient. It is this interpersonal consideration rather than the pastness of events per se that determines the use of the detached *passé simple* form; in conversation, the same events normally would be expressed with the "involving" present perfect tense form, projecting and reflecting a quite different set of participant relationships.

Waugh studied written data, but in spoken grammar, the fact that communication is face-to-face (or at least, in the case of phone talk, in real time to a real listener) clearly also affects grammatical choices that construct and reflect participant relationships. One such feature of the real-listener relationship is tentativeness and indirectness, a politeness strategy that minimizes imposition and threat to face (Brown & Levinson, 1987). This often manifests itself in tense and aspect choices that have traditionally been proscribed in pedagogical grammar, such as the use of progressive forms with verbs considered to be unamenable to progressive contexts, for example, *want, like, have to,* and so forth. Progressive forms of these verbs may indeed be rare or nonexistent in written data, but are by no means rare in spoken, as in Examples 7 and 8, in which the speakers seem to be adopting an indirect or nonassertive stance.

Examples 7 and 8

   7. [Telephone inquiry to travel agent]

Customer: Oh, hello, my husband and *I are wanting* to go to the Hook of Holland next weekend.

   8. [Speakers in a business meeting]

Speaker 1:   So all of that. You see, when you devolve power as they did with the divisional structures, just all went off and did their own thing. And unfortunately *we're having to sort of come back* from that and say, well is that the most cost effective, because we've got to cut our costs.
Speaker 2:   Yeah.

Here, once again, we have a case for separating spoken and written grammar, and for making sure that our spoken grammar reflects the range of tense and aspect choices open to speakers to create appropriate interpersonal meanings.

The meanings created by tense and aspect choices may also be textually oriented. Such is often the case in oral narrative, in which speakers exercise considerable liberty in tense and aspect choice for the dramatization of events, or for their foregrounding and backgrounding. A considerable literature exists on tense and aspect in spoken narrative; for example, see Wolfson (1978, 1979) and Schiffrin (1981) for English. For other languages, see, for example, Silva-Corvalán (1983) (Spanish), Soga (1983) (Japanese), and Paprotté (1988) (Greek). This is not to say that written narratives do not also exercise freedom with tense and aspect choices (see McCarthy, 1995, for some instances of this), but, once again, the distribution of such choices is different in the written and spoken modes, and the variation and rate of change from one form to another tends to be more intense in spoken narratives. Example 9 illustrates some of the typical spoken patterns.

Example 9

Speaker 1 is telling a story about how difficult it was to buy his favorite ice cream, called *Magnum,* in a small, provincial English town.

> **Speaker 1:**   So *we're looking* in there and *we can't find* any Magnums so *we turn round* and *he actually interrupts* his phone call to say you know what you looking for and *we said* have you got any Magnums [Speaker 2: Mm] and *he sort of shook his head* in a way as to say no you know we don't get such things it was a complete rejection [Speaker 3: Yeah] and we, *we sort of took a step* back from the thing and *there it was* labeled Magnum.

Such variation (here between simple past and so-called historic present) is by no means random or unmotivated, but coincides with important segments of the narrative, in which listeners are, as it were, taken in and out of the story-world in real time, as though they are participating in the drama themselves.

The point to be made here about spoken grammar is that a wide range of strategies is available to speakers to create and reinforce relationships and to involve or detach their listeners, and that the verb-phrase morphology plays a key role in signaling these functions. The pedagogical grammar of the spoken language must therefore ensure that the full functional range of choices is described and made available to learners, who should not be artificially restricted by proscriptive (and incomplete) rules based only on written data.

Voice is also more subtle and varied in the grammar of everyday conversation than most teaching materials would have learners think. There is, naturally, a focus on the core *be*-passive in contrast to the active voice. However, when we look at a large amount of conversational data we see that, as already noted in the section "Phrasal Complexity," the *get*-passive, massively more frequent in spoken data than in comparable amounts of written data, adds a further layer of choice, reflecting speakers' perceptions of good or bad fortune, or newsworthiness. In fact, the picture is even more complicated than that in spoken data, with the *be-* and straight *get*-passives of the type discussed in the section "Phrasal Complexity" forming just two points on a gradient or cline of passiveness that involves other *get*-constructions and *have* in a variety of configurations of agent and recipient roles (on the notion of a passive gradient in English, see Svartvik, 1966). Some examples follow.

Examples 10–16

10. You see, if ever you *get yourself locked out* . . .
11. Rian *got his nipple pierced* and it was so gross.
12. She *got me to do* a job for her, fencing.
13. Right we've got to *get you kitted out*.
14. The tape seems to have *got stuck* . . .
15. When the police came, they called a local garage and *had two recovery vehicles free my car.*
16. Our next-door neighbor's house was broken into again and he *had a few things stolen.*

Not only do Examples 10 to 16 display different syntactic patterns (e.g., reflexive and nonreflexive objects, presence or absence of infinitive *to*), but they also display different nuances of representation, with 10 suggesting some sort of responsibility on the part of the recipient, 14 being somewhat indeterminate as between an event and a state, 15 and 16 differing in terms of volition, and so forth. The clear lesson is that a spoken grammar will devote detailed attention to such complex phenomena, which might otherwise be underplayed in a grammar source only from written examples.

POSITION OF CLAUSE ELEMENTS

Pedagogical grammars naturally look for the most robust guidelines for the user, and rules about the positions of clause elements are extremely useful. The positions for adverbials are one such area where recurrent errors by learners are flagged and/or warned against. The *Collins-COBUILD English Grammar* (Collins-COBUILD, 1990, pp. 282–285), although stressing the flexibility of adverbial positioning in the clause, gives the basic positions as final, initial, and medial (between subject and verb), and a warning that, for some English speakers, split infinitives (e.g., *To boldly go* . . .) are unacceptable. Eastwood (1994, p. 265) more directly warns against incorrect placement of adverbials between verb and direct object (e.g., *She speaks very well English.*). However, in certain spoken and written registers, most notably journalism, this latter "rule" is regularly contradicted in examples such as 17.

Example 17

Mr. [name] said he will fight *vigorously* attempts to extradite him to Britain. (BBC Radio 4 news, 3.8.98)

Moreover, in casual conversation in English, there is evidence that positioning is even more flexible, brought about by the exigencies of real-time synthesizing. For example, adverbials may occur after tags, and adverbs not normally considered amenable to final placement in written text regularly occur clause-finally.

Examples 18–21

18. Spanish is more widely used isn't it *outside of Europe?*
19. I was worried I was going to lose it and I did *almost.*
20. You know which one I mean *probably.*
21. [Speaker is talking about his job] It's a bit panicky but I've not got any deadlines like you have *though.*

The lesson here would seem to be that ordering of elements in the clause is likely to be different in spoken and written texts because of the real-time constraints of unrehearsed spoken language and the need for clear acts of topicalization and suchlike to appropriately orientate the listener. It is no surprise, therefore, that we find phenomena such as fronted objects to be much more frequent in conversation than in written texts, as well as emphatic placement of adverbials in first position.

Examples 22 and 23

22. *Those pipes* he said he's already disconnected; *the others* he's going to disconnect.
23. *The eighteenth* it starts.

Even more notable in spoken data, however, are the occasions when content matter is placed outside of the core clausal positions, in the form of what have traditionally been determined left- and right-displaced or left- and right-dislocated elements, or pre-posed and post-posed elements. Although left-dislocated elements are most typically single noun phrases, these can fulfill a variety of functions outside of the conventional clause structure.

Examples 24–28

24. *Paul,* in this job that he's got now, when *he* goes into the office *he's* never quite sure where he's going to be sent.
25. *A friend of mine, his* uncle had the taxi firm when we had the wedding.

26. *His cousin in Beccles, her boyfriend,* his parents bought *him* a Ford
     Escort for his birthday.
27. I mean typically, *an American,* you shake hands with an American,
     tell them your name and immediately they'll start using it.
28. Well, *this little story I was going to tell you about,* I was on holiday with
     an elderly friend of mine in Butlins, Barry Island, South Wales, as
     you know, and she asked me . . .

Examples 24 through 28 show that the preplaced noun phrases can provide content for the subject (24), an attribute of the subject (25), or the
object (26), can merely flag up an entity and repeat it in the upcoming
clause (27), or can simply provide a broad topical framework not necessarily repeated in any subsequent element (28). Left-dislocated phenomena
have been documented in a variety of languages (see, e.g., Aijmer, 1989;
Geluykens, 1989, for English, French, and Italian; Geluykens, 1992, for English; Blasco, 1995, for French; Rivero, 1980, for Spanish), and it is clear that
such choices reflect concern on the part of the speaker to bring the listener
into the appropriate frame or schema for understanding the upcoming
clause (often from a person or entity known to the listener to the new person or entity that is to be the topic). One only has to think how "unspeak-
able" and difficult to process similar clauses can be if uttered with the kinds
of embedding often found in formal written styles (e.g., *His cousin in Beccles'*
boyfriend's parents bought him . . .) to appreciate the naturalness of these phenomena in everyday talk. They pass without notice; conversational participants do not consider them aberrant, though they do not easily fit into the
conventional bounds of the clause (hence the recourse to terminology such
as "dislocation," an issue we return to later in the section "Metalanguage").
    Likewise, after conventional clause elements have been exhausted, fur-
ther linguistic matter may arise on the record, as in Examples 29 and 30.

Examples 29 and 30

29. And *he*'s quite a comic *the fellow,* you know.
30. [Talking about someone who has just had the disease, shingles] *It*
     can leave you feeling very weak, it can, though, apparently, *shingles,*
     can't it.

Here, noun phrase content is left until the end, as it were. Why should
this be so? Corpus evidence suggests that these right-dislocated elements
have a strong evaluative function, and usually occur in contexts in which
speakers are expressing judgments, opinions, stance, and so forth (Aijmer,
1989; McCarthy & Carter, 1997). It would be wrong, therefore, to dismiss
such patterns as "performance phenomena," or "afterthoughts" (see
Fretheim, 1995, for a good discussion).

Our criterion here for a spoken grammar must therefore be that elements that occur in unusual word orders as compared to written texts, and elements that do not fit easily into the conventional clause structure, should not be relegated to a dusty corner of the grammar, but should be accorded proper attention, because they play key textual and interpersonal roles in conversation. That such features are not peculiar to English[3] (on right-dislocation see Ashby, 1988, 1994, on French; Heilenman & McDonald, 1993, on French; Fretheim, 1995, on Norwegian) and may well be universal should not tempt us to assume they will simply be automatically assimilated or transferred, and learners may need to be made explicitly aware that such patterns are licensed and perfectly normal in the target language. Exposure to written data alone or absence of reference to such features in pedagogical grammars can only reinforce the prejudice that they are aberrations or irregularities of some sort.

CLAUSE COMPLEXES

In the first of our 10 criteria, we raised the problem of units of description, and mentioned the issue of subordination. It is often difficult to assign to a clause the label "subordinate". This is particularly so with what are conventionally termed nonrestrictive *which* clauses. Tao and McCarthy (1998), in a study of a corpus of British and American spoken texts, found that the majority of such clauses were evaluative in function, as typified by Example 31.

Example 31

I can't angle it to shine on the music stand, and the bulb's gone, *which doesn't help.*

They also found that many such clauses occurred after a pause, or after feedback from a listener.

Example 32

Speaker 1:   Well actually one person has applied.
Speaker 2:   Mm.
Speaker 1:   *Which is great.*

---

[3]We are often questioned as to whether right-dislocations are a peculiarity of British English, but they certainly occur in U.S. English, as an example from National Public Radio's *Morning Edition* demonstrates: *It's the mattress money of choice, the greenback is.* (On how Russian people hoard U.S. dollars: 8.25.98.)

In both cases, the *which* clause seems more like a second main clause (indeed, *which* could be substituted by *and that* in both cases, with no loss of meaning, to produce unequivocal "main" clauses). Speakers seem sometimes to recognize this fact, and main–subordinate "blends" occur.

Example 33

> **Speaker 1:** Nearly a hundred quid a week. But that's the average there, you know.
>
> **Speaker 2:** Mm.
>
> **Speaker 1:** *Which it's all relative I suppose.*

In the spoken language, clause complexes need reassessment in terms of what is to be considered main and what subordinate. This principle applies not only to *which* clauses but most notably also to clauses introduced by *because/'cos*, where the same indeterminacy applies (for a good discussion of these issues of subordination, see Schleppegrell, 1992).

Other types of clause complexes are rare in everyday conversation, even though they might be quite evident in written texts. This applies to several types of combinations of main and nonfinite subordinate clauses, such as those in Examples 34 and 35.

Examples 34 and 35

> 34. Both airports were clearly identified as to country, *it* be*ing* explicitly stated that Airport X lacked both radio and tower. (Cambridge International Corpus)
>
> 35. First *staged* at the Glasgow Citizens in 1994, and *described* by Williams as being a "comedy of death", the play sees Everett cast brilliantly against type as the rich dying widow Flora Goforth. (*The Observer*, November 26, 1992, p. 3)

Once again, corpus evidence strongly argues for a reexamination of the types of clause complexes found in spoken and written language and the need for rethinking the accepted descriptions of main and subordinate clauses.

UNPLEASING ANOMALIES

The title of this section refers to the fact that, in examining everyday spoken data, the researcher often encounters features that go against the grain, either of the researcher's own notions of acceptability or of more general feelings among educated users of the language. Occasionally, aberrations do occur in spoken performance (as they do in writing), but there is a difference between on-off oddities and recurrent, patterned usage distributed across a wide range of speakers and contexts in a corpus designed to reflect a broad demographic and social spectrum, as the CANCODE corpus is. When such patterns become so recurrent that they cannot just be ignored, one has to assimilate them into the grammar. We have already mentioned *which* clause blends that challenge the usual rule of nonreduplication of the subject (Example 33); these are by no means rare, and pass unnoticed in conversation. Example 36 is a further example.

Example 36

X's has had to be delayed because his teeth were slow coming, er, coming down, er, *which* fair enough, *that* was just one of those things, it was unavoidable.

Even more widespread are utterances that seem to contain "double negatives," but which are natural and common in the speech of all social and regional groups.

Examples 37 and 38

37. It should fit there, cos it's *not* that big I *don't* think.
38. **Speaker 1:** We probably won't see much wildlife.
    Speaker 2: *Not* without binoculars we *won't*.

Both Examples 37 and 38 occur in comment clauses, and this may be significant in opening the option of apparent double negativity. It is such potential correlations that spoken grammarians have to take into account when attempting to explain grammatical choices that defy traditional written norms, rather than dismissing the spoken examples as aberrant.

Another kind of apparent anomaly that recurs on the corpus across a wide range of speakers is conditional clause complexes that challenge the rule that excludes a modal verb from the conditional clause.

Example 39

If *I'd have* stopped I probably would have wondered what she was going to say. (Instead of *if I had stopped* . . .)

The important criterion here for a spoken grammar is that "irregularities" and anomalies that may go against the grammarian's instincts concerning correctness or acceptability should first be checked as to their distribution across speakers and contexts. When a sufficient number of examples from different speakers in different contexts suggest that a feature is normal and widespread, then it should be entered in the grammar, even though it may still be deemed unacceptable in more formal contexts or in writing.

LARGER SEQUENCES

In a recent study, McCarthy (1998, chap. 5) looked at grammatical patterns spanning several sentences or whole paragraphs in written texts and several clauses and/or speaker turns in spoken texts. Based on earlier research, such as that of Zydattiss (1986) and Celce-Murcia (1991), McCarthy's work looked at how sequential patterns of verb tense and aspect varied between spoken and written texts. In some cases, the patterns were the same in both modes, as with the *used to*-plus-*would* sequence, where, in both written and spoken texts, initial *used to* provides a contextual frame for the interpretation of subsequent uses of *would* as "past habitual":

Example 40

Speakers 1 and 2 are describing how they took part in a consumer survey that involved a remote computer automatically ringing their home telephone to collect data in the middle of the night.

> **Speaker 1:** They *used to* you know ring up early hours of the morning, well you *would,* the phone *wouldn't* ring, they *'d* ring that computer.
> **Speaker 2:** And they *'d* read it.
> **Speaker 3:** Yeah.
> **Speaker 2:** And it *'d* go through the phone.

Exactly the same sequence occurs in literary texts, as McCarthy (1998, p. 99) demonstrates. However, a common written (and formal spoken) pattern in news texts, involving initial *be to*-plus-*will,* as in Example 41, is extremely rare in everyday conversation outside of formal contexts such as meetings.

Example 41

ELECTRICITY CHIEFS TO AXE 5,000

> Five thousand jobs *are to* be axed by electricity generating firm National Power, it was announced yesterday. Smaller power stations *will* close but bosses pledged no compulsory redundancies over the next five years. (*Daily Mirror,* July 7, 1990, p. 2)

The same functional sequence of broad reference to determined future events followed by details seems to have as its nearest equivalent in spoken language in the sequence *going to*-plus-*will.*

Example 42

Speaker 1 is a health service worker informing Speaker 2 about a new "patient's handbook" that they are producing.

Speaker 1:   I'm sort of chairing the working group, em [laughs] a document that, that it's official name *is going to* end up being something like Patient Handbook [Speaker 2: Yeah] but at the moment it, it's lovingly known as the alternative Gideon [Speaker 2: [laughs]] you *'ll* find it on the locker next to the bed or something, yeah.

Observation of extended patterns such as these naturally depend on the willingness of the grammarian to look beyond the bounds of the sentence (or the immediate speaker turn in spoken texts), in other words to take a discourse-grammar perspective (Hughes & McCarthy, 1998). The criterion we wish to press home here is that grammatical patterns exist across longer stretches of text, and that we must take a discoursal perspective that goes beyond the sentence or immediate utterance to establish the degree of overlap or otherwise in such patterns in written and spoken language.

THE COMPARATIVE CRITERION

This criterion follows directly from the previous section. So far in this chapter we have emphasized difference, that a spoken grammar is in some crucial ways quite a different animal from a written one. The strong form of such a view is misleading, however. Quite clearly, much grammar overlaps between spoken and written, and it would be a disservice to our learners to have them believe that everything has to be learned from square one when the speaking-skills component of the syllabus comes on stream. What is needed is a thorough examination of a spoken corpus side by side with a good, balanced, written one, so that relevant differences can be revealed and entered into the grammar wherever necessary. An example of this might be a comparison of conjunctions as they occur in a spoken corpus and a written one. A pedagogical grammar entry might resemble Fig. 4.1.

Some conjunctions are particularly associated with written or spoken registers and particular positions in those registers. For example, *on the contrary* is very rare in informal conversation. In written English it is more common and usually occurs in front position (or much less frequently in mid-position):

> *He had no private understanding with Mr. X. On the contrary he knew very little of him.*

On the other hand occurs frequently in both spoken and written language. But the concessive adverb *then again* (always in front position) is much more frequent in spoken than written:

> *If it had been at the bottom of a councillor's street then I don't think it would ever have been built. But then again that goes on all the time.*

Other conjunctions more common in written than spoken language include *accordingly, moreover, furthermore, duly, therefore, as a consequence,* and *in the event.*

Other conjunctions more common in spoken than written language include *what's more, as I say, because of that,* and *in the end.*

FIG. 4.1   Linking in written and spoken English.

By the same token, there should be some way of indicating (perhaps as the default condition) areas of the grammar that do not differ from the written usage (e.g., the *used to*-plus-*would* pattern illustrated in a previous section). The comparative criterion is thus a practical one, designed to lessen the load and learning fears for the learner confronting a spoken grammar for the first time. However, a final point needs to be made in relation to written corpora: It is relatively easy to incorporate newspapers and other journalistic texts into a corpus because of ease of availability, access on the Internet, and so forth, but a good written corpus should be as widely sourced as possible to include the kinds of texts people read as a matter of daily routine (not just quality newspapers). This would include mass mailings, tabloid news, magazines, Web pages, E-mails, signs, notices and advertisements, and so forth. Some of these types of written discourse have evolved or are evolving more toward spoken styles, and it may be that the traditional conventions of written grammar, as based on highly literate authors, are not necessarily as highly represented in such text types as we might think. Research with such a balanced corpus might yield a better picture of the cline of usage that exists between formal, literary, and technical texts at one extreme, and casual conversational ones at the other (see Biber, 1988, for an excellent example of such comparative research).

METALANGUAGE

Throughout this chapter we have struggled, in some places more visibly than others, with a metalanguage that has not always been up to the task of describing the phenomena we would wish to embrace in a spoken grammar. This has been particularly noticeable in the discussions on units and on subordinate and main clauses, where we have often used scare quotes to hide our unease with the terminology. A metalanguage inherited from written-based grammars brings with it its own metaphors and assumptions, which can often create dissonance when applied to spoken data. Nowhere was this more apparent for us than in the section that discusses left- and right-dislocated elements. For one thing, we are unhappy with the notion of "dislocation" or "displacement," because it suggests either that something has been moved or that it is not in its rightful place. We see no evidence in real contexts that anything is in an abnormal position or that real language users have any problems with such forms when they occur. And yet we are at a loss to find a better term to describe the phenomena. In a book in which we offer extracts from the CANCODE corpus for class use, we suggest *heads* (or *topics*) and *tails* as appropriate metaphors for left- and right-dislocation, respectively (Carter & McCarthy, 1997, pp. 16, 18), but many may find these terms equally unsatisfactory. What we are in no doubt about is that the metaphors of "left" and "right" are page-driven (and even, for that matter, Western-alphabet page-driven, because other major world writing systems compose their pages vertically or from right-to-left), and totally inappropriate to spoken language, which has no *left* or *right*, only a *now*, a *before*, and a *next*. In this respect, the metaphor of pre- and postposing, as used by Hallidayan grammarians, is slightly less misleading. We do not consider the discussion of metalanguage to be a splitting of hairs: Metaphors are powerful, and the metaphor of the page as the repository of language is an overbearing one in our western cultures. Now that we can investigate language other than on the page (though admittedly, corpus linguists still tend to work with transcripts rather than original audiotapes), we urgently need to evolve a shared metalanguage among the applied linguistic professions that will adequately give form to our understandings of the grammar of everyday talk. Our ninth criterion for a spoken grammar is, therefore, a careful reflection on the metalanguage to be used, and an attempt to devise one that can communicate the special characteristics of the grammar of speech.

NATIVE AND NONNATIVE USERS

Our final criterion relates to the notion of authority in grammatical description. Put simply, the issue is: Who is to be the voice of authority with regard to a spoken grammar? The question arises because, in the past, societies have looked to their most highly literate members (usually great writers) in the quest for the establishment of standards of correctness in grammar. No such obvious authorities exist for the grammar of conversation. Equally, we have to take into account that, whereas in writing language users tend to strive toward standard norms within any linguistic community (such that in English, for instance, there are standard written norms embracing the United Kingdom, rather than a northern British, say, or west-country norm), in informal speech variety is of the essence (in the case of Britain there are indeed northern and west-country styles of speaking, along with many others). Variety in this case also includes phonological variation, and this can affect grammatical items as much as lexical ones (e.g., the various British pronunciations of the negative form of *I am*:/ɑɪ ɑ:nt/, /ɑɪ elnt/, /ɑɪ aemnt/). The evidence of a spoken corpus is only as reliable as the design of the corpus, and thus, as we have already alluded, great care must be taken to ensure that any entry in the spoken grammar is represented in a wide range of speakers of any broad-based linguistic community as defined by the grammarian for practical purposes (e.g., North American English, Mexican Spanish, Swiss German).

However, in the case of widely used languages such as English, Mandarin Chinese, or Spanish a further question arises, and that is: Should the spoken grammar of a language be that of the speakers of the original, colonizing language, or should it be that of its present-day users? This issue is particularly acute in the case of English, which has taken over as lingua franca in numerous domains across the globe, such that it is no longer controversial to speculate that its native speakers are in a minority among the total number of its daily users. There are extreme answers to the question posed, and some less extreme. One extreme answer is to say that one norm is required, and that that norm should emanate from the dominant colonizing community (candidates for which, in different parts of the world, in the case of English, would be British, American, or Australian varieties). This answer is quite understandably offensive to many highly proficient or near-native users of English in communities where robust local varieties have evolved (e.g., Malaysian English). Another extreme answer is to say that a spoken grammar should be as varied as its users. Clearly there are both practical and theoretical problems here; this would require a massive collection of data beyond the resources of most organizations (though the International Corpus of English (ICE) corpus project at present comes the closest to achieving this aim; see Nelson, 1996), and it is theoretically very difficult to delimit the boundaries of varieties (we have suggested how difficult it is simply to delimit a variety called "British spoken English"). Compromise solutions include targeting those nations where a language such as English has official status and is in daily use, but such a solution excludes the millions of business and professional users of English who communicate in our new global village in spoken English. The most realistic solution, at least for the present, would seem to be to have a variety of spoken corpora (some country-based, some more regionally or globally based, some native-speaker, some nonnative, some mixed, etc.), which could be cross-compared to establish a core set of grammatical features in wide international usage.

Shifting the balance away from the native speakers of colonizing communities has important implications for the basic concept and status of the native speaker. Just as a corpus of nonnative speaker speech will contain a wide range of speakers of varying degrees of proficiency, so too will any native-speaker corpus, and it becomes more difficult and complicated to decide who are the most "expert" users of a language like English, since many nonnative users will clearly be more proficient communicators and users of English than many native speakers. We thus alter the focus and enter the territory of *expert users* of a language as those to whom we may look as models, regardless of their status as native or nonnative speakers. We have no easy way at the moment of distinguishing who these users are; we have no spoken equivalent of an international literary canon of English. Nor perhaps should we even consider going down that path if we wish to be truly democratic in our description of English, in which case we are left with the (probably limited) resources of whatever corpora are available to us, and reliance on statistical evidence across groups of users (native and nonnative), without evaluation of their expertise as users, as to what should and should not be included in a more internationally motivated grammar of spoken English.

Our tenth criterion thus leaves us with more questions than answers, but it is no less important for that. The point to be underscored here is that the spoken language raises more immediate questions about the authority of its users than does the written, and where languages have become international lingua francas, the question of variation will almost certainly be uppermost. It is one that corpus linguistics can only partially solve, and one that raises as many ideological questions as linguistic ones.

CONCLUSION

The need to investigate spoken grammars is, we believe, an urgent one within the language teaching profession. Already committed as most of us are to a communicative methodology that stresses the importance of speaking skills, any well-evidenced information about how people actually use grammar in everyday talk must be a bonus to us. What is more, in a world where communications are developing so rapidly, it can only be a matter of years before anyone, anywhere in the world, can speak directly to anyone else in real time, easily and cheaply. In that world, spoken language, and the mastery of lingua franca (whether it be English or whatever replaces it) will be an empowering skill. We have argued that spoken grammar highlights the textual and interpersonal aspects of messages because of its face-to-face nature; it would be a severe injustice if we, as a profession, refused to investigate its grammar, or closed our eyes to what we can know about how real speakers use it in everyday life in order to help our learners become better global communicators. Our 10 criteria are probably not the only possible ones, and readers are invited to add their 11th or 12th. However, the 10 we have discussed have served the present authors as useful constraints in our own research and our applications of that research in the practical arena (see Carter, Hughes, McCarthy, 1999). We certainly view the design and implementation of spoken grammars as one of the most challenging areas in the practice of language teaching today.

REFERENCES

Aijmer, K. (1989). Themes and tails: The discourse function of dislocated elements. *Nordic Journal of Linguistics, 12,* 137–154.

Ashby, W. (1988). The syntax, pragmatics, and sociolinguistics of left- and right-dislocations in French. *Lingua, 75,* 203–229.

Ashby, W. (1994). An acoustic profile of right-dislocations in French. *French Language Studies, 4,* 127–145.

Biber, D. (1988). *Variation across speech and writing.* Cambridge, UK: Cambridge University Press.

Blasco, M. (1995). Dislocation et thématisation en français parlé. *Recherche sur le Français Parlé, 13,* 45–65.

Brown, P., & Levinson, S. (1987). *Politeness: Some universals in language usage.* Cambridge, UK: Cambridge University Press.

Carter, R. A., Hughes, R., & McCarthy, M. J. (1998). Telling tails: Grammar, the spoken language and materials development. In B. Tomlinson (Ed.), *Materials development in language teaching* (pp. 67–86). Cambridge, UK: Cambridge University Press.

Carter, R. A., Hughes, R., & McCarthy, M. J. (1999). *Exploring English grammar in context.* Cambridge, UK: Cambridge University Press.

Carter, R. A., & McCarthy, M. J. (1995a). Discourse and creativity: Bridging the gap between language and literature. In G. Cook & B. Seidlhofer (Eds.), *Principle and practice in applied linguistics. Studies in honour of H. G. Widdowson* (pp. 303–321). Oxford: Oxford University Press.

Carter, R. A., & McCarthy, M. J. (1995b). Grammar and the spoken language. *Applied Linguistics, 16,* 141–158.

Carter, R. A., & McCarthy, M. J. (1997). *Exploring spoken English.* Cambridge, UK: Cambridge University Press.

Carter, R. A., & McCarthy, M. J. (1999). The English *get*-passive in spoken discourse: Description and implications for an interpersonal grammar. *English Language and Linguistics, 3,* 41–58.

Celce-Murcia, M. (1991). Discourse analysis and grammar instruction. *Annual Review of Applied Linguistics, 11,* 135–151.

Chappell, H. (1980). Is the *get-passive* adversative? *Papers in Linguistics, 13*, 411–452.

Collins-COBUILD. (1990). *Collins-COBUILD English grammar.* London: HarperCollins.

Eastwood, J. (1994). *Oxford guide to English grammar.* Oxford: Oxford University Press.

Fretheim, T. (1995). Why Norwegian right-dislocated phrases are not afterthoughts. *Nordic Journal of Linguistics, 18*, 31–54.

Geluykens, R. (1989). The syntactization of interactional processes: Some typological evidence. *Belgian Journal of Linguistics, 4*, 91–103.

Geluykens, R. (1992). *From discourse process to grammatical construction: On left-dislocation in English.* Amsterdam: John Benjamins.

Halliday, M. A. K. (1961). Categories of the theory of grammar. *Word, 17*, 241–92.

Halliday, M. A. K. (1991). Corpus studies and probabilistic grammar. In K. Aijmer & B. Altenberg (Eds.), *English corpus linguistics* (pp. 30–43). London: Longman.

Halliday, M. A. K. (1992). Language as system and language as instance: The corpus as a theoretical construct. In J. Svartvik (Ed.), *Directions in corpus linguistics* (pp. 61–77). Berlin: Mouton de Gruyter.

Heilenman, L. K., & McDonald, J. L. (1993). Dislocated sequences and word order in French: A processing approach. *Journal of French Language Studies, 3*, 165–190.

Hockett, C. (1986). Grammar for the hearer. In G. McGregor (Ed.), *Language for hearers* (pp. 49–68). Oxford: Pergamon.

Hughes,, R. & McCarthy, M. J. (1998). From sentence to discourse: Discourse grammar and English language teaching. *TESOL Quarterly, 32*, 263–287.

Itkonen, E. (1980). Qualitative vs. quantitative analysis in linguistics. In T. Perry (Ed.), *Evidence and argumentation in linguistics* (pp. 334–366). Berlin: Mouton de Gruyter.

Lerner, G. H. (1991). On the syntax of sentences-in-progress. *Language in Society, 20*, 441–458.

McCarthy, M. J. (1995). Conversation and literature: tense and aspect. In J. Payne (Ed.), *Linguistic approaches to literature* (pp. 58–73). Birmingham: University of Birmingham, English Language Research.

McCarthy, M. J. (1998). *Spoken language and applied linguistics.* Cambridge, UK: Cambridge University Press.

McCarthy, M. J., & Carter, R. A. (1995). What is spoken grammar and how should we teach it? *ELT Journal, 49*, 207–218.

McCarthy, M. J., & Carter, R. A. (1997). Grammar, tails and affect: Constructing expressive choices in discourse. *Text, 17*, 405–429.

Nelson, G. (1996). The design of the corpus. In S. Greenbaum (Ed.), *Comparing English worldwide: The International Corpus of English* (pp. 27–35). Oxford: Oxford University Press.

Nesbitt, C., & Plum, G. (1988). Probabilities in a systemic-functional grammar: The clause complex in English. In R. Fawcett & D. Young (Eds.), *New developments in systemic linguistics: Vol. 2, Theory and applications* (pp. 6–38). London: Pinter.

Palmer, H. E., & Blandford, F. G. (1969). *A Grammar of spoken English* (3rd ed.). Cambridge, UK: Heffer.

Paprotté, W. (1988). A discourse perspective on tense and aspect in standard modern Greek and English. In B. Rudzka-Ostyn (Ed.), *Topics in cognitive linguistics* (pp. 447–505). Amsterdam: John Benjamins.

Rivero, M. (1980). On left-dislocation and topicalisation in Spanish. *Linguistic Inquiry, 11*, 363–393.

Schiffrin, D. (1981). Tense variation in narrative. *Language, 57*, 45–62.

Schleppegrell, M. (1992). Subordination and linguistic complexity. *Discourse Processes, 15*, 117–131.

Silva-Coryalán, C. (1983). Tense and aspect in oral Spanish narrative: Context and meaning. *Language, 59*, 760–780.

Soga, M. (1983). *Tense and aspect in modern colloquial Japanese.* Vancouver: University of British Columbia Press.

Svartvik, J. (1966). *On voice in the English verb.* The Hague: Mouton.

Swan, M. (1995). *Practical English usage.* Oxford: Oxford University Press.

Tao, H., & McCarthy, M. J. (1999, July). *Redefining non-restrictive* which-*clauses, which is not an easy thing.* Paper presented at the Speech and Writing Conference, University of Nottingham, 1999.

Waugh L. (1991). Tense-aspect and hierarchy of meanings: Pragmatic, textual, modal, discourse, expressive, referential. In L. Waugh & S. Rudy (Eds.), *New vistas in grammar: Invariance and variation* (pp. 241–259). Amsterdam: John Benjamins.

Wolfson, N. (1978). A feature of performed narrative: The conversational historical present. *Language in Society, 7,* 215–237.

Wolfson, N. (1979). The conversational historical present alternation. *Language, 55,* 168–182.

Zydatiss, W. (1986). Grammatical categories and their text functions—some implications for the content of reference grammars. In G. Leitner (Ed.), *The English reference grammar: Language and linguistics, writers and readers* (pp. 140–155). Tübingen: Max Niemeyer Verlag.

APPENDIX: CANCODE PUBLICATIONS (1994–2000)

Carter, R. A. (1997). Grammar, the spoken language and ELT. In D. A. Hill (Ed.), *Milan, 95: English language teaching* (pp. 26–32). Rome: British Council.

Carter, R. A. (1997). *Investigating English discourse: Language, literacy and literature.* London: Routledge.

Carter, R. A. (1997). Speaking Englishes, speaking cultures, using CANCODE. *Prospect, 12*(2), 4–11.

Carter, R. A. (1998). Orders of reality: CANCODE, communication and culture. *ELT Journal, 52,* 43–56.

Carter, R. A. (1999). Common language: Corpus, creativity and cognition. *Language and Literature, 8*(3), 1–21.

Carter, R. A. (1999). Standard grammars, standard Englishes: Some educational implications. In A. R. Bex & R. Watts (Eds.), *Standard English: The continuing debate* (pp. 17–43). London: Routledge.

Carter, R. A., & McCarthy, M. J. (1995). Discourse and creativity: Bridging the gap between language and literature. In G. Cook & B. Seidlhofer (Eds.), *Principle and practice in applied linguistics* (pp. 303–321). Oxford: Oxford University Press.

Carter, R. A., & McCarthy, M. J. (1995). Grammar and the spoken language. *Applied Linguistics, 16,* 141–158.

Carter, R. A., & McCarthy, M. J. (1997). *Exploring spoken English.* Cambridge, UK: Cambridge University Press.

Carter, R. A., & McCarthy, M. J. (1997). Written and spoken vocabulary. In N. Schmitt & M. J. McCarthy (Eds.), *Vocabulary: Description, acquisition, pedagogy* (pp. 20–39). Cambridge, UK: Cambridge University Press.

Carter, R. A., & McCarthy, M. J. (1999). The English get-passive in spoken discourse: Description and implications for an interpersonal grammar. *Journal of English Language and Linguistics, 3,* 41–58.

Carter, R. A., Hughes, R., & McCarthy, M. J. (1998). Telling tails: Grammar, the spoken language and materials development. In B. Tomlinson (Ed.), *Materials development in L2 teaching* (pp. 67–86). Cambridge, UK: Cambridge University Press.

Carter, R. A., Hughes, R., & McCarthy, M. J. (2000). *Exploring grammar in context.* Cambridge, UK: Cambridge University Press.

Hughes, R., Carter, R. A., & McCarthy, M. J. (1995). Discourse context as a predictor of grammatical choice. In D. Graddol & S. Thomas (Eds.), *Language in a changing Europe* (pp. 47–54). Clevedon, UK: BAAL/Multilingual Matters.

Hughes, R., & McCarthy, M. J. (1998). From sentence to grammar: Discourse grammar and English language teaching. *TESOL Quarterly, 32*, 263–287.

McCarthy, M. J. (1994, August). English idioms in use. *Language Teacher* (Tokyo), *18*(8), 17–18.

McCarthy, M. J. (1994). Vocabulary and the spoken language. In H. P. Longo (Ed.), *Atti del seminario internazionale di studi sul lessico* (pp. 119–130). Bologna: Clueb.

McCarthy, M. J. (1994). What should we teach about the spoken language? *Australian Review of Applied Linguistics, 2*, 104–120.

McCarthy, M. J. (1995). Conversation and literature: Tense and aspect. In J. Payne (Ed.), *Linguistic approaches to literature* (pp. 58–73). Birmingham, UK: English Language Research.

McCarthy, M. J. (1998). *Spoken language and applied linguistics.* Cambridge, UK: Cambridge University Press.

McCarthy, M. J. (1998). Talking their heads off: The everyday conversation of everyday people. *SELL,* vol. 0:107–128.

McCarthy, M. J. (1998). Taming the spoken language: Genre theory and pedagogy. *Language Teacher, 22*(9), 21–23.

McCarthy, M. J. (1999). Turning numbers into thoughts: Making sense of language corpora technology and observing language. *Language Teacher, 23*, 25–27.

McCarthy, M. J. (1999). What constitutes a basic vocabulary for spoken communication? *SELL, 1*, 233–249.

McCarthy, M. J. (1999, April). What is a basic spoken vocabulary? *FELT Newsletter, 1*, 7–9.

McCarthy, M. J. (in press). Captive audiences. The discourse of close contact service encounters. In J. Coupland (Ed.), *Small talk.* London: Longman.

McCarthy, M. J. (in press). *Issues in applied linguistics.* Cambridge, UK: Cambridge University Press.

McCarthy, M. J., & Carter, R. A. (1994). *Language as discourse: Perspectives for language teaching.* Harlow, UK: Longman.

McCarthy, M. J., & Carter, R. A. (1995). Spoken grammar: What is it and how do we teach it? *ELT Journal, 49*, 207–218.

McCarthy, M. J., & Carter, R. A. (1997). Grammar, tails and affect: Constructing expressive choices in discourse. *Text,17*(3), 231–252.

McCarthy, M. J., & O'Dell, F. (1999). *English vocabulary in use. Elementary level.* Cambridge, UK: Cambridge University Press.

McCarthy, M., & Tao, H. (1999). Understanding non-restrictive *which* clauses in spoken language, which is not an easy thing. *Language Sciences.*

Stanfield, C. (1996). English as she is spoke (conversation with CANCODE researcher Jean Hudson). *Cambridge Language Reference News, 2,* 2.

Grammar and Communication: New Directions in Theory and Practice[1]

Martha C. Pennington
University of Luton, UK

INTRODUCTION

Traditional grammars are unreal. Since ancient times, treatises and teachings on the subject of grammar have consisted of formal descriptions and prescriptions of sentence structure formulated to maintain a conservative, standardized register of language in close alignment with the written form (Crystal, 1995, p. 192). As part of this long-standing tradition, grammars of English (and other languages of Europe) have been built around sentence structures abstracted from an artificially standardized Latin model as applied to written language (Lyons, 1969, sec. 1.2). Traditional grammars have thus evolved as idealized, static, abstract, and artificial impositions that bear a distant relationship at best to the structure of the languages they purport to describe. They are therefore entirely inappropriate to the practical communicative needs of today's language students.

Is it any wonder that students of language—and often their teachers—find the subject of grammar to be esoteric and difficult? In my experience as a language teacher and program administrator, I have dealt with a large number of students who complained that their instruction in grammar was dry and seemingly irrelevant (for similar observations, see Crystal, 1995,

---

[1] This paper was presented in abbreviated form at a colloquium on the teaching of grammar held at the TESOL Conference, New York City, March 10, 1999.

pp. 190–192). In my experience as a teacher educator, I have found that required modules on grammar are often the most hated and feared among language teachers and prospective teachers—even more than those on research methods! New perspectives on grammar and the teaching of grammar are needed to bring it back from the margins and into the heart of language and the language teaching profession where it belongs. For grammar is nothing more or less than the organizing principles of a linguistic or (broader) communicational system, without which, there is no system.

SOME NEW APPROACHES

The nontraditional approaches of Communicative Language Teaching (e.g., Munby, 1978; Widdowson, 1978) and Functional Grammar (e.g., Halliday, 1985; Wilkins, 1976) have gone some way toward addressing the problem of lack of relevance and meaningfulness of traditional grammar and grammar teaching. Communicative Language Teaching has sought to address the gap in traditional language teaching between grammar and usage by a focus on the communicative process and the negotiation of meaning between participants. The communicative approach has, however, sought to fill this gap indirectly, as it does not necessarily include a systematic treatment of grammar, even one defined in communicative terms. In fact, many adoptions of "communicative" approaches represent an essentially structural-situational approach (Richards & Rodgers, 1986, pp. 34 ff.) that is, traditional grammar with "communicative enhancements."

Nor is the gap adequately filled by functional grammar, which, though representing an important advance in tying grammar to meaningful functions, is still essentially a classificatory system based on static, sentence-level, writing-based grammar (Rutherford, 1987, pp. 66–67). This is true even of the work of the premiere functionalist of the present day, M. A. K. Halliday, who observes (see, e.g., Halliday, 1985, pp. xxii–xxv, 201–202) that even his own grammatical descriptions represent essentially "product" views of language based on a grammatical tradition derived from analysis of written language. This is not to deny that Halliday's work has had a major positive influence on linguistics and language pedagogy (see, e.g., Lock, 1995, for a recent pedagogically oriented treatment) and has also been highly influential on the work of other linguists, in particular, the Birmingham school from which the Incremental Grammar developed by Brazil, highlighted in the present work, derives.

There is a need for fresh orientations to the system of grammar based on the reality of language learning and use that will give renewed purpose to the teaching of grammar. The purpose of this chapter is to explore current trends in linguistic description and theory in relation to language learning and communication as a basis for pedagogical recommendations. Four recent treatments of language are described with implications drawn for language teaching. These are Minimalism (Chomsky, 1995), Incremental Grammar (Brazil, 1995), Action Grammar (Clark, 1996), and Relevance Theory (Sperber & Wilson, 1986/95).

It should be noted at the outset that the four works examined here vary greatly in their orientations to language and may in fact be incompatible in certain respects. First of all, only Chomsky (1995) and Brazil (1995) are explicitly attempting to provide linguistic grammars; Clark's (1996) concern is with language use, and Sperber and Wilson (1995) have a focus on communication in general. Of the two grammarians, Brazil has a focus on performance—specifically, on speech—whereas Chomsky is concerned with competence, or the innate mechanisms and knowledge of language, a "cognitive system" or "module," as opposed to a "performance system" (Chomsky, 1995, p. 2). His orientation to grammar is therefore of a more abstract sort than that of Brazil, who seeks to capture the dynamics of spoken language as it is being generated. Brazil's focus on linguistic performance—specifically, on spoken language—means that the type of grammar he wishes to construct is essentially different from Chomsky's program of describing linguistic competence. In fact, Brazil, in the Hallidayan tradition from which his work derives, does not separate performance from competence. Like Brazil, Clark and Sperber and Wilson are concerned with the process of communication, although unlike Brazil, they have no specific concern to produce a linguistic grammar.

In spite of their greatly varying approaches to language and some opposing features, these four schools of thought, each in their separate ways, capture important facts about language that are potentially relevant for language teachers. Rather than advocating one or the other school of thought over the others, the attempt is made here to overview each of them on its own terms and, on this basis, to draw implications for language teaching. Given the wide range of orientations reviewed, any implications drawn will necessarily be of a general sort.

MINIMALISM

Minimalism, or the *Minimalist program,* was originated by Noam Chomsky and followers (e.g., Chomsky, 1995; Radford, 1997a, 1997b) as a new research program within the Universal Grammar (UG) approach to language. Most of the work in Minimalism presupposes a strong foundation in linguistics, particularly in syntax. One introduction to UG and Minimalism that should be accessible to language teachers with only a basic background in linguistics is provided by Cook (1997, chap. 11). A more extensive account, which those with some grounding in linguistics should find reasonably accessible, is that of Radford (1997b).

In Minimalism, the aim is to provide the simplest possible Universal Grammar, that is, the minimal grammar that can account for language acquisition as well as for the differences among languages. Consistent with this goal, Minimalism focuses on (a) the basic principles that the grammars of all languages must satisfy and (b) the ways in which these principles are realized in different languages.

The most basic principle of the grammars of human language is that of *Hierarchical Structure.* An assumption of the Minimalist approach is that in "the formation of syntactic structures . . . categories are combined in a *pairwise* fashion to form larger categories. One consequence of this is that phrases and sentences have an intrinsically **binary** structure" (Radford, 1997a, p. 97; emphases as in the original), in which one element is the *head* of the construction. Such an assumption means that complex syntactic structures can be built from simple two-part structures, which are easier for the human mind to process than other types of structures (Yngve, 1996). An example is a prepositional phrase such as *in the school* built in steps, first by combining, or *merging,* determiner *the* plus noun *school,* then by merging the preposition (*in*) with (*the school*).

An important basic principle of Minimalism is that of *Economy of Structure.* According to this principle, there is no level or type of structure in the grammar that is not absolutely necessary for describing the specialized cognitive system that is human language. This principle makes Minimalist grammars different not only from traditional grammars but also from earlier forms of UG, which often contained descriptively convenient extra layers of structure. The principle of Economy, if followed, guarantees that Minimalist grammars will be "optimal" systems, given the realities of human language.

Languages are the same in their principles; they are also the same in being structured according to a set of parameters. However, they differ in the values, or *settings,* of these parameters. A *parameter* is a "macroproperty" of language that determines other, less general, properties of language. Each macroproperty or parameter is a dimension of variation across languages that has a specific value in a particular language. In language learning, parameters are said to be set to one or another value based on the child's exposure to input from a particular language. In this view, learning a language involves setting a series of cognitive "switches" that "trigger" the setting of other switches and lower level linguistic features in cascading ("domino") fashion.

Consistent with other aspects of the Minimalist program, parameters are generally binary, that is, there are two choices for setting the values of each one. As one type of parameter, in the binary branching structures that are the basic units of syntax, heads may be in first or second position. Some languages characteristically have the head—for example, a preposition within a prepositional phrase—second (e.g., Turkish, Japanese), whereas others characteristically have the head first (e.g., English).

Parameters are set in early childhood as part of (normal) first language acquisition. The ability to reset these—as in the case in which a person abandons the mother tongue when becoming immersed in a culture where a different language is primary, or to learn a second set of parameter settings, as in the case of becoming bilingual—apparently declines with age.

The most significant source of variation among languages is the *lexicon*. The lexicon contains lexical items and grammatical morphology, which can be thought of as lexical elements that are bound to categories of "free" elements such as verbs and nouns, and subsets of these such as concrete nouns (*book, table, pen*, etc.) and stative verbs (*be, seem, live*, etc.). The composition of the grammatical structures of the Minimalist grammar is based on details of the lexicon, as the properties of individual lexical items are the determining factor as to which items can combine. Thus, collocation is an important aspect of the Minimalist program.

Consistent with the concern for differentiating language universals from language-specific facts, the orientation of Minimalist grammar suggests a contrastive pedagogy for the lexicon. Both interlingual and intralingual comparison and contrast can be fruitfully carried out, as a way for the learner to gain an understanding of the relevant semantic distinctions and classes of the target language. The parameter settings of the target language might also be taught by comparison and contrast with a particular language or languages known to the learners. In fact, a pedagogical principle of comparison/contrast is generally consistent with the Minimalist program emphasis on binarity.

INCREMENTAL GRAMMAR

What I will refer to as Incremental Grammar is based on the University of Birmingham tradition linked to the work of Michael Halliday, specifically, the approach of David Brazil as described in his *A Grammar of Speech* (1995). This is a highly readable book that can provide direction for a dynamic orientation to the teaching of grammar, particularly for those teachers who are familiar with a Hallidayan analytical framework and terminology.

Brazil's Incremental Grammar can be seen as extending or rethinking Hallidayan grammar to provide a "process" account of how people deploy linguistic resources in real time to achieve their communicative purposes. Incremental Grammar focuses on the step-by-step construction of speech over time, with Hallidayan functional grammar (taken in the broadest sense, including intonation) providing options for building incrementally from one element to the next. In place of clauses or sentences as the object of analysis, it substitutes "purpose-oriented increments of speech" (p. 37). If any of the resulting structures are the same as a sentence in traditional grammar, this is purely accidental.

Brazil (1995) starts from "a view of language as something happening" (p. 10) that makes him reject hierarchical, constituent structure approaches to grammar:

> Although some kinds of discourse can undoubtedly be analysed in accordance with a constituent-within-constituent model, it is less clear that such a model is necessary. . . . The constituent parts of events of many kinds can, of course, be perceived to partake in this kind of relationship; but at least some of those events might be equally amenable to description along increment-by-increment lines. (p. 6)

Incremental Grammar is a process and processing view of grammar that seeks to model the way people produce speech "piecemeal and in real time" (p. 21), from one moment to the next. This is done by a *chaining* of linguistic elements (e.g., nouns, verbs) to form *increments* of speech driven towards fulfilling a communicative purpose.

Discourse chains are constructed of "used" language, by which Brazil means spoken language used in pursuit of a purpose or function, within the broad domain of "the management of human affairs" (p. 26). Such used language generally involves a speaker in relation to another person, both parties cooperating to continue a discourse until a communicative purpose is achieved. Both parties are cooperative in "that speakers make the best judgements they can manage as to present communicative needs and do the best they can to satisfy them; and listeners in their turn assume that what they hear is designed to match those needs" (p. 31).

A chain is made up of two or more elements occurring in sequence. Each permissible chain contributes to forming an increment of a certain type, that is, with a certain purpose, such as a *telling* increment. The shortest possible chain that could be a telling increment is a noun followed by a verb, connecting to the following states:

Initial State → N → Intermediate State → V → Target State (p. 48)

According to this view, a communicator begins in an initial state with an intention to communicate something and an idea of how to do so, based on a perception of what the hearer knows. The speaker selects an initial element, for example, a noun such as *that man*, with the intention of building from this to a target state. A speaker will continue adding elements to previously produced elements until a target state is reached. For example, the speaker might add the element *is waving* (V) to *that man* (N), which with suitable intonation contour completes a chain that constitutes a basic telling increment. With a different verb, for example, *says* or *wants*, the chain would not count as a completed telling increment, because these verbs require objects to complete their meaning.

> Chains can be interrupted by *suspensions*, which add new information out of sequence: For instance, since the production of chain-initial N always entails a commitment to produce a following V, anything else which happens to occur will amount only to a putting-off of the obligation to produce that V. Although in the case of
>
> This woman finally asked her
>
> the adverbial element *finally* occurs "unexpectedly" after initial N, its occurrence neither cancels nor modifies the expectation of a following V that the N has set up. In other words, the Intermediate State after the intruding or suspending adverbial element is exactly the same as the state which preceded it. (Brazil, 1995, p. 63)

In our example, the speaker might add *over there* to *that man*, generating the chain *that man over there*. This chain does not (yet) achieve a target state but rather maintains an *intermediate state*, which may then be modified to become a target state by the addition of a finite verb such as *is waving*, with proclaiming intonation.

Proclaiming (falling) intonation signals achievement of target states and thus completion of discourse units (i.e., increments), whereas *referring* (rising) intonation signals ongoing development of discourse units. If, for example, a basic NV chain is produced with proclaiming intonation, a target state has been achieved, meaning that either the speaker's overall communicative purpose or some subpart of it has been achieved, as in:

$$\searrow$$

Proclaiming Intonation   *I'm going.*

If, however, *I'm going* is spoken with referring intonation, this signals the speaker's intention to continue the chain, as in:

$$\nearrow \qquad\qquad\qquad \searrow$$

Referring Intonation   *I'm going, (and I won't return.)*

In addition to simple chains such as N-V or N-V-N, there are various types of *extensions* that can be employed to continue a chain after a target state has been achieved—for example, a nonfinite verbal element. Chains may be continued beyond the basic requirement for meaningfulness if the speaker's purpose has not yet been fulfilled. In our example, the speaker's primary purpose might not be to inform the hearer that *that man over there is waving* but rather to give a reason for that behavior. If so, the speaker would continue adding elements to the discourse chain that would constitute further increments—for example, a telling increment beginning with *because* that would clarify the speaker's purpose in drawing the hearer's attention to the man waving, such as, *That man over there is waving because I asked him to*. Depending on the speaker's purpose, the discourse-chain might be extended by other types of increments, for instance, asking increments, as in:

$$\nearrow \qquad\qquad\qquad\qquad \searrow$$

That man over there is waving because I asked him to.

$$\nearrow \quad \nearrow \quad \nearrow \quad \nearrow$$

Do you remember last week when I told you I had a man I wanted you to meet?

$$\searrow \qquad \searrow \quad \nearrow \quad \searrow$$

Well, that's him: that's Greg. Come on over and I'll introduce you.

As this example shows, speakers' purposes in talking and their means for achieving them are often complex and become clear only as a discourse unfolds.

A chain begun by one speaker may also be continued by other speakers to fulfill their purposes. For example, a first speaker may ask a question to get an answer, but the intended respondent may not know the answer or may otherwise fail to complete the exchange in the way the speaker intended, such as by responding with a question, such as *Why do you ask that?* In such a case, the respondent initiates a new discourse chain that can be expected to progress in a different direction from that initiated by the original speaker. Eventually, the first speaker may (or may not) be able to return to the original question and have it answered, thus satisfying the delayed communicative purpose with which the discourse was begun. It is not uncommon for some communicative purposes to remain unsatisfied or to change in the course of an interaction. The content and direction of a discourse is unpredictable and can never be determined in advance.

Not only the structures but also the meanings of linguistic elements are determined by context. Brazil speaks of the "here-and-now" and "oppositional" character of spoken language that is exploited in the creation of meaning in real-time communication. When people talk, they create references "for the nonce," through deixis (e.g., *this, that*) and pronouns (e.g., *I, you, him*) whose reference is determined by the context of speech. They also build up meaning as much by what they do not include in their frame of reference as by what they do include. In the words of Brazil (1995):

> Seen in this light, the communicative value of the word can be said to depend upon the circumstances under which it is used. Instead of thinking of meaning as a property which is inherently attached to the word, we can focus upon the way people use words—and, indeed, other linguistic items—to create oppositions, as in "friend not relative," "friend not merely acquaintance," which are of relevance to whatever communicative purpose is presently being pursued. (p. 35)

Brazil also notes the importance of intonation in helping to convey the speaker's intended communicative purpose in context.

Brazil's approach focuses attention on the rationale behind a speaker's choice of linguistic means within the functional categories of grammar (noun, verb, etc.). In so doing, he attempts to capture the dynamic of grammar as a means of achieving communicative purposes. A grammar based on purposeful communicative increments requires an understanding of the purposes that human communication can fulfill and does fulfill in specific instances. Incremental Grammar is then a *situated* grammar emphasizing the interactive and context-dependent nature of linguistic structure and meaning, and implicating the speaker's planning and in-process decision making that allows communication to proceed. An Incremental Grammar pedagogy would thus be strategy- and practice-oriented, raising learners' awareness of the linguistic means available for fulfilling specific communicative purposes and developing their skill in making and implementing communicative choices while producing speech.

ACTION GRAMMAR

What I will refer to as *Action Grammar* is an approach developed by the psycholinguist Herbert H. Clark in his elegant book, *Using Language* (Clark, 1996). Clark's book builds a new synthesis based on the sociology of language tradition of Goffman and Schegloff (e.g., Goffman, 1971, 1981; Schegloff, 1979, 1980) combined with the "language in use" tradition of modern philosophers of language such as Austin, Grice, and Searle (e.g., Austin, 1962; Grice, 1957, 1982; Searle, 1969, 1980), and the more recent outgrowths of this latter tradition in Levinson's pragmatics (e.g., Levinson, 1983) and Sperber and Wilson's cognitively oriented Relevance Theory (e.g., Sperber & Wilson, 1995). In its clear and comprehensive presentation of the facts of human interaction and language use, Clark's book should prove a valuable reference for language teachers.

Clark (1996) begins from a view of language as one of the means by which humans carry out purposeful actions:

> What people do in arenas of language use is take actions. At a high level of abstraction, they negotiate deals, gossip, get to know each other. At a lower level, they make assertions, requests, promises, apologies to each other. In doing that, they categorize things, refer to people, and locate objects for each other. At yet a lower level, they produce utterances for each other to identify. And at the lowest level, they produce sounds, gestures, writing for each other to attend to, hear, see. These at least are the actions of speakers and addressees in the primary layer of language use. Strikingly, all these actions appear to be joint actions—an ensemble of people doing things in coordination. (pp. 17–18)

Thus, "speaking and listening are not independent of each other. Rather, they are participatory actions, like the parts of a duet, and the language use they create is a joint action, like the duet itself" (p. 20).

Similar to Brazil, Clark places conversational discourse at the center of linguistic analysis and description. Face-to-face conversation, which he sees as the basic setting for language use, is defined by the following characteristics:

Copresence:	The participants share the same physical environment.
Visibility:	The participants can see each other.
Audibility:	The participants can hear each other.
Instantaneity:	The participants perceive each other's actions at no perceptible delay.
Evanescence:	The medium is evanescent—it fades quickly.
Recordlessness:	The participants' actions leave no record or artifact.
Simultaneity:	The participants can produce and receive at once and simultaneously.
Extemporaneity:	The participants formulate and execute their actions extemporaneously, in real time.
Self-Determination:	The participants determine for themselves what actions to take when.
Self-Expression:	The participants take actions as themselves. (pp. 9–10)

Other settings for language use, such as letter writing or lecturing, may share some characteristics with conversation but will also have different defining features.

Clark also makes observations similar to those of Brazil about the unpredictability of conversational discourse:

> Conversations aren't planned as such. They emerge from the participants' attempts to do what they want to do . . . . The result is often a conversation that looks orderly even though each step of the way was achieved locally and opportunistically. Much of the structure of conversations is really an emergent orderliness. (p. 351)

Part of this unpredictability is a result of the situated nature of interaction, in which "meaning and understanding are created around particular events" (p. 13).

> Another aspect of unpredictability is the "multi-layering" of spoken discourse: The primary layer . . . represents actual people doing actual things. Higher layers represent other domains, often hypothetical, that are created only for the moment. It often takes many different roles, such as actor and stenographer, to create and support them. (p. 17)

In the extra domains created by multilayering, speakers can take on different temporary roles such as might involve speaking for or imitating another (e.g., in quoting, reporting, or narrating). They may represent shifts in frame of reference or persona by changes in register, as when a parent interlaces conversation to a visiting friend with remarks to a nearby child who demands attention from time to time, or by changes in language, as when a bilingual shifts frame of reference or persona when moving between a vernacular ("low") language and an institutional ("high") language in some forms of code-switching (Pennington, 1998). The multilayering property is a central aspect of language use of all types, and all competent speakers—even children—are aware of and make use of such layering of discourse.

To a greater extent than Brazil, Clark (1996) stresses that communication is (a) a means for achieving other purposes and (b) a species of joint human activity. He notes that:

> The tight link between language use and joint activities has been a source of confusion. Many phenomena have been treated as features of language use when they are really features of the joint activities in which the language is being used. These phenomena include coordination, cooperation, conventions, turns, closure, joint projects, opportunistic actions, and the accumulation of common ground. (pp. 387–388)

The joint activities that language use helps to fulfill range widely across communities of speakers: "Most joint activities depend on norms, practices, skills, and expectations that are shared by communities of expertise— Scots, physicians, baseball aficionados—and that cover everything from how to shake hands or deal cards to how to show deference or display emotion" (p. 388).

Grammars of language in real use must therefore be interactive in nature and relative to specific discourse communities and their communicative practices. They must show linkages within larger structures of human interaction and norms of joint activity that incorporate modes of behavior besides language. A detailed study of the many and varied types of joint activities in which humans participate is thus the basis for a fully adequate account of language.

RELEVANCE THEORY

Relevance Theory has been developed by Dan Sperber, Deirdre Wilson, and their followers as a general theory of human communication and information processing. The best known treatment is that of their book, *Relevance: Communication and Cognition*, originally published in 1986 and in a second edition in 1995 (Sperber & Wilson, 1995). A clear overview is also available in an article published in 1986 and 1987 (Wilson & Sperber, 1986). A general sense of Relevance Theory can be gained as well by perusing the introductory (literature review or background) sections of articles in the past few years of *Journal of Pragmatics*, which seems to have become increasingly focused on Relevance Theory and the development of its implications for language, communication, and cognition.

Relevance Theory starts from the realization that understanding a speaker's meaning requires much more than parsing a sentence and matching form to meaning:

> Many linguists have assumed without question that the code model of pragmatics is correct. It is easy to see why. There is no doubt that utterance interpretation involves an element of decoding: the grammar of a natural language just is a code which pairs phonetic and semantic representations of sentences, and there is no doubt that understanding an utterance involves recovering the phonetic representation of the sentence uttered and decoding it into the associated semantic representation. However, . . . there is more to understanding an utterance than merely recovering the semantic representation of the sentence uttered: there is a gap between the semantic representations of sentences and the thoughts communicated by utterances. (Wilson & Sperber, 1986, pp. 36–37)

In any act of communication, there is always less than full information between speaker and hearer:

> The existence of indeterminacies in interpretation suggests a fundamental inadequacy in the code model of communication. Where indeterminacy is involved, it seems that the most that communication can achieve is to bring about some similarity between the thoughts of the communicator and her[2] audience. (Wilson & Sperber, 1986, p. 37)

Relevance Theory focuses on the interaction of prior knowledge with utterance structure in the interpretation and production of language, with grammar providing options for cueing underlying meaning (Sperber & Wilson, 1995).

In using language, speakers provide some signals for hearers as to their thoughts or intentions, and hearers seek to interpret these, based on their knowledge of language and other things. Communication involves a process of inferencing in which a hearer seeks to interpret the speaker's intentions based on prior knowledge, a view of the current communicative situation, and perceptions of signals provided by the speaker, some of which are linguistic. These signals serve as evidence of the speaker's thoughts:

> On . . . an *inferential* account, communication is achieved not by coding and decoding messages, but by providing evidence for an intended hypothesis about the communicator's intentions. Communication is successful when the audience interprets the evidence on the intended lines. Failures in communication result from misinterpretation of the evidence provided. Indeterminacy results from the fact that a single utterance may provide evidence for a range of related hypotheses, all similar enough to the thoughts the communicator wanted to convey. (Wilson & Sperber, 1986, p. 39)

As an example, consider a speaker's utterance of *Why is the window open?* By asking the question, the speaker directs attention to the hearer and suggests that a reason is needed as to why the window is open. In so doing, she implies both (a) that some response from the hearer is expected and (b) that the window should under normal circumstances, that is, those without special reasons attached to them, not be open. In one context, the speaker may intend this question to cue the fact that she does not have information that she assumes the hearer has about the reason for or the cause of the window being open. In such a case, the speaker might be satisfied with an informative response giving a reason or cause, such as:

---

[2]A convention within Relevance Theory is to refer to the speaker as *she* and the hearer or audience as *he*. This convention is adopted in this section.

The air conditioning broke down.

The front door was locked and I didn't have my key.

In a context in which the speaker has some control over the hearer's actions, the speaker might intend the question *Why is the window open?* to elicit an action response from the hearer, that is, to get him to close the window. In some cases, the speaker might intend the hearer to interpret this utterance as a reprimand, on the assumption that the hearer should not have let the window be open because of some prior shared knowledge between speaker and hearer (e.g., if the speaker had complained before about the window being left open). As these many possible interpretations show, only in a specific context can a particular speaker intention become manifest, that is, be deduced or revealed as the most relevant possible meaning within that context (Sperber & Wilson, 1995).

In the view of Relevance Theory, speakers seek to provide the most relevant evidence for hearers to draw the inferences they want them to draw; for their part, hearers form hypotheses about the implicit import of utterances by seeking the most relevant interpretation of the signals provided. In consequence, communication operates on a principle of *relevance.* Indeed, "human communication *tends* to be organised so as to maximise relevance" (Sperber & Wilson, 1995, p. 262; emphasis as in original). Wilson and Sperber (1986) then suggest:

> If humans pay attention only to relevant information, a communicator, by claiming an audience's attention, creates an expectation of relevance. She creates a presumption, in particular, that the information she is attempting to convey, when processed in a context she believes the audience to have accessible, will be relevant enough to be worth the audience's attention. (p. 45)

There are "three ways in which new information can interact with, and be relevant in, a context of existing assumptions: by combining with the context to yield contextual implications; by strengthening existing assumptions; and by contradicting and eliminating existing assumptions" (Wilson & Sperber, 1986, p. 43). In these three different ways, an utterance, as a type of new input provided by a speaker to an audience, has *contextual effects.* These contextual effects are then defined in terms of relevance, in that "new information is relevant in any context in which it has contextual effects, and the greater its contextual effects, the more relevant it will be" (Wilson & Sperber, 1986, p. 43). The search for relevance is ultimately related to memory and perceptual limitations, and thus economy, as hearers process information in the smallest number of steps, or at the least depth, possible. This means that "speakers should make their utterances easy to understand: in our terms, . . . speakers should make the contextual effects of their utterances easy to recover" (Wilson & Sperber, 1986, p. 44).

Communication is a process of negotiating meaning, that is, a mutually agreed or overlapping set of understandings with the same force and implicational meaning. This process is easier when speaker and hearer share language, culture, and communicational history. Problems arise when speakers produce utterances that are ambiguous, that is, which are consistent with different assumptions and interpretations, or when speaker and hearer do not share the same assumptions or context of utterance (as when they have little common background). For example, if a person comes into a room and says, *I got it!* anyone who has had no prior contact with or knowledge of the person will probably assume that the utterance is not relevant to them, or that it is too vague or ambiguous to be interpreted or to be worth the effort to try to process. If a person who hears this utterance wants to interpret it, he may try, even if it seems hard to do. In such a case, the person wishing to process the utterance will try to maximize its relevance for him, that is, to give it an interpretation that makes the most relevant links to his contextual assumptions.

At the other extreme, there may be a person or persons in the room who would know exactly what the speaker meant by an utterance on a particular occasion of *I got it!* A person who understood this minimal utterance would presumably be someone who knew, most likely based on previous communication with the speaker or others close to her, that she was trying to obtain or hoping to receive (*get*) a particular "something" to which *it* could refer (e.g., a particular job, a letter of acceptance, a long-awaited gift, the solution to a problem). For the person who had that prior knowledge, *I got it!* might be both a sufficient and an efficient act of communication in the sense of clearly indicating the speaker's intended meaning in an "economical" way, that is, by use of the fewest possible words. To the extent that this is true, the speaker has maximized the relevance of her utterance for the particular audience that was in fact able to interpret it.

The possibility of such a clear interpretation in this as in other cases is prefaced on the shared context between the speaker and the intended audience. Where such a shared context does not exist, the speaker must make her intention clear by more explicit or extensive signaling. In place of a simple *I got it!* the speaker might spell out her state of mind, as in: *I'm so relieved. I've been waiting all week for a very important letter and it has finally arrived.* In between this detailed statement and the brief *I got it!* are intermediate degrees of explicitness, such as *The letter came, finally!* or *I got the letter!* or *That letter I was so worried about—I got it!* Each of these utterances would be tailored to a particular audience, based on the speaker's assumptions about what information would be most relevant and efficient to convey her intention to that audience. The speaker makes this judgment within a particular context of assumptions about the world and about what the audience knows, and based on what the speaker wants the audience to know of her intentions, some or all of which she may try to keep hidden (i.e., for purposes of secrecy or deception).

Like Incremental Grammar and Action Grammar, Relevance Theory stresses the context-dependent nature of communication, as speakers customize their utterances to their intended audiences in the effort to maximize relevance and efficiency, and hearers expect relevance when interpreting speakers' utterances. It also reinforces the theme brought out in the discussion of Action Grammar of the joint work performed by participants to a communicative encounter. However, whereas Incremental Grammar focuses primarily on the speaker and Action Grammar focuses on the cooperative work of speaker-hearer ensembles, Relevance Theory emphasizes the distributed roles and reciprocal responsibilities of speaker and hearer in the process of communication. To a greater extent than the other orientations, Relevance Theory centers on the hearer—both directly, as the one who interprets utterances, and indirectly, as the speaker's projection of the intended audience's mental context of utterance. Relevance Theory therefore suggests an emphasis in teaching on the process of interpreting and not only producing utterances.

A SYNTHESIS: COLLOCATIONAL, CONSTRUCTIVE, CONTEXTUAL, AND CONTRASTIVE GRAMMAR

All of these orientations represent attempts to develop an account of language that accords as closely as possible with the way people actually learn and use language. Looking across all four of the reviewed perspectives on language and communication, a synthesis can be derived for pedagogy. The characteristics of a pedagogical grammar as derived from the discussion presented here are that it be *collocational, constructive, contextual,* and *contrastive.*

The Grammar Should Be Collocational. This means that the grammar should be built on collocational relations between individual lexical items and, to the extent possible, subcategories of these, rather than starting from the higher and more abstract level of syntactic structures. Much more time than is usually spent in grammar teaching should be devoted to semantic structure of the lexicon and of connected discourse, and to the way words are selected to fulfill contextual requirements.

The Grammar Should Be Constructive. A constructive grammar is one that builds structure bit by bit, from the simplest elements and by the most transparent procedures that most closely model the way language is learned and used. A constructive grammar would offer learners a way to build communication out of elements that can be continually added in sequence to form discourse-level chains. Language use would be instructed as a problem-solving activity carried out in time, with communicative decisions at one moment linked to those that precede and follow. Instruction would thus focus on the strategic operations of planning and decision-making, review and assessment, and how these result in the initial production and the continual development and repair of utterances.

The Grammar Should Be Contextual.   In a contextual grammar, elements and structures are taught in relation to their context. Syntactic and lexical choices are explicitly related to pragmatic ones, and these are in turn explicitly related to higher discursive and nondiscursive purposes, and to social and cultural facts about different languages. The focus is on discourse, and on the joint action of speaker and hearer in the creation and negotiation of meaning. Through their joint action, the speaker and hearer create a temporary communicative interface, or common shared cognitive environment, within which they can carry out their intended purposes.

The Grammar Should Be Contrastive.   A contrastive grammar involves drawing the learner's attention to contrasts and criterial differences between the target and other languages (e.g., the different use in French and English of the definite article or the simple past and present perfect tenses) and between sets of similar features and items of the target language (e.g., the simple past and present perfect tenses in English or sets of lexical items with overlapping meaning, such as *watch/look/see*, which have different collocational relations). In explicating the characteristics of the target language in relation to other languages known to the learners, a new contrastive pedagogy can draw on the notion of parameter settings as developed within the Minimalist and larger UG frameworks. Learners can in this way be introduced to the minimal differences between languages, as a starting point for considering the more extensive differences that stem from individual lexicons and the meaning of individual words.

THE PLACE OF THE NEW GRAMMARS IN APPLIED LINGUISTICS AND GRAMMAR TEACHING

Most of the features of the proposed "new grammars" can be found elsewhere. At the same time, the proposed pedagogical features are unique in some respects.

Collocation

Those working in corpus linguistics address the importance of collocation as a principle for building real texts (Biber, Conrad, & Reppen, 1998; McCarthy, 1998). However, linguists have only begun to realize how much of language is captured in collocation rather than "syntax." As Willis (1994) observes:

> A concern with the transmission of abstract sentence patterns teaches nothing about the meanings and use of particular words. Indeed it can obscure the function of words like *would* by implying that the meaning is given by a particular structural configuration rather than residing in the word itself . . . . Too much time has been given to presenting learners with target structures which are simply the sum of their parts. Too little time has been given to looking at the items which make up those structures. (p. 65)

A similar point is made by Hubbard (1994), based on a review of non-transformational theories of grammar that provide alternatives to Chomsky's "Standard Theory":

> [M]uch of the grammatical structure of English is directly linked to the logical structure of lexical items. This means that it may be more useful to think of introducing substructures through common words than as syntactic formulas with words as convenient placeholders. Doing so would yield a lexically driven grammar. (p. 65)

The implication of the present discussion is that grammar pedagogy should devote far more attention than has been done in the past to lexical relations and the meaning of individual words, both individually and in context, in determining grammatical choices.

Context

Many approaches to language teaching that have arisen in the last half-century have stressed the importance of context. The idea of teaching grammar in context is the basis of the situational linguistics of Firth (1968), the notional syllabus (e.g., Wilkins, 1976), as well as the English for Specific Purposes (ESP) approach (e.g., Robinson, 1980), and various communicative grammars (e.g., Leech & Svartvik, 1975). What is new here is (a) the tie to action, (b) the dynamic aspect, and (c) by implication, speaker-hearer interaction. Rather than function-based, the type of grammar proposed here is more essentially interaction-based. It is in this sense like the type of pedagogical discourse grammar proposed by Hughes and McCarthy (1998) as "[focused] first and foremost on the people involved in producing the language sample, their relationships, and the ideas that they are conveying rather than merely on a section of text as a setting for a grammatical structure" (p. 281).

Constructivity

The most original feature of the present discussion is perhaps that of constructivity. This feature in a sense takes us back to the early days of machine processing of language that was Chomsky's inspiration but which led him to reject linear (finite state) grammars as incapable of handling sentence processing (Chomsky, 1957). Chomsky's demonstration of this impossibility has been widely accepted; it was, however, called into question by his contemporaries in information processing at MIT, such as Victor Yngve and Gilbert Harman (see, e.g., Harman, 1963) and by scholars at Penn such as Aravind Joshi (e.g., Joshi, 1972) who were in close touch with Zellig Harris, Chomsky's teacher. In his recent book, Yngve (1996) has stressed the advantage of minimal depth of processing, particularly, binary branching structures, for generating linguistic strings; and Chomsky himself has moved increasingly to simple structures.

In addition, new accounts of language universals such as that of Hawkins (1999) are being advanced as having more to do with processing limitations than innate parameters, and processing models of language acquisition are gaining ground rapidly. Many now believe that innate perceptual processing mechanisms can account for first language acquisition and the development of grammar without an independent grammar module (for discussion, see Bates, 1997); and Ellis (1996) has advanced the argument that serial processing is a primary mode of language acquisition.

What is unique in the present context is the notion that the serial processing that builds utterances is targeted, that is, it is directed at achieving communicative purposes. Thus, a constructive grammar must be both left-right (bottom-up) and right-left (top-down) in operation, checking the element-by-element production of words in sequence against an ultimate goal or higher purpose that one or more speakers are cumulatively fulfilling. The two aspects of processing build a communicative structure, or discourse, by selecting a next element that fits with what has gone before and at the same time helps to advance the discourse toward completing the participants' intended purpose.

Contrast

The principle of contrast may at first appear to revive the discredited tradition of contrastive analysis. It differs from the latter approach, however, in advocating the teaching of contrast at a deep systemic level, such as in terms of parametric oppositions that determine widespread differences among languages, or semantic properties that place lexical items into contrasting and complementary sets. It also differs from the tradition of contrastive analysis in advocating a principle of contrast for teaching both interlingual and intralingual structural and lexical properties.

The present orientation to contrast can be related to the British Language Awareness Movement (James, 1994). James (1994) describes the work of the Language Awareness scholars as building pedagogical interfaces between languages by explicit comparison and contrast: "Unlike classical contrastive analysis, with their morbid preoccupation with [native language] interference, these scholars have been looking for ways to build bridges between [native language] and [foreign language] ignorance" (p. 210). As he relates, scholars "are now beginning to write contrastive analyses in which the contrasts are not seen as separate and unconnected linguistic accidents, but as related by implication: two surface contrasts are related to and shown to be reflexes of the same underlying contrast" (p. 213). Such work represents promising applications of contrastive analysis for language pedagogy. The orientation to contrast developed here can also be related to the pedagogy of "consciousness-raising" (e.g., as developed by Rutherford, 1987) or "input-processing" (VanPatten, 1996).

CONCLUSION

Traditional grammars, in relying on a written language norm filtered through an ancient language and in privileging the sentence as the essential unit of analysis, have described language in terms of an abstract ideal rather than as a central aspect of human behavior. This chapter has reviewed four prominent theoretical and descriptive orientations to language and communication, each of which offers alternatives to this traditional view and insights that may be of value to language pedagogy. Assuming that new theoretical orientations in linguistics are built on an accumulation of findings, it would seem that each of the four orientations presented—Minimalism, Incremental Grammar, Action Grammar, and Relevance Theory—offers a considerable advance over traditional grammar. It is therefore important that we in applied linguistics and language teaching attempt to draw out the practical implications of these orientations for our pedagogy. This has been done in the present case by extracting four conditions that new pedagogical grammars must satisfy: They should be collocational, constructive, contextual, and contrastive.

I have called here for a realistic grammar in the sense of reflecting language acquisition and use. After more than 2,000 years of traditional grammar, and notwithstanding the insights of Communicative Language Teaching, it is time to turn the attention of the field of language teaching back to the structural area of language, but with new points of view. Clearly, we have some catching up to do, so that grammatical pedagogy can be modeled more closely on what is known about language and communication more generally. It is hoped that the review and suggestions presented here might give some ideas for the design of new grammar books and courses for the millennium. Under the optimistic assumption that there is progress in human history, we can also hope that the knowledge contained in any such books and courses will not be with us for another two thousand years but will rather be recognized as only the most recent step along the path by which grammatical pedagogy will continue to evolve in relation to our descriptions and theories of language.

REFERENCES

Austin, J. L. (1962). *How to do things with words.* Oxford: Oxford University Press.

Bates, E. (1997). On language savants and the structure of the mind. *International Journal of Bilingualism, 1,* 163–179.

Biber, D., Conrad, S., & Reppen, R. (1998). *Corpus linguistics: Investigating language structure and use.* Cambridge, UK: Cambridge University Press.

Brazil, D. (1995). *A grammar of speech.* Oxford: Oxford University Press.

Chomsky, N. (1957). *Syntactic structures.* The Hague: Mouton.

Chomsky, N. (1995). *The minimalist program.* Cambridge, MA: MIT Press.

Clark, H. H. (1996). *Using language.* Cambridge, UK: Cambridge University Press.

Cook, V. (1997). *Inside language.* London: Arnold.

Crystal, D. (1995). *The Cambridge encyclopedia of the English language.* Cambridge, UK: Cambridge University Press.

Ellis, N. C. (1996). Sequencing in SLA: Phonological memory, chunking, and points of order. *Studies in Second Language Acquisition, 18,* 91–126.

Firth, J. R. (1968). *Selected papers: 1952–59.* (F. R. Palmer, Ed.). London: Longman, Green & Co.

Goffman, E. (1971). *Relations in public.* New York: Harper and Row.

Goffman, E. (1981). *Forms of talk.* Philadelphia: University of Pennsylvania Press.

Grice, H. P. (1957). Meaning. *Philosophical Review, 66,* 377–388.

Grice, H. P. (1982). Meaning revisited. In N. V. Smith (Ed.), *Mutual knowledge* (pp. 230–243). London: Academic Press.

Halliday, M. A. K. (1985). *An introduction to functional grammar.* London: Arnold.

Harman, G. H. (1963). Generative grammar without transformation rules: A defense of phrase structure. *Language, 39,* 594–616.

Hawkins, J. A. (1999). Processing complexity and filler-gap dependencies across grammars. *Language, 75,* 244–285.

Hubbard, P. L. (1994). Non-transformational theories of grammar: Implications for language teaching. In T. Odlin (Ed.), *Perspectives on pedagogical grammar* (pp. 49–71). New York: Cambridge University Press.

Hughes, R., & McCarthy, M. (1998). From sentence to discourse: Discourse grammar and English language teaching. *TESOL Quarterly, 32,* 263–287.

James, C. (1994). Explaining grammar to learners. In M. Bygate, A. Tonkyn, & E. Williams (Eds.), *Grammar and the language teacher* (pp. 203–214). New York: Prentice Hall.

Joshi, A. K. (1972). How much hierarchical structure is necessary for sentence description? In S. Ploaetz (Ed.), *Transformationelle analyse: Die transformationstheorie von Zellig Harris and ihre entwicklung* (pp. 389–398). Frankfurt am Main: Athenaeum.

Leech, G., & Svartvik, J. (1975). *A communicative grammar of English.* London: Longman.

Levinson, S. C. (1983). *Pragmatics.* Cambridge, UK: Cambridge University Press.

Lock, G. (1995). *Functional English grammar for language teachers.* New York: Cambridge University Press.

Lyons, J. (1969). Intervention in "Formal logic and natural language." *Foundations of Language, 5,* 269.

McCarthy, M. (1998). *Spoken language and applied linguistics.* Cambridge, UK: Cambridge University Press.

Munby, J. (1978). *Communicative syllabus design.* Cambridge, UK: Cambridge University Press.

Pennington, M. C. (1998). Perspectives on language in Hong Kong at century's end. In M. C. Pennington (Ed.), *Language in Hong Kong at century's end* (pp. 3–40). Hong Kong: University of Hong Kong Press.

Radford, A. (1997a). *Syntactic theory and the structure of English: A minimalist approach.* Cambridge, UK: Cambridge University Press.

Radford, A. (1997b). *Syntax: A minimalist introduction.* Cambridge, UK: Cambridge University Press.

Richards, J. C., & Rodgers, T. S. (1986). *Approaches and methods in language teaching.* New York: Cambridge University Press.

Robinson, P. (1980). *ESP (English for specific purposes).* Oxford: Pergamon.

Rutherford, W. E. (1987). *Second language grammar: Learning and teaching.* London: Longman.

Schegloff, E. A. (1979). Identification and recognition in telephone conversational openings. In G. Psathas (Ed.), *Everyday language: Studies in ethnomethodology* (pp. 23–78). New York: Irvington.

Schegloff, E. A. (1980). Preliminaries to preliminaries: "Can I ask you a question?" *Sociological Inquiry, 50,* 104–152.

Searle, J. R. (1969). *Speech acts.* Cambridge, UK: Cambridge University Press.

Searle, J. R. (1980). The background of meaning. In J. R. Searle, F. Kiefer, & M. Bierwisch (Eds.), *Speech act theory and pragmatics* (pp. 22–43). Dordrecht: Reidel.

Sperber, D., & Wilson, D. (1986/1995). *Relevance: Communication and cognition.* (2nd ed.). Oxford: Blackwell.

VanPatten, B. (1996). *Input processing and grammar instruction: Theory and research.* Norwood, NJ: Ablex.

Widdowson, H. G. (1978). *Teaching language as communication.* Oxford: Oxford University Press.

Wilkins, D. A. (1976). *Notional syllabuses.* Oxford: Oxford University Press.

Willis, D. (1994). A lexical approach. In M. Bygate, A. Tonkyn, & E. Williams (Eds.), *Grammar and the language teacher* (pp. 56–66). New York: Prentice Hall.

Wilson, D., & Sperber, D. (1986). Outline of relevance theory. In H. O. Alves (Ed.), *Encontro de Linguistas Acta.* University of Minho, Braga, Portugal. Also published in *Notes on Linguistics, 39,* 5–24 (July 1987).

Yngve, V. H. (1996). *From grammar to science: New foundations for general linguistics.* Amsterdam/Philadelphia: John Benjamins.

II

Classroom Approaches
to Grammar Teaching

Part II introduces approaches to grammar teaching that promote aware-ness of form-meaning relationships while retaining a focus on accuracy-building. A common theme in these six chapters is the need to show learn-ers the living, dynamic nature of grammar as opposed to static, rule-based instruction insisting on only one "right way." The authors achieve this by use of pragmatic analysis of the meaning expressed by different forms, dis-course functions of grammar structures, several types of task-based activi-ties, authentic texts to provide context, and invented sentences to promote awareness of form-function relationships.

Diane Larsen-Freeman articulates the section theme clearly in the title of her chapter, "The Grammar of Choice." Larsen-Freeman asks teachers to rethink prescriptive approaches to grammar teaching, emphasizing that grammar is not a rigid set of forms to be taught solely for accuracy, but rather is a way for learners to express their personal thoughts and voice in their choice of syntax. Different propositions, Larsen-Freeman suggests, can be formulated in a great variety of ways, and learners can be taught that their choice of grammar structures can have various pragmatic implications. She gives examples of constructing syntax to show different attitudes, to express power, and to establish identity, speech acts where grammar choice can be used to express widely differing pragmatic stances, even when propositional content is identical. She presents sentences illustrating that choice of the present tense rather than the past can show psychological closeness. Other sentences show the use of modals for register—use of *could* being more polite than *can* when making requests. Additional sentences present examples of third-person indefinite forms used for expressing tact, moderation, and hedging. Pedagogical activities are presented that raise learners' awareness of options in using syntax to construct meaning, for example, learners choos-ing among different accurate grammar forms expressing the same proposi-tional meaning, followed by a discussion of the implications of their choice.

In line with Larsen-Freeman's discussion of the pragmatic functions of grammar, Marianne Celce-Murcia's chapter, "Why It Makes Sense to Teach Grammar in Context and through Discourse," provides a rationale for teaching grammar in context. Her teaching suggestions include several points of grammar representing structures important for teaching English. There are two examples for each structure, such as the uses of *must* versus *have to, have got to* and *I do too* versus *so do I* for speech, and the past perfect tense and *it*-clefts for writing. Her argument illustrates why a discourse-based, context-embedded approach to teaching grammar is pedagogically superior to a decontextualized sentence-level approach, not only for the exemplified structures but for most imaginable grammar points. Celce-Murcia also briefly presents a method of discourse analysis that teachers and researchers can use for implementation of the curriculum focusing on contextual analysis. Her pedagogical approach is based on a simple heuristic; namely, that well-selected, authentic examples of language use that are contextually and discursively representative of the grammar point in focus should be the basis for grammar instruction. The tasks and activities that the teacher develops should exploit and build on the target forms in the example texts, and when students actively engage in comprehension, analysis, and elaboration of the exemplars, they reach a point where they can move toward receptive and productive use of the target grammar points in their own discourse and for their own communicative purposes in context.

In "Structure-Based Interactive Tasks for the EFL Grammar Learner," Sandra Fotos presents a task-based approach to grammar instruction for the English as a foreign language (EFL) situation and for the English as a second language (ESL) classroom where learners must achieve high levels of accuracy. She recommends a three-part grammar lesson, starting off with formal instruction on the target grammar structure, pointing out rules for its use, followed by performance of structure-based communicative tasks that either require use of the structure to complete the activity or present the grammar point itself as a problem that must be solved. Task performance is followed by a discussion of the lesson, followed by communicative activities containing the target structure. Examples of both types of tasks are presented and discussed, to enable teachers to develop course/program-specific tasks. Fotos rejects suggestions by ESL authors regarding the design of purely communicative tasks addressed to "real life" needs by noting that use of such tasks is predicated on abundant out-of-class exposure to the target language—entirely lacking in the EFL situation—and emphasizing that the "real life" needs of EFL learners are not the development of communicative skills necessary for daily life in the target culture but rather the development of accuracy for passing entrance examinations and achieving high scores on proficiency tests such as the Test of English as a Foreign Language (TOEFL).

Rod Ellis furthers the discussion of classroom approaches to grammar in his chapter, "Methodological Options in Grammar Teaching Materials." He presents pedagogical suggestions for grammar teaching developed from a critical analysis of six ESL/EFL grammar practice textbooks. Ellis examines three aspects of instructional methodology: the way grammar structures are presented, the nature of the examples used to illustrate the structures, and the activities students are asked to perform. Looking at units for teaching the Present Continuous Text, Ellis checks (1) whether the structure was presented through an explicit lesson or required the learner to discover rules; (2) whether the examples provided were contrived or authentic, were isolated sentences or were presented in context, and were examples of oral or written language; and (3) whether the learners were required to produce sentences containing the target structure, perform reception activities showing that they understood the sentences, or judge whether sentences were correct. His examination indicates that textbook methodology is generally characterized by explicit description of structures and controlled production practice, an approach differing little from that used for decades. In contrast, based on what is currently known about Second Language Acquisition (SLA), Ellis recommends a discovery approach to grammar learning using receptive tasks requiring processing of input, thus calling attention to use of the target form in context. Such tasks also require learners to solve grammar problems in ways that develop awareness of how form is linked to meaning.

Also moving beyond traditional textbook approaches, Eli Hinkel advocates the use of authentic language texts and models to establish form-meaning relationships and to build accuracy in uses of tenses in writing. In "Teaching Grammar in Writing Classes: Tenses and Cohesion," she notes that grammar teaching is usually viewed as the development of accuracy, whereas writing instruction is more directed toward organization skills. She argues for the inclusion of a strong grammar component within the writing syllabus. Hinkel presents research indicating that accuracy, particularly in the use of tenses, is a major determinant of L2 writing rating procedures, yet notes the general lack of tense instruction in writing pedagogy. To remedy this, she recommends use of authentic examples for a discourse-based examination of form-meaning relationships in written tenses. Analysis of such authentic material provides the learners with written discourse examples of the use of adverbial markers and tense inflections to denote time, past tense reporting that is also true for the present, the use of present tense models for reporting events in both past and present, and other problematic tense uses. Hinkel also examines tense shift in various genres of academic writing, which many ESL learners need to master, and suggests that examination of authentic material can raise learners' awareness of use in context and allow them to apply formal knowledge gained from grammar instruction to the understanding of text cohesion.

6

The Grammar of Choice[1]

Diane Larsen-Freeman
School for International Training, Brattleboro, Vermont

INTRODUCTION

Many teachers (and students) believe grammar to be a linguistic strait-jacket. They think that grammar consists of arbitrary rules of a language, to which speakers must adhere or risk the penalty of being misunderstood or of being stigmatized as speaking an inferior or inadequate form of the target language. It is easy to understand why grammar is viewed in this manner. Many of us have felt the despair of receiving a paper back from a language teacher filled with red marks related to the form of what we had written, not to the content that we had worked so hard to express. Also, speaking the standard dialect of a language accurately does provide speakers with access to opportunities they might otherwise be denied. I recall the late Carlos Yorio's sharing with me his challenge in helping his students, many of whom were New Yorkers and spoke English fluently, learn to speak Standard English accurately so that they would have more options for employment. Indeed, grammar does relate to formal accuracy, and there is a cost to those who fail to adhere to it.

However, there is another side to grammar, a side to which I seem much called upon to draw attention these days. I no doubt have accepted this mission in part because some of my professional interests lie in better

---

[1]This chapter was first delivered as a paper at the International TESOL Convention, Seattle, March 1998.

understanding grammar and finding ways to help teachers do the same. As we know, teachers teach subject matter the way that they conceptualize it. The purpose of this chapter, then, is to challenge the common misconception that grammar has to do solely with formal accuracy (Larsen-Freeman, 1995). I do believe that if grammar were better understood, not only would it be taught and learned better, but also the rich potential of its system would be admired, thus enhancing attitudes toward grammar. Teachers and their students would appreciate how inextricably bound up with being human grammar is. For rather than being a linguistic straitjacket, grammar affords speakers of a particular language a great deal of flexibility in the ways they can express propositional, or notional, meaning and how they present themselves in the world.

For this volume, then, I am not going to discuss views of grammar from a theoretical linguistics or a second language acquisition research perspective. I have recently written about these matters elsewhere (Larsen-Freeman, forthcoming a, 2001b). Instead, in this chapter, I will first examine and then define grammar in a way that reflects a different orientation from what grammar normally takes in the minds and materials of English as a second language/English as a foreign language (ESL/EFL) teachers. Second, I will provide a number of examples that illustrate the flexibility of the system. Finally, I will address pedagogical concerns.

A DEFINITION

As I have already suggested, it is true that grammar relates to linguistic form, about which speakers have little choice. As we see in Example 1, when using the verb *be*, English speakers need to use *am* for first person singular subjects and *are* for first person plural subjects. *Children* is the irregular plural form of *child*. Attributive adjectives precede nouns in English, so we say *a fragrant meadow*, not *a meadow fragrant*.

  1. I am → We are

     one child → two children

     A fragrant meadow → *A meadow fragrant

There are, however, two departures from the usual way of thinking about grammar that I want to encourage in this chapter. First, the rules illustrated in Example 1 constitute a very minimal set, concerning such things as the form of the verb so that it agrees with its subject, the form of a plural common count noun, and adjective-noun word order. Second, even within this restricted set of rules, a choice exists. A speaker or writer must decide when to use these forms. Another way to say this is that grammar not only consists of rules governing form; grammatical knowledge consists of knowing when to use the forms to convey meanings that match our intentions in particular contexts.

Let me return to the three common examples of grammar rules shown in Example 1 to demonstrate that even at this very basic level, we have a choice of forms to use. Consider the contrast between *I am* and *We are*. This distinction seems straightforward enough; however, even while holding the propositional meaning constant, there is still room for choice, depending on how I, as the speaker, want to position myself vis-à-vis my audience:

2. I am speaking about the grammar of choice this afternoon.

   We are speaking about the grammar of choice this afternoon.

Either of these statements would be acceptable if I were addressing an audience on the topic of a grammar of choice. With the first option, I would be reflecting my agency in the act of speaking. With the second option, I would still be doing the speaking; however, my choice of the second option would signal my intention to make my audience feel more included in the event, perhaps to promote solidarity between us.

Sometimes, even with the same subject, a choice of verb form exists. I could say:

3. My family *is* coming over for dinner on Sunday.

Or some dialects of English, British English, for example, will permit the plural form of the *be* verb with the subject *family*:

4. My family *are* coming over for dinner on Sunday.

The choice between a singular or plural verb will indicate that the speaker is thinking of *family* either as a particular unit of people (Example 3), or as a collection of individuals that comprise the unit (Example 4). The duality of number property is a feature of a certain category of nouns, called collective nouns, of which the noun *family* is a member.

Now, how about the example having to do with plural formation? Well, it is hard to imagine when I might choose *children* over *child* other than to express the notional meaning of plurality, but suppose that I had chosen an informal synonym for the word *child*. What if I had said *kid*, for instance?

5. One kid → Two kids

?My kid is home sick from school today.

My kids are home sick from school today.

Many English speakers are uncomfortable referring to a single child as *kid* but find *kids* to be perfectly acceptable for talking about more than one child. They feel that *kid* has a pejorative connotation that *kids* does not. When needing to talk about one child, they would avoid using the term *kid* by finding a more acceptable alternative such as *son* or *daughter*. Although admittedly this oddity might be an idiosyncracy of this particular noun, it does illustrate my point that our choice of grammar structure makes a difference in more than simple accuracy of form.

What then about the rule of grammar that says in English an attributive adjective precedes the noun? Actually, it is in fact possible for attributive adjectives to follow a noun in English when they are clausally derived:

6. That meadow fragrant with the smell of newly mown hay reminds me of my youth.

Such a position can ascribe a different quality to the adjective from when it is in prenominal position, however. Bolinger (1967) points out that prenominal adjectives tend to reflect more permanent characteristics of a noun, whereas adjectives in postnominal position reflect temporary characteristics. Thus, if I talk about *that fragrant meadow*, I am speaking of a characteristic of the meadow, whereas in Example 6, when the adjective follows the noun, I am relating the feature of fragrance to a specific event (Celce-Murcia & Larsen-Freeman, 1999).

For the purpose of this chapter, I will treat only choices of the sort illustrated in Examples 2 and 5. Although Examples 3 and 6 also reflect choices, the choices they offer have to do with a choice of meaning—am I conceiving of a collective noun as a whole unit or as a unit comprised of a number of individuals? Am I conceiving of a noun as having a permanent attribute or only a temporary one? The choice of grammatical form clearly signals a difference in notional meaning in these examples. This is the sort of choice that exists among the various verb tense-aspect combinations, the choice of article, preposition, phrasal verb, and so forth. Learning which forms express the meaning they intend clearly represents a formidable challenge for ESL/EFL students and must be dealt with in a systematic fashion (Larsen-Freeman, 1990, 1991, 1994). But this type of challenge is also more commonly recognized. And thus, for the remainder of this chapter, I want instead to deal with the sort of choice represented by Examples 2 and 5. In these examples the propositional content, or what is sometimes called the notional or representational meaning, remains the same no matter which option I select. There is a difference, though, and the difference to me is a difference in the pragmatic meaning or use.

Our students will be judged for the way they say something as much as the forms they use and the propositional meaning they express. And as listeners our students will have to learn to draw inferences as to a speaker's intentions based on the forms the speaker chooses to use. I am not suggesting that we judge our students' performance against native speaker norms (Cook, 1999), and it does not make sense for all students to aspire to such norms. I do believe, however, that it is the students who must (and will) decide how they wish to position themselves as speakers of English and that we should help them understand the linguistic options before them in order to do so. Thus, an understanding of when or why to use a particular grammatical form should be part of an ESL/EFL teacher's understanding of grammar so as to avoid the teacher's giving students easy answers in the moment that contribute to confusion later on and so that students understand that they have a choice and what the consequences are of making a particular choice.

The purpose of this chapter, then, is to talk about a grammar of choice.[2] A more complete definition of grammar requires that we see that it is what enables our students to use the language accurately, meaningfully, and appropriately (Larsen-Freeman, 1991). This understanding entails by necessity our recognition that grammar consists of forms that have meaning and use. It is the use dimension, the one that includes what linguists refer to as pragmatics or discourse factors, that I wish to explore for the remainder of this chapter.[3]

CHOICE OF GRAMMAR STRUCTURES

Although I will by no means exhaust the inventory of choices I can make with regard to the social use of grammatical structures, for the purpose of illustration, I will treat three broad categories—attitude, power, and identity—and

---

[2]After I submitted my abstract, I discovered that R. A. Close (1992) also discussed the idea of there being choice in grammar. Although his notion and mine stem from the common concern that grammar needs to be seen as much more than a body of static rules about form, the main difference between our two positions is that he uses the term "Grammar as Choice" to deal mainly, although not exclusively, with choices of what I am calling propositional meaning, where I am using the term "a grammar of choice" to refer to the choices of pragmatic use.

[3]It is important to recognize that what I am dealing with in this is only one type of use challenge, one involving social-functional factors. There is another type of use challenge, concerning the appropriate use of grammar structures in discourse (see Celce-Murcia, 1991; 1992; Hughes & McCarthy, 1998; Larsen-Freeman, 1992).

list a number of sometimes overlapping subcategories within each. Let me (us?) now look briefly at each to appreciate the grammatical choices we have as speakers of English, even when the propositional meaning is more or less held constant.

Attitude

Psychological Distance.   Consider the following example from Riddle (1986):

> 7. Anne: Jane just bought a Volvo.
>
> John: Maureen *has* one.
>
> Anne: John, you've got to quit talking about Maureen as if you were still going together. You broke up three months ago.

Anne chides John for his continued attachment to Maureen. She infers that John still feels psychologically close to Maureen because he has reported her ownership of a Volvo using the simple present tense. Notice that John could have stated the same propositional content using the past tense even though Maureen's ownership of the Volvo still obtains (i.e., *Maureen had one*). If he had in fact done so, he might have avoided the rebuke from Anne.

Of course, attitudes can be signaled not only by psychological proximity but also by psychological distance. For example, a speaker "may wish to mark something that is physically close (for example, a perfume being sniffed by the speaker) as psychologically distant" (Yule, 1996, p. 13):

> 8. I don't like *that*.

In this analysis, the demonstrative pronoun *that* does not convey physical distance; in fact, contrary to what ESL/EFL students are often taught, the referent for *that* is physically proximate. Nevertheless, the speaker wishes to establish psychological distance and thus selects *that* presumably to indicate disapproval.

Assessment.   Closely related to the subcategory of psychological distance is one of assessment. It is an old trick of academic discourse that one can "distance" oneself from the claims of others by employing certain lexical forms (e.g., *so-called; allegedly*). Grammatical forms can be used in this way as well. The following example is taken from Batstone (1995, p. 197):

> 9. Smith (1980) *argued* that Britain *was* no longer a country in which freedom of speech *was* seriously *maintained.* Johnson (1983), though, *argues* that Britain *remains a* citadel of individual liberty.

Batstone points out that the past tense in this example is used to assess Smith's argument as being no longer worthy of current interest, whereas Johnson's argument is held to be of real and continuing relevance (hence the present tense). The contrast in tenses, then, is being used to express the writer's assessment of the respective arguments. As I have just mentioned, assessment can also, of course, be conveyed lexically. As Batstone acknowledges, had the writer used the verb *demonstrated* rather than *argued* to report Smith's position, our perception of the writer's viewpoint might have been different.

Politeness.   While we are illustrating the various subtle "social uses" of the present and past tenses, we should treat the matter of politeness. It is well known that with the social-interactional use of the modal verbs, when a choice exists, the modal that was historically marked for past tense (e.g., *could*) is considered more polite than the historical present tense form (e.g., *can*).

10. Could you help me with my homework?

Can you help me with my homework?

However, the use of the past tense for politeness extends beyond the use of modal verbs:

Did you want something to eat?

is considered a more polite offer than

Do you want something to eat?

Much to the chagrin of many an ESL/EFL teacher left to explain to perplexed students why the past tense is being used for a present time offer— and is the offer really meant to be sincere when it is couched in the past? The past tense is not being used for past time, of course, but rather to indicate some distance, to make the offer less direct, and therefore more polite.

A parallel opposition exists for the choice between the two determiners *some* and *any* in an offer:

11. Would you like some cake?

Would you like any cake?

The use of *some* is more polite because its use is more likely when an affirmative answer is anticipated (Celce-Murcia & Larsen-Freeman, 1999; Close, 1992).

Of course, the association of a positive attitude with *some* and a negative attitude with *any* contributes to use more than simply making an offer more or less polite. Green (1989, p. 135) claims that the first sentence in Example 12 could be a bribe, whereas the second could be a threat:

12. If you eat some bread, I'll cook hamburgers all week.

    If you eat any bread, I'll cook hamburgers all week.

Moderation. Third person indefinite forms can be used to moderate potential accusations in a way that second person forms cannot because of the latters' directness. Compare the definite second and the indefinite third person forms in this example from Yule (1996, p. 11):

13. You didn't clean up.

    Somebody didn't clean up.

The speaker of both sentences may well have known who made the mess, but the use of the third person indefinite pronoun *somebody* makes the issue somehow more impersonal and therefore less direct/more moderated.

Tact. Another way to show tact involves the use of negative equatives. In general, when making comparisons it is considered more tactful to use negative equatives rather than comparatives when the adjective has negative polarity. For example, in Example 14, the negative polarity adjective *dumb* is very rude in the comparative, whereas its positive polarity counterpart in a negative equative is considered more indirect and less rude (Celce-Murcia & Larsen-Freeman, 1999).

14. Moe is dumber than Curly.

    Moe is not as intelligent as Curly.

Deference. Again, closely related to this discussion is the question of deference signaled grammatically. Close (1992) offers the following minimal pair:

15. I hope you will come and have lunch with me.

    I am hoping you will come and have lunch with me.

Close (1992) notes:

Both are right but they are not equal in the effect they might have on the hearer. . . . My own explanation is that a busy self-important man might feel [the first one] to be too presumptuous, and refuse the invitation, but [the second] flatteringly deferential and accept; while someone else to whom the invitation was given might feel that [the first] was definitely meant, and accept with pleasure, but [the second] to be uncertain and not sufficiently pressing. The speaker's attitude—dictatorial or deferential, positive or uncertain—can certainly be an important factor in these cases. (p. 64)

Power

Close says that it is the speaker's attitude that conditions the choice between the two sentences in Example 15. The issue of showing deference to another might just as easily fit into the second category I have created, one that I call power. Critical discourse analysis is concerned with issues of power imbalances in society, and analysts who practice it examine discourse for the subtle yet influential way in which power can be conferred on certain participants at the expense of others. Stubbs (1990, as cited in Batstone [1995]), for example, finds it significant that in South African newspaper accounts dealing with events surrounding the release of Nelson Mandela, agency is often ascribed to Blacks by making them the subject of the clause, when reporting acts of violence. Here is an example from a newspaper report:

16. "Jubilant Blacks clashed with police. . . ."

The same propositional content could have been conveyed if the roles of the subject and object had been reversed (i.e., *Police clashed with jubilant Blacks*). Since such texts are not ideologically neutral, it seems that the order chosen was intended to assign responsibility to Blacks.

Importance.   While I am dealing with the issue of the conferral of agency/subjecthood, it is worth bringing up the case of the so-called symmetrical predicates. Contrary to some linguists' claims, it has been found that the two versions of symmetrical predicates are not in fact equivalent—that depending on the importance of the noun phrases, one form over another is preferred.

Here is an example of a test item from Sher (1975, as reported in Celce-Murcia, 1980) that demonstrates the nonequivalency:

Suppose it was discovered that Shakespeare did not write his plays alone. Someone named Smith helped him, although the real genius did come from Shakespeare. How would you describe the relationship?

17. a. Shakespeare wrote with Smith.

  b. Smith wrote with Shakespeare.

  c. No preference

Sher found that a statistically significant number of respondents chose b, fewer chose a, and even fewer chose c—the answer if the predicates were truly symmetrical. It seems that most respondents favor the option that would afford the more important agent end-focus position.

Gender. Relevant to a discussion of power imbalances is the well-attested difference between the speech of men and women. One of the ways the difference manifests itself is in the use of intensifiers. Sargent (1997) speculates that women make more use of intensifiers than men out of a concern that they are not going to be heeded. Thus, Example 18 is more likely to be uttered by a woman than by a man.

18. It's really a very nice spot.

Assertiveness. Another issue related to power has to do with how assertively someone voices his or her opinons. Consider the following from Green (1989, p. 134):

19. I don't think Sandy will arrive until Monday.

   I think Sandy won't arrive until Monday.

The first sentence illustrates what has been called the negative transportation construction (Lakoff, 1969; Horn, 1971, 1978 [cited in Green, 1989]), in which the negative has been transported from the clause it conversationally negates, as depicted in the second sentence in Example 19. The "transportation" of the negative can occur with a certain class of verbs and adjectives. Although both sentences communicate the same propositional meaning, sentences such as the first, with the transported negative, are hedged, that is, "they represent weaker claims, apparently by implicating rather than asserting the relevant negative proposition" (Green, 1989, pp. 134–135).

Presumptuousness. Then, too, certain forms in the language carry with them certain presuppositions. For example, Celce-Murcia and Larsen-Freeman (1999) point out that one use of uninverted questions is when the speaker expects confirmation of a presupposition. Using an uninverted question thus suggests that the person asking the question knows the other person well enough to predict the other's answer.

20. Worker to supervisor: You're going to the dance?

Although in all likelihood the question in Example 20 is an innocent comprehension check, the use of the uninverted form carries with it an affirmative presupposition—i.e., that the answer will be "yes." As such, the use of a question with this form suggests that the person asking the question knows the other person well enough to anticipate the listener's answer. If such intimacy does not exist, wording a question in this way may seem presumptuous.

Conviction. Green (1989) states the following, which supports my main premise in this chapter:

> In fact there are truth-conditionally equivalent alternatives to practically every describable condition, and to the extent that this is true, the alternatives will tend to have different pragmatic values. It would not be too surprising to discover that even constructions such as the [ones in Example 21] (Bolinger 1972) differ systematically in their use, reflecting different assumptions of the speakers, for example, that [the second member of the pair] implies a stronger conviction on the part of the subject. (p. 139)

21. I know that it's raining.

    I know it's raining.

Thus, although the *that* complementizer is syntactically optional, Green suggests it has a pragmatic role to play.

Identity

Henry Widdowson (1996) wrote that "although individuals are constrained by conventions of the code and its use, they exploit the potential differently on different occasions for different purposes. . . . The patterning of a person's use of language is as naturally distinctive as a fingerprint" (pp. 20–21). Widdowson's observation relates to how we use language to establish and maintain personal identity. There are a number of contributing factors to identity development that I have included in this broad category.

Personality. In interesting doctoral dissertation research, Roger Putzel (1976) administered the Myers-Briggs personality indicator to a group of male graduate students. He also interviewed each student at the time of the text. He later transcribed the interview and correlated the patterns of language used with the results of the personality test. Putzel found a number of significant correlations between the grammar the students used and their personality types. To offer just one example, here is the usage pattern for English auxiliary verbs Putzel found.

22. *Sensing, Thinking, Judging Introverts Intuitive, Feeling Extroverts*

    I could   I might   I would I should   I will   I am going to

Putzel explains his data as follows:

(1) STJ's [students who were categorized as sensing, thinking, judging personality types] create hypothetical or uncertain situations [thus they use a lot of modal verbs], (2) introverts express a sense of obligation (presumably internally generated) [thus they use *should* a lot], and (3) NFP's [intuitive, feeling personality types] are concerned with getting on to the future [thus they often use *will*]. The correlation of *I am going to* with Extraversion further testifies to the NFP's future orientation because extroverts are nearer to NFPs than introverts. (p. 134)

Putzel sums up these findings by noting that words suggesting caution, restraint, and control are associated with the Thinking and Sensing personality. Words evincing impulse and divergence correlate with the Intuiting and Feeling personality (p. xi). Our grammar shows even when we are unaware of it!

Age.   It is well known that language use is age-graded. Adolescents in particular are known to adopt a special argot to distinguish themselves from the adults they have not yet become. Most obviously these are lexical items—*cool* springs readily to mind. But there are other linguistic markers that give one's age away. Languages change, and younger speakers may adopt innovations in speech that older people resist. These include grammar structures. For example, I still say that

23.   Someone graduates from high school.

But among younger speakers, I often hear:

Someone graduates high school.

Then, too, *babysit* is for me an intransitive verb. Younger speakers, however, use it transitively:

I am going to babysit this weekend. (intransitive)

I am going to babysit him this weekend. (transitive)

Origin.   Speakers are born into dialect communities. Particular pronunciation, word choices, and even grammatical patterns are associated with particular dialects. I'll never forget when I learned of the existence of the modal sequence in Example 24, a characteristic of a particular dialect of North American English spoken in the southern part of the United States. The sequence seemed to violate all rules of acceptable modal verb syntax that I had ever learned. It made semantic sense though, certainly as much as my modal plus phrasal modal sequence *I might be able to.*

24. I might could go.

Of course, the converse also applies. People can choose not to use their native dialect features in order to avoid identifying themselves with a particular dialect. Many speakers become bidialectal, switching between the two depending on with whom they are interacting and for what purpose.

Status.   Certain speech norms have a higher social status than others. These norms sometimes have to do with the use of particular grammatical forms. Stalker (1989) cites the hapless native English speakers who tend to forget the high-status norms, which they are apt to use infrequently, or they grow confused about what is "right." "We know that there is a right way and a wrong way to use *like* and *as*," Stalker affirms, "but we cannot remember which is which" (p. 188).

25. It tastes good like/as it should.

Such confusion breeds linguistic insecurity, which in turn inclines many to avoid any syntactic frame that might call for us to choose between two forms. Others, of course, conform to the prescriptive rules for English, taking pride in speaking English "properly" and in the status they garner for doing so.

Group Membership and Discourse Communities.   Just as young people adopt a special age-graded argot to make themselves distinctive and to achieve solidarity with others of the same age, so do all speakers enter into different groups and discourse communities quite readily, and with each, take on a new identity kit (Gee, 1990). We learn to speak as members of our discourse community. Within each discourse community, there are certain norms about what constitutes appropriate ways of speaking or writing. To illustrate the point, here is a parody of an educational administrator and a teacher describing the same pheonomenon (Celce-Murcia & Larsen-Freeman, 1999). An administrator might say:

26. Prior to the administration of the assessment instrument, a skills-level analysis must be conducted to ascertain the critical level of pre-paredness of the target population.

Whereas a classroom teacher might say:

Before we give the test, we'd better find out if these particular students are ready for it.

As I indicated at the outset of this chapter, I have chosen only some of the ways that grammar patterns vary in their use. I certainly also should point out that many of the other systems of language play roles here. Certainly phonological factors contribute to dialects, particular lexical choices mark membership in different discourse/speech communities, and there are many other ways of conveying attitudes besides the use of grammar structures. Sometimes what is not said is as indicative of attitude as what is said. For example, a teacher who writes a letter of recommendation for a student in which the teacher's highest praise is for the student's penmanship leaves the recipient of the letter to infer a great deal about the individual for whom the letter was written, not all of it favorable.

PEDAGOGICAL CONSEQUENCES

Before making some brief comments on the specific pedagogical implications for the grammar of choice, it is important that readers appreciate that although some of what I have discussed in this chapter relates to subtleties that might only be considered potential items for an advanced-level syllabus, I have tried to make the case that there is very little givenness in language—that choices abound.[4] Indeed, every grammatical structure we produce in language has both a meaning and a use. Every time I speak, I am attempting to match my meaning or pragmatic intention with particular language forms for particular reasons. At the risk of repetitiveness, I should say that when we think of grammar, we should think of three dimensions: form, meaning, and use. In what follows, however, I will confine my remarks only to the use dimension.[5]

First of all, I think it bears saying that the old teacher standby "It depends" in answer to a student's question of "Should I say A or B?" is a very legitimate response. Students who are seeking a decisive answer are understandably dissatisfied with this one. However, such a response is an honest attempt to reflect the fact that the choice of a particular structure is dependent both on the intended meaning and on how the speaker construes the situation at the moment of speaking. As Close's interpretation of Example 15 demonstrates, multiple interpretations are possible. Of course,

---

[4]Of course, there may be a large inventory of fixed and semifixed lexicalized items that native speakers draw on for the sake of fluency (e.g., Pawley & Syder, 1983), so it is not true to say that at every juncture I have a choice. However, no matter what the size of the linguistic unit, these same dimensions of form, meaning, and use will apply.

[5]The pedagogical consequences of a grammar of choice are more fully illustrated in the ESL student series *Grammar Dimensions* (forthcoming) and the ESL teacher text *The Grammar Book: An ESL/EFL Teacher's Course* (Celce-Murcia & Larsen-Freeman, 1999).

I should hasten to add that the teacher should not leave the student's question at that. The student should be helped to see as clearly as possible and in a level-appropriate manner what each option entails. Often teachers and students think that questions about grammar should have one right answer. This is, however, certainly not the case.

Not all of these distinctions should be taught, of course. We can inform our students that a particular form is associated with a particular dialect without teaching it for production. Nevertheless, there are distinctions among these I have illustrated that do enable students to express meaning in the way they choose, and which would therefore be candidates for instruction. Much of the initial instruction might be of the consciousness-raising sort, without any explicit output practice. Students might be asked to engage in a consciousness-raising task in which they make a choice about which of two or three forms they might use on a given occasion, questions of the type illustrated by Example 17 from Sher. Their options should be accurate grammatical forms conveying similar propositional meaning. Subsequently, students should receive feedback on their choices. Later, during more communicative practice, students can be given situations in freer activities, such as role plays, and asked to use the grammar appropriate to the occasion and to the way that they would position themselves in that role. In this way, little by little, students will begin to understand the choices that are available to them and to learn the consequences of their choices.

In conclusion, far from being a linguistic straitjacket, grammar is a flexible, incredibly rich, system that enables proficient spreakers to express meaning in a way appropriate to the context, to how they wish to present themselves, and to the particular perspective they wish to contribute. Although accuracy is an issue in grammar, so is meaningfulness and appropriateness of use. A better way to conceive of grammar for pedagogical purposes, then, might be as a grammar of choice.

REFERENCES

Batstone, R. (1995). Grammar in discourse: Attitude and deniability. In G. Cook & B. Seidl-hofer (Eds.), *Principles and practice in applied linguistics: Studies in honour of H. G. Widdowson* (pp. 197–213). Oxford: Oxford University Press.

Bolinger, D. (1967). Adjectives in English: Attribution and predication. *Lingua, 18,* 1–34.

Celce-Murcia, M. (1980). Contextual analysis of English: Application to TESL. In D. Larsen-Freeman (Ed.), *Discourse analysis in second language research* (pp. 41–55). Rowley, MA: Newbury House.

Celce-Murcia, M. (1991). Discourse analysis and grammar instruction. *Annual Review of Applied Linguistics, 11,* 135–151.

Celce-Murcia, M. (1992). A nonhierarchial relationship between grammar and communication. Part 2. In J. E. Alatis (Ed.), *Georgetown University round table on languages and linguistics 1992* (pp. 166–173). Washington, DC: Georgetown University Press.

Celce-Murcia, M., & Larsen-Freeman, D. (1999). *The grammar book: An ESL/EFL teacher's course* (2nd ed.). Boston: Heinle & Heinle.

Close, R. A. (1992). *A teacher's grammar: The central problems of English.* Hove, UK: Language Teaching Publications.

Cook, V. (1999). Going beyond the native speaker in language teaching. *TESOL Quarterly, 33*, 185–209.

Gee, J. (1990). *Social linguistics and literacies: Ideology in discourse.* Bristol, PA: Falmer.

Green, G. (1989). *Pragmatics and natural language understanding.* Hillsdale, NJ: Erlbaum.

Hughes, R., & McCarthy, M. (1998). From sentence to discourse: Discourse grammar and English language teaching. *TESOL Quarterly, 32*, 263–287.

Lakoff, R. (1969). A syntactic argument for negative transportation. In R. J. Binnick, A. L. Davison, G. M. Green, & J. L. Morgan (Eds.), *Papers from the Fifth Regional Meeting of the Chicago Linguistic Society* (pp. 140–147). Chicago: Department of Linguistics, University of Chicago.

Larsen-Freeman, D. (1990). Pedagogical descriptions of language: Grammar. *Annual Review of Applied Linguistics, 10*, 187–195.

Larsen-Freeman, D. (1991). Teaching grammar. In M. Celce-Murcia (Ed.), *Teaching English as a second or foreign language* (pp. 279–295). New York: Newbury House.

Larsen-Freeman, D. (1992). A nonhierarchial relationship between grammar and communication. Part 1. In J. E. Alatis (Ed.), *Georgetown University round table on languages and linguistics 1992* (pp. 158–165). Washington, DC: Georgetown University Press.

Larsen-Freeman, D. (1994). Second language pedagogy: Grammar. In *The encyclopedia of language and linguistics* (Vol. 7, pp. 3752–3756). Oxford: Elsevier Science.

Larsen-Freeman, D. (1995). On the teaching and learning of grammar: Challenging the myths. In F. Eckman, D. Highland, P. Lee, J. Mileham, & R. Rutkowski Weber (Eds.), *Second language acquisition theory and pedagogy* (pp. 131–150). Hillsdale, NJ: Erlbaum.

Larsen-Freeman, D. (Forthcoming a). Grammar. In R. Carter & D. Nunan (Eds.), *An ELT companion.* Cambridge, UK: Cambridge University Press.

Larsen-Freeman, D. (2001b). *Teaching language: From grammar to grammaring.* Boston: Heinle & Heinle.

Pawley, A., & Syder, F. (1983). Two puzzles for linguistic theory: Nativelike selection and nativelike fluency. In J. Richards & R. Schmidt (Eds.), *Language and communication* (pp. 191–226). London: Longman.

Putzel, R. (1976). *Seeing differently through language: Grammatical correlates of personality.* Unpublished doctoral dissertation, University of California, Los Angeles.

Riddle, E. (1986). The meaning and discourse function of the past tense in English. *TESOL Quarterly, 20*, 267–286.

Sargent, M. (1997, November). *The interaction of language and gender.* Paper presented at the TESL conference, Halifax, Nova Scotia.

Stalker, J. (1989). Communicative competence, pragmatic functions, and accommodation. *Applied Linguistics, 10*, 182–193.

Widdowson, H. (1996). *Linguistics.* Oxford: Oxford University Press.

Yule, G. (1996). *Pragmatics.* Oxford: Oxford University Press.

Why It Makes Sense to Teach Grammar in Context and Through Discourse

Marianne Celce-Murcia
University of California, Los Angeles

INTRODUCTION

All naturalistic learning of first and second languages takes place in context and at the level of discourse rather than the abstract sentence level. When learners can comprehend and reproduce an utterance such as *I'm hungry*, the contextual meaning generally involves much more than the literal meaning of the sentence (see Celce-Murcia & Olshtain, 2000). If a child utters this to his mother on coming home from school, it is a request for food. If the same child utters it after having completed his lunch, the utterance is a complaint and a request for additional food. A beggar uttering these words in the street is requesting money rather than food. If a guest says these words on arriving for dinner, it may well signal an indirect compliment, "I've eaten very little today in anticipation of a wonderful meal," in addition to conveying the literal meaning of the utterance.

These differing interpretations of one surface utterance demonstrate that knowing the literal and decontextualized meaning of an utterance and being able to produce it with grammatical accuracy are only a part (some would say a small part) of being able to use the utterance appropriately in a variety of communicative contexts. One needs contextual knowledge (pragmatic knowledge regarding participants, purpose, topic, etc.) in addition to knowledge of grammar and lexis to be able to do this.

Contextual knowledge often interacts with another type of knowledge—discourse knowledge—which takes into account what has already been mentioned and what is most likely to be mentioned next. Knowledge of the unfolding discourse (or cotext) interacts with contextual knowledge when speakers choose articles in English, for example. Speakers make different presuppositions about what listeners know and share with them when they choose between utterances like Examples 1 and 2:

1. I saw the dog outside just now.

2. I saw a dog outside just now.

The first utterance presupposes that there is one specific dog that both the speaker and listener(s) can identify because of knowledge they share. The second utterance presupposes that the dog the speaker saw is unfamiliar either to the speaker, or the listener, or both of them. If the dog is unfamiliar to the speaker but presumed to be familiar to the listener, the speaker's talk might continue with, "Is it yours?" or "Is it your neighbor's?" However, if the dog is also presumed to be unfamiliar to the listener, the speaker might continue, "It was very friendly and tried to play with me and follow me in the house." Thus, the article the speaker initially selects (*a* versus *the*) establishes presuppositions, and the cotext that unfolds, which is often coconstructed by the interlocutors, gives us further information about who knew what. If the initiating speaker had said (1) above without making the correct presuppositions, the interlocutor might have responded by saying, *What dog?* This would in turn signal to the first speaker that an erroneous presupposition had been made and the wrong article had been used.

In formal linguistics, grammar is typically described and studied as context-free knowledge. This fits well with Chomsky's innateness hypothesis (Chomsky, 1968), which holds that all normal newborn humans are hard-wired for Universal Grammar and predisposed to learn whatever natural language(s) they are exposed to in the course of their cognitive development. This is not the only theory of how people learn first (or second) languages, however; another proposal is the language socialization hypothesis (Ochs, 1988), which holds that the grammar one acquires and uses as one develops cognitively and socially is highly constrained in terms of local social and cultural expectations and is shaped by local experiences over time rather than by an abstract universal and innate mechanism.

This author tends to side with the language socialization hypothesis and holds that grammar in a first or second language is acquired through the learner's repeated and meaningful experience with contextualized discourse, in which grammar is a structural resource that may or may not get explicitly analyzed by the learner as she or he observes and/or engages in meaningful interaction. What has convinced me of this position is the fact that so few "rules" of English grammar can be applied and used without reference to context. A few context-free rules that I have been able to think of are as follows:

- Verbs and verb phrases following prepositions must take the gerund form.
- Reflexive pronoun objects must agree in person, number, and gender with their subjects.
- Determiners must agree in number and noun type (count/mass) with their head nouns.

Other rules that some have proposed as context-free such as "subject-verb agreement" and "*some-any* suppletion" have been challenged by Reid (1991) and Lakoff (1969), respectively, who argue that these two grammar rules are not context free but meaning dependent. Certainly, the majority of grammatical problems that English as a second language/English as a foreign language (ESL/EFL) teachers have to deal with are not context free but rather clearly functionally motivated:

- Article usage (choice of definite, indefinite, or zero article)
- Choice of tense-aspect form
- Using past or present tense versus a modal auxiliary
- Choice of active versus passive voice
- Choice of a statement form or an interrogative form
- Choice of a syntactically affirmative form or a negative form
- Putting the indirect object after the verb or after the direct object and in a prepositional phrase (for ditransitive verbs that allow alternation)
- Putting the particle after the verb or after the direct object (for separable phrasal verbs)
- Using unmarked word order versus a marked construction such as "*it*-cleft" or "wh-cleft," and so forth

Using grammar entails making a series of decisions about when and why to use one form rather than another. Obviously, one needs to know the formal options (or be able to approximate them adequately) to make these decisions in an effective manner. Yet, if one's goal is communication, it seems even more important to be able to deploy forms effectively—even if the forms are partly inaccurate—than it is to use perfectly accurate forms inappropriately. Thus, the man who can ask, "What you want?" when a complete stranger walks into his house is more effective pragmatically than the bookworm who can say "I'd like to buy that horse" perfectly in 10 different languages but who ends up buying a mule because he does not know the difference between a horse and a mule. In the final analysis, context-free knowledge is of less value than contextualized knowledge. And when we speak of teaching grammar in context, we mean teaching grammar through context-embedded discourse rather than through abstract, context-free sentences.

As a final bit of background, let me make clear what I mean by "grammar" and "discourse." Grammar is by far the easier term to define. For me it includes syntax (word order), morphology (grammatical inflections on words), and function words (structurally important words like articles, prepositions, pronouns, auxiliary verbs, etc.).

Discourse is harder to define. A formal definition of "discourse" might specify that it is a coherent unit of language consisting of more than one sentence; a functional definition might characterize discourse as language in use (Schiffrin, 1994). However, neither definition is adequate on its own. Discourse in context may consist of only one or two words as in *stop* or *no smoking.* Alternatively, a piece of discourse can be hundreds of thousands of words in length, as some novels are. A typical piece of discourse is somewhere between these two extremes. Furthermore, the notion of "sentence" is not always relevant, especially if we are analyzing spoken discourse, and the phrase "language in use" is so general that it is almost meaningless. The best definition of discourse that we have been able to formulate (see Celce-Murcia & Olshtain, 2000) combines the formal and functional perspectives, that is, discourse is an instance of spoken or written language that has describable internal relationships of form and meaning that relate coherently to an external communicative function or purpose and a given audience/interlocutor. Furthermore, the external function or purpose can only be determined by taking into account the context and the participants (i.e., all the relevant social and cultural factors).

CONTEXTUAL ANALYSIS

Language pedagogy consists of far more than teaching grammar through discourse. However, for those teaching situations in which the teacher feels it would be desirable or necessary to focus on grammar (and to teach it through discourse), where can the teacher turn for the necessary background information? The work of functional grammarians such as Givón (1993), Halliday and Hasan (1976, 1989), and Thompson (1978, 1985)—although very valuable—does not yet give teachers a complete account of how grammar functions at the discourse level. Thus, for many years I have been training my graduate students to answer their own questions and solve their own problems by doing contextual analysis (Celce-Murcia, 1980a, 1990). This is an approach in which the researcher uses at least 100 tokens of a target form or structure (complete with contextual information and cotext) to begin making useful generalizations about where the target form occurs (or does not occur), what it means, and why it is used (or not used) by a given speaker/writer in a given piece of dixcourse. Today large commercially available on-line corpora not only greatly facilitate the data collection process but also allow for greater generalization of findings. (See Biber, Conrad, & Reppen (1998) and Kennedy (1998) for further information.)

When doing a contextual analysis, we begin by looking at form and distribution and then move on to meaning and use by taking relevant contextual information and the entire cotext into consideration. The grammar examples discussed in this chapter all involve research projects carried out by my graduate students and/or myself using contextual analysis and language corpora.

TEACHING GRAMMAR THROUGH SPOKEN DISCOURSE

What is the difference between the modal auxiliary *must* and the phrasal modals *have to (hafta)* and *have got to (gotta)?* Melrose (1983), in a contextual analysis of these forms, discovered that most native speakers of American English use *must* in their speech primarily for expressing present and past inferences, or what linguists often refer to as the epistemic use of *must:*[1]

> *You must have the wrong phone number.*

> *John must have been teasing when he said that.*

The form *have to* is used by Americans mainly to express externally motivated and internally motivated necessity in their speech:

> *You have to fill out this form before the doctor sees you.*

> *Excuse me. I have to go to the restroom.*

---

[1]There is an emphatic use of *must* that is not inferential. It is spoken mainly by females in the context of making a recommendation but did not occur in Melrose's data: for example, *You simply must try the cheesecake. It's fabulous.*

Melrose examined a database with equal proportions of spoken and written discourse[2] and found only two spoken tokens of *must* expressing necessity (in contrast to dozens of tokens of *have to*). Her results seem to reflect a dialect difference of sorts between British and American English, because British speakers appear to use *must* much more frequently in their speech to signal necessity than do Americans, who would tend to use *have to* instead (*COBUILD Dictionary*, 1987):

I must come over and see you.

Ok, I'll talk to him if I must. (p. 951)

According to Melrose, rather than having any discrete meaning, *have got to*—in contrast to *must* or *have to*—is used in speech but not in writing by Americans to express either inference or necessity with special urgency and affect (real or feigned):

You gotta be kidding.

You've gotta lend me $20.00, Sam. I'm broke!

The findings from Melrose's study give us and our students guidelines on how Americans typically use these forms and why native speakers seem to find utterances from nonnative speakers such as the following to be a bit odd, given that *have to* (or *have got to*) is much more typically used than *must* in such conversational necessity-based contexts:[3]

? You must exercise more to lose some weight.

? I must go to the restroom.

The second grammatical problem in spoken American English that we will examine here is the use of coordinating tag forms like *I do too* in contrast to inverted tags like *so do I*. Many reference grammars and ESL/EFL teaching materials cite sentence-level examples and claim that these forms are equivalent:

---

[2]Melrose's corpus consisted of oral data such as *The White House Transcripts* and available transcripts of radio talk shows, whereas her written data covered a variety of genres. See Melrose (1983) for detailed specification of the corpus.

[3]Part of the perceived oddness of such directives with *must* is undoubtedly the fact that the speaker does not have the status vis-à-vis the interlocutor to issue such a strong directive. The first example would be okay if a doctor said it to a patient, for example.

John loves strong coffee, and I do too.

John loves strong coffee, and so do I.

There are also parallel uninverted and inverted patterns for negated sentences:

John doesn't like brussels sprouts, and I don't either.

John doesn't like brussels sprouts, and neither do I.

Although these sentences do seem very similar, through an examination of the occurrence and use of these forms in discourse, Celce-Murcia (1980b) reveals that there are many differences. The *too/either* tags permit the addition of new information in the predicate, whereas the inverted *so/neither tags* do not:[4]

My brother plays second base, and he pitches too.

*My brother plays second base, and so does he pitch.

Another difference is that when these forms are abbreviated to the minimum and used in rejoinders only the *too/either* version is possible:

A: I'm sorry the Chicago Cubs lost the game.

B: Me too![5]

The *so/neither* forms do not have such minimal abbreviated variants:

A: I'm sorry the Chicago Cubs lost the game.

B: *So me.

A third difference in distribution is that the *too/either* forms are strongly preferred over the *so/neither* forms when these forms are preceded by a logical connector (Shayne, 1975):

---

[4]This study involved use of oral data that included the transcripts in Carterette and Jones (1974) and written data that included news reports and editorials as well as fiction. For further specification, see Celce-Murcia (1980b).

[5]The negative equivalent of *me too* varies. It can be *me either* or *me neither*. When the latter is used, I feel this is simply a sign that the rejoinder is negative, not an indication that the inverted tag is being abbreviated.

Macy's offers lots of bargains, although . . .

(a) so does Gimbel's.

(b) Gimbel's does too. (This form is strongly preferred by native speakers.)

Celce-Murcia (1980b) also found that in environments where native speakers were expressing some negative affect or negative evaluation, the inverted *so/neither* forms were strongly preferred over the more neutral *too/either* tags. Exemplars such as the following occurred:

"You're a (expletive deleted), and so's your old man!"

A: I get up at 6 A.M. every day!

B: So what? So do I!

When asked, native speakers agreed that these utterances would lose some of their emotionally charged and highly negative message if the speakers had said: *and your old man is too* or *So what? I do too.*

Thus, although the uninverted *either/too* tags are more versatile than the inverted *so/neither* tags, there are important differences at the discourse level that make it very misleading for teachers and textbooks to present these structures as if they were perfect paraphrases of each other. In fact, for the majority of tokens occurring in naturalistic discourse, it is not possible to substitute one of these tag types for the other. This is why it is very important to provide learners with authentic discourse samples to illustrate all of the contextually dependent grammatical rules they are expected to learn.

TEACHING GRAMMAR THROUGH WRITTEN DISCOURSE

My first example for written discourse is the use of the past perfect tense in written narrative. This tense has typically been explained at the sentence level as having two different meanings (see also chaps. 7, 9, and 27 in Celce-Murcia & Larsen-Freeman, 1999):

1. Past counterfactual (in certain embedded or subordinate clauses)

   I wish I'd said that (= I didn't say that.)

   If John had studied, he would have passed the test. (=John didn't study.)

   She collected the test before I had finished it. (=I didn't finish the test.)

2. The event marked with past perfect occurred prior to another event/ act:

When he arrived, I had finished eating. (eating occurred before arriving)

He said that he had read the book. (reading occurred before saying)

However, there is another use of the past perfect that can be understood only with reference to discourse. Consider the following text (target form has been italicized):

> The students sat in the bleachers of Pauley Pavilion, watching the faculty enter in their caps and gowns. Dignitaries continued to arrive while the band played a festive melody for the onlookers. To the cheers of the crowd, President Clinton came in and took his assigned seat on the podium . . . UCLA's 75th anniversary celebration *had begun*. (*UCLA Daily Bruin*, May 24, 1994)

This text defies a sentence-level description appealing to past counterfactuality or a prior happening. Instead, in this text the past perfect seems to signal a climax or an author's coda of sorts. By using the past perfect, the writer of this article is saying, somewhat dramatically, "Pay attention; this is why I'm telling you this story." Because the past perfect is a marked tense (in contrast to the simple past, which is used for the rest of the narrative), authors can use the past perfect to signal some important climax, breakthrough, or discovery with respect to their narrative. Here are two more texts of this type:

> In the 1980s researchers at Stanford University were trying to teach American Sign Language to Koko, a female gorilla. Koko was well cared for and was surrounded by interesting objects. Her caretakers continually exposed her to signs for the food and toys in her environment. Koko particularly loved to eat bananas and play with kittens. One day Koko was hungry but couldn't find any bananas. She went to the researcher and made a good approximation of the sign for "banana." Koko was immediately rewarded with a banana, but even more important, the research team knew that Koko *had made the connection* between a sign and the object it represented. (author data)

> The "Rent" story began in the summer of 1992, when Larson, riding his bike down 4th Street in the East Village, passed the New York Theatre Workshop, which was a mess with a major renovation. "He stuck his head in the door," says James Nicola, the artistic director of NYTW. He looked in and thought, "This is perfect." What was perfect was the extraordinary NYTW stage, 40 feet wide and 30 feet deep in a house that had 150 seats . . .

> The next day Larson cycled back and dropped off a tape of songs he had written for "Rent," all sung by him. "I listened to a couple and immediately knew this was a rare and gifted songwriter," says Nicola. The four-year process of creating "Rent" *had begun*. (*Newsweek*, May 13, 1996, p. 58)

Note that the verbs used in the past perfect in such texts are quite limited in terms of their lexical aspect; they are punctual verbs and verb phrases that signal the moment when something happened: Something had begun/started, a discovery/breakthrough had occurred/been made, and so forth. Again, these are not sentence-level uses of the past perfect, but a discourse-level use that can only be conveyed to learners through exposure to and engagement with appropriate authentic texts.[6]

The second construction in written discourse that I shall use as an illustration is the *it*-cleft, for example, *It was John who broke the window.* Kim (1988) shows that such sentences are about twice as frequent in written as in spoken discourse; I believe this distribution reflects the fact that in spoken discourse one can signal the same message more economically via prosody, for instance, *JOHN broke the window.* In any case, it is important to note at the outset that writers use *it*-clefts for two different purposes (Prince, 1978):

Stress focus: The constituent following *it*+be receives emphasis, thereby signaling a contrast between this constituent and all other possibilities, as in the example above, *It was John (and no one else) who broke the window.* The presupposed part, *who broke the window*, is known information in this type of *it*-cleft.

Information focus: The relative clause contains new information in this type of *it*-cleft, but the constituent following "*it*+be" is repeated or anaphoric (i.e., known) information, for example, *It was there that Joe and Mary met for the first time.*

Kim's corpus-based analysis[7] reveals that *it*-clefts occur most frequently in written genres such as historical narrative, persuasive discourse, and journalistic writing.

In what follows I give two examples of the stress focus type of *it*-cleft, one each from *Time* and *Newsweek:*

---

[6]The examples of the past perfect used to mark a coda in written discourse do not come from a specific corpus. They are examples of a salient pattern that I have noted and collected over several years after the pattern came to my attention. It would be useful to check the frequency and distribution of this pattern in a written corpus.

[7]Kim (1988) used a sizable corpus—see Kim (1988) for further specification—of spoken and written American English to examine the distribution and functions of *wh*-clefts and *it*-clefts at the discourse level, so I have simply used his findings to select representative examples for this chapter.

It was Cole who chose Fargo as the microcosm for the debate on federal benevolence and intrusion. Says Duffy, who wrote the story, "She saw it as a fascinating mix of frontier and front page. Then she dissected the town until she knew more about it than Fargoans. Late last week, needing an anecdote, she ran down to a local bowling alley, did three interviews and delivered a freshly minted kicker for the story inside an hour." (*Time*, May 22, 1995, p. 4)

This was the fourth paragraph of a five-paragraph article titled "To our readers," which discussed two *Time* correspondents, Michael Duffy and Wendy Cole. The article was obviously more about Cole than Duffy, since she is the topic of four of the five paragraphs, including the one above. The placement of Cole in the information focus of the paragraph using a marked *it*-cleft signals that she will be the topic of the paragraph and also provides stylistic variation with the other three paragraphs about Cole, which begin: *Cole has . . . , Wendy has . . . , Cole found . . . .*
Here is the second example of a stress-focus it-cleft:

The president believes the press is driving the impeachment train. "They [the Republicans] think you're with 'em," he said with a smile. "As long as they think you all [the media] are with 'em, they'll keep on going." Actually, most Washington pundits would be satisfied to end the mess now with a plea bargain, censure and a fine. . . . *It's* the GOP leadership that wants to push the pedal all the way down. They're depressingly close to gassing the country into another six to nine months of Monica, polls be damned. The House Judiciary Committee, whose GOP members come from conservative Clinton-hating congressional districts, is all but certain to vote impeachment—along party lines. (*Newsweek*, Oct. 5, 1998, p. 36)[8]

The above paragraph is the seventh of a nine-paragraph essay, titled, "They Always Get It Right," which is a quote from President Clinton about what he feels is the wisdom of the American people. The marked *it*-cleft occurs in the middle of the paragraph to convey with some emphasis the writer's opinion that the GOP leadership (not the media or Washington pundits) was intent on dragging out impeachment proceedings against Clinton.

---

[8]The two sentences I have omitted from the middle of this paragraph (*Newsweek*, 1998) are an aside from the author that appear in parentheses:

(I'd like Clinton also to undertake a couple of hours a week of community service as a penance. If he can find time for illicit sex, he can find time to volunteer—with no cameras—in a school or homeless shelter.) (*Newsweek*, Oct. 5, 1998, p. 36)

Although interesting, this aside did not seem relevant to the overall structure of the paragraph and thus it was omitted from the excerpt used in this chapter.

In both of the above cases the contrastive meaning inherent in the use of the *it*-cleft is clear. Notice that in the two following examples no such contrast is conveyed in the topic constituent of the information focus *it*-clefts, both of which occur in two successive paragraphs in a three-page article in the *Los Angeles Times,* titled "On the Road Through Morocco, Family Style":

> Although it was quite intimidating to our kids (and their parents) at first, we soon began adapting to the square's bizarre rhythm. Musicians, magicians, acrobats, folk healers, fire eaters, storytellers, snake charmers, monkey trainers, tooth extractors, hustlers, beggars and, of course, those who merely observe this amazing scene are among the crowd that converges here as the sun sets each evening. *It's then* that dozens of small mobile eateries are set up on the periphery, serving everything from traditional Moroccan lamb stew to couscous and pastries to steamed lamb heads replete with their most coveted delicacy, the eyeballs.
>
> *It was* this latter food item that convinced us we would eat in a bona fide restaurant, Dar Marjana, about five minutes from the square. There, an elderly, bent-over man in a djellaba, or long robe, greeted us with a lantern in hand and led us down a dark, narrow alleyway opening onto a beautiful courtyard ringed by knee-high tables. (*Los Angeles Times,* Oct. 4, 1998, p. L20)

In these two paragraphs from the middle of a fairly long travel section article, the two information focus *it*- clefts occur (1) in the last sentence of the first paragraph and (2) in the first sentence of the second paragraph. In both cases, the element in focus is anaphoric known information (i.e., *then* is coreferential with *as the sun sets each evening* and *this latter food item* is coreferential with *steamed lamb heads replete with their most coveted delicacy, the eyeballs).* The respective relative clauses in these two *it*-clefts convey new information:

1. that dozens of small mobile eateries are set up
2. that convinced us we would eat in a bona fide restaurant

The writer could have worded these sentences differently; however, she chose to use information focus *it*-clefts to introduce stylistic variety and (hopefully) maintain reader interest at this midpoint in the narrative about her family's travels.

Note that although the stress-focus, contrastive *it*-clefts could conceivably be taught and practiced at the sentence-level, such a strategy would be impossible for teaching the use of information-focus *it*-clefts, which make use of known information as the focused element in order to introduce new information in the relative clause.

A PEDAGOGICAL APPROACH

It would take too much space to show you how I would teach each of the four grammar points discussed above, so I will take just one point, the past perfect tense in written narrative, to illustrate the type of teaching strategy I use when teaching grammar through discourse.

In my own ESL classes and in ESL tutorials, I have used texts like the three authentic texts presented above for the past perfect (i.e., the texts about the UCLA anniversary, Koko, and *Rent*) to use initially for reading comprehension. Students ask questions about any words or structures that are unclear and then orally summarize the stories for me in their own words. Then, I ask the students to work in groups to answer questions like these about the three texts:

1. Where does the past perfect tense occur in these texts?
2. What other tense(s) occur(s)?
3. What is the function in the texts of the sentence with the past perfect tense?
4. What kind of verb takes the past perfect in such a text?

Once the groups have come up with their explanations, we discuss them and use the best of the suggested explanations as the grammar explanation for this phenomenon (revising it, if necessary).

As the final step, I ask the students to try to think of some past event they are familiar with that involves some important climax, result, or turning point that one might want to mention and emphasize at the end of a narrative about the event. I ask them to write their own short narratives (in groups or individually) in the simple past—using the past perfect for the somewhat dramatic climax.

When I tried this strategy with a class of fairly advanced ESL students, many of them wrote good narratives; the best one, titled "The Rosetta Stone," was written by a student majoring in archeology, and I'd like to share it with you (it has been edited for minor morphological and spelling errors and could now be used as an additional example text):

"The Rosetta Stone"

Before 1800 no one knew how to read Egyptian hieroglyphics. In 1799 arche-ologists found a basalt tablet in the town of Rosetta, Egypt, which later was called the Rosetta Stone. This tablet was important because it contained the same message written in Egyptian hieroglyphics, in Egyptian Demotic script, and in Greek. Because the researchers already knew how to read Demotic script and Greek, they were able to figure out the meaning of the hieroglyph-ics for the first time. The code *had* finally been *cracked*.

CONCLUSION

What has become increasingly clear to me in my ongoing studies of English grammar and my attempts to teach it is that we can explain only part of English grammar at the sentence level (sometimes we can explain a significant part, as with the counterfactual and prior-event meanings of the past perfect; sometimes we can explain very little at the sentence level, as with articles and information-focus *it*-clefts). To fully understand any form or construction, we must also understand how it functions at the discourse level. This is true even for structures we can describe at the sentence level, because teachers (and learners) still need to know in what discourse genres and contexts such sentences normally occur. Once we change our perspective from sentence level to discourse level, we are in a position to teach grammar both as a resource for creating discourse in context and as a resource for using language to communicate—both receptively and productively. This is what most of us are in fact trying to do when we teach language, so contextualized discourse-level analyses of English grammar that supplement and go beyond existing sentence-level accounts have the potential to enrich and transform the way we teach grammar and the way our students learn grammar. I hope my examples have helped illustrate this new analytical and pedagogical perspective for you. In my opinion, it offers a long overdue supplement—if not a radical alternative—to sentence-level grammar instruction.

ACKNOWLEDGMENTS

I would like to acknowledge that this chapter reflects very noticeably my collaborations over the years on the teaching of grammar with Diane Larsen-Freeman and Elite Olshtain. I have drawn heavily on examples, texts, and ideas used in these collaborative efforts; however, any errors or shortcomings in this chapter are mine alone.

REFERENCES

Biber, D., Conrad, S., & Reppen, R. (1998). *Corpus linguistics: Investigating English structure and use.* Cambridge, UK: Cambridge University Press.
Carterette, E., & Jones, M. (1974). *Informal speech.* Berkeley: University of California Press.
Celce-Murcia, M. (1980a). Contextual analysis of English: Application to TESL. In D. Larsen-Freeman (Ed.), *Discourse analysis in second language research* (pp. 41–55). Rowley, MA: Newbury House.
Celce-Murcia, M. (1980b). A discourse analysis of *I do too, so do I.* In J. Povey (Ed.), *Language policy and language teaching: Essays in honor of Clifford Prator.* Los Angeles: English Language Services.

Celce-Murcia, M. (1990). Data-based language analysis and TESL. In *Proceedings of the Georgetown round table on languages and linguistics 1990* (pp. 245–259). Washington, DC: Georgetown University Press.

Celce-Murcia, M., & Larsen-Freeman, D. (1999). *The grammar book: An ESL/EFL teacher's course* (2nd ed.). Boston: Heinle & Heinle.

Celce-Murcia, M., & Olshtain, E. (2000). *Discourse and context in language teaching.* New York: Cambridge University Press.

Chomsky, N. (1968). *Language and mind.* New York: Harcourt, Brace, and World.

COBUILD English Dictionary. (1987). London: Collins.

Givón, T. (1993). *English grammar: A function-based approach.* Amsterdam: John Benjamins.

Halliday, M., & Hasan, R. (1976). *Cohesion in English.* London: Longman.

Halliday, M., & Hasan, R. (1989). *Language, context, and text: Aspects of language in a social-semotic perspective.* Oxford: Oxford University Press.

Kennedy, G. (1998). *An introduction to corpus linguistics.* Harlow, UK: Addison Wesley Longman.

Kim, K-H. (1988). *A discourse analysis of cleft and pseudo-cleft constructions in American English.* Unpublished master's thesis, University of California, Los Angeles.

Lakoff, R. (1969). Some reasons why there can't be any *some-any* rule. *Language, 45,* 608–615.

Melrose, S. (1983). Must *and its periphrastic forms in American English usage.* Unpublished master's thesis, University of California, Los Angeles.

Ochs, E. (1988). *Culture and language development.* Cambridge, UK: Cambridge University Press.

Prince, E. (1978). A comparison of *wh*-clefts and *it*-clefts in discourse. *Language, 54,* 883–906.

Reid, W. (1991). *Verb and noun number in English: A functional explanation.* London: Longman.

Schiffrin, D. (1994). *Approaches to discourse.* Oxford: Basil Blackwell.

Shayne, J. (1975). *I do too* versus *so do I.* Unpublished English 215 paper, University of California, Los Angeles.

Thompson, S. (1978). Modern English from a typological point of view: Some implications of the function of word order. *Linguistische Berichte, 54,* 19–35.

Thompson, S. (1985). Grammar and written discourse: Initial vs. final purpose clauses in English. *Text, 5,* 56–84.

Structure-Based Interactive Tasks for the EFL Grammar Learner

Sandra Fotos
Senshu University, Tokyo, Japan

Although this chapter addresses the use of task-based grammar instruction in the English as a foreign language (EFL) classroom, many considerations also apply to classrooms in English as a second language (ESL) settings where learners particularly need to build grammatical accuracy. Structure-based tasks designed to promote awareness of target grammar forms are presented as useful pedagogy for providing communicative reinforcement of instructed grammar points, an important consideration because grammar teaching is characteristic of many EFL classrooms and of academic ESL programs as well. Procedures for the creation of course-specific structure-based tasks are also discussed.

THE NEED FOR EXPLICIT GRAMMAR TEACHING

As mentioned in the Introduction to this volume, input-enhanced communicative syllabuses that focus on *form* rather than *forms* have been recommended by some researchers as an effective way to introduce grammatical points. Such syllabuses present grammar points indirectly and have been termed "analytic" (Long & Crookes, 1992; Wilkins, 1976), in contrast with "synthetic" syllabuses, which are structure based. In analytic communicative syllabuses, grammar forms are introduced through carefully designed activities but are not usually instructed formally. The underlying premise here (Long, 1991; Skehan, 1996) is that learners will be able to unconsciously analyze aspects of the target language when required to by the nature of the communicative activity. Research supporting this view (see reviews in N. Ellis, 1995; Long & Robinson, 1998) maintains that learners can successfully notice, then process, linguistic structures that have been introduced to them within purely communicative contexts, particularly if there is a deliberate enhancement of the communicative input to draw learners' attention to the target structure, for example, by "flooding" communicative material with numerous usages of the structure (e.g., Trahey & White, 1993) or by making the structures obvious by highlighting.

Such an approach has been termed *implicit* grammatical instruction because there is no overt mention of the target grammatical point (Ellis, R., 1997). This approach, however, is dependent on learner access to abundant in-class communicative material containing the target forms, and also assumes that learners are exposed to outside communicative input to support their continued awareness. These requirements present several difficulties, particularly in the EFL situation.

Problems with Purely Communicative Approaches

A first issue in the implementation of communicative approaches in general has been the development and sequencing of communicative instructional material. Although ostensibly meaning focused and lacking formal instruction, many "communicative" textbooks are, in fact structure based, proceeding from easy to difficult grammar forms and lexical items, even if the target forms are not directly taught through a formal lesson. In addition, most of these textbooks do not supply extensive communicative material containing target structures, thus, the teacher must generate additional activities and integrate them into the syllabus while maintaining required materials. This is problematic in situations where class time is limited or teachers are required to use the same textbook and give identical examinations based on those texts. Here the development and accommodation of extra communicative material to allow students to notice particular forms is extremely difficult.

Second, purely communicative methodology has had only marginal impact on the overall teaching of English throughout the globe (Skehan, 1998), where the dominant pedagogy continues to involve a structural syllabus and grammar translation. Many English language programs attached to universities within the ESL situation also maintain a structural focus because learners expect this type of instructional format and feel that they cannot achieve the necessary proficiency gains to exit the program and enter regular academic classes without explicit, teacher-led instruction.

In addition, there is recent empirical evidence demonstrating that explicit instruction is necessary to promote high levels of accuracy in the target language, even when communicative opportunities to encounter target forms are abundant. Researchers have found that learners benefit from formal instruction prior to meaning-focused activities because such instruction helps them activate their previous knowledge of the target structures and promotes their attention to the forms they will encounter (e.g., Cadierno 1995; Ellis, R., 1995, 1998; Lightbown, 1992; Lightbown & Spada, 1990; Robinson, 1996; White, 1991). It must be noted, however, that this suggestion was made several decades before by cognitive psychologist David Ausubel (Ausubel, Novak, & Hanesian, 1978) and is widely used in general education. It is called the Advance Organizer.

According to Ausubel, learning a second language is similar to learning another set of symbols for familiar meanings. The main act is establishing equivalency between the new symbols and the meaningful symbols already stored in the mind through the prior language. Thus, new material should be connected to existing ideas in the learner's cognitive structure to facilitate the construction and organization of form-meaning relationships. This is achieved through use of the Advance Organizer, the presentation of introductory material ahead of the learning task and at a higher level of abstraction. The Advance Organizer explains and integrates the material to be learned with previously learned material, establishing the relationship between new and old knowledge. This consideration is support for explicit grammar instruction prior to performance of communicative activities containing the instructed point.

New research also indicates that meaning-focused exposure to grammar forms previously taught in a formal grammar lesson significantly increases learner accuracy in use of these forms. A study of more than 40 ESL classrooms in Canada found that learners from communicative classes in which teachers gave brief grammar explanations and corrected learner errors showed greater accuracy in use of the target forms than learners from communicative classrooms without such intervention. Similar results have been reported in investigations of feedback on learner errors (Carroll & Swain, 1993), adverb placement (White, 1991), and question formation (White, Spada, Lightbown, & Ranta, 1991). Such communicative exposure to instructed grammar points has been called "consolidated acquisition" (Lightbown, 1992), and has been suggested to facilitate the processing of the new forms.

In addition to formal instruction before meaning-focused activities, postactivity feedback correcting errors and pointing out how the target form has been used in context has also been recommended (Carroll & Swain, 1993; Ellis, R., 1994, 1997; Fotos, 1998; Skehan, 1998; White, 1991). Such summative activities also assist in processing the new information and integrating it with previous knowledge.

The Three-Part Grammar Lesson

Thus, there is a strong case for a grammar lesson that has the following three parts: (1) explicit grammar instruction, preferably at the beginning of the lesson; (2) communicative activities containing many usages of the instructed form; and (3) summary activities to focus learners' attention on the grammar form they were instructed on and then encountered communicatively.

In the next section, the use of tasks as pedagogy within this three-step model of grammar teaching is outlined. It is be suggested that grammar task performance can instruct learners, increase their awareness of the target forms, and provide reinforcement for noticing how instructed features are used in meaning-focused contexts.

TASK–BASED APPROACHES TO LANGUAGE INSTRUCTION

Although tasks have been used in the field of general education for many decades and have been essential research instruments for psychological, anthropological, sociological, and organizational research, it is only since the 1980s that tasks have become prominent in second/foreign language learning. At this time a number of researchers and curriculum developers proposed that second/foreign languages could be effectively taught through a task-based approach (Crookes & Gass, 1993a, 1993b; Dickins & Woods, 1988; Long, 1991; Long & Crookes, 1992; Nunan, 1989, 1993; Prabhu, 1987; Robinson, 1996; Skehan, 1996, 1998), and some have even called for syllabuses consisting entirely of tasks.

The Rationale for Task Use

Support for task-based approaches to language instruction comes from the theoretical assumptions that interaction is fundamental to language acquisition and that both learner comprehension and production play significant roles in interaction (Ellis, R., 1994, 1997; Nunan, 1993). Tasks can supply the learner with target language input that is rich in communicative usages of problematic target structures, and task performance provides opportunities for the type of learner interaction suggested to promote language acquisition; that is, opportunities to produce the target language and receive feedback on the productions. Such feedback has been suggested to be particularly important because it enables learners to "notice the gap" between the target language they want to produce and the limitations of their current interlanguage (Carroll & Swain, 1993; Kowal and Swain, 1994; Swain & Lapkin, 1998), thus encouraging "pushed output" (Swain, 1985; Swain & Lapkin, 1998), a term referring to learners' efforts to modify their output in the direction of increasingly targetlike forms after they have received feedback that their previous utterances were not well understood.

There have been a number of studies of learner talk during task performance (summarized in R. Ellis, 1997), and such talk is often called "negotiated interaction" because learners "negotiate meaning" with each other by asking and answering questions to assist their understanding. The types of negotiation will be discussed in more detail in a following section. Other investigations comparing the talk produced by tasks to that from teacher-fronted lessons (e.g., Pica, 1997; Pica & Doughty, 1985; Rulon & McCreary, 1986) indicate that learners produce more in pairs/groups, tend to use longer utterances, are more relaxed and less anxious about using the TL (Target Language), yet do not tend to speak any less grammatically than in teacher-fronted participation patterns. It was therefore suggested by several researchers (Ellis, N., 1995; Fotos, 1994; Fotos & Ellis, 1991; Loschky & Bley-Vroman, 1990, 1993) that it might be possible to construct interactive, problem-solving tasks that would provide both grammar instruction and communicative interaction.

At this point, however, it must be noted that some researchers (e.g., Long, 1991; Skehan, 1998) suggest that focus on specific grammar forms, whether through traditional instruction or through task performance, would probably not lead to a restructuring of the learner's internal linguistic system. Rather, a purely communicative task-based approach determined by analysis of the learners' real-world needs for communicative functions in the target language would be more successful in promoting the necessary amounts of meaningful interaction to result in language acquisition.

However true this might be for the ESL situation (which remains to be determined), this consideration is not valid for the EFL situation for two reasons. First, access to communicative TL, both inside and outside the classroom, is extremely limited. Therefore, EFL learners cannot receive enough communicative input to allow them to acquire uninstructed target language forms. Second, EFL learners do not have the same real-world needs for specific communicative functions in the target language as ESL learners do. Rather, they need to pass the English portion of entrance examinations for high school or college, or to obtain high scores on proficiency measures such as the TOEFL (Test of English as a Foreign Language) for study abroad. Thus, their real-world needs involve mastery of grammar structures that will be tested and the attainment of accuracy in their use.

Consequently, this chapter rejects such purely communicative task-based approaches in favor of a combination of formal instruction supported by performance of structure-based interactive tasks and summative activities at the end of the lesson.

The following section presents different task definitions, task types, and task features.

Task Definitions, Classifications, and Features

Definitions. A number of definitions of "task" have been proposed since task use became a focus for language instruction (see the summary in Nunan, 1993). In 1983, Long defined a task as "a piece of work or activity from everyday life, undertaken for self or other, done freely or based on reward." In 1987, Prabhu defined communicative tasks as interactive activities that require learners to negotiate meaning and to arrive at an outcome. Pica, Holliday, Lewis, and Morgenthaler (1989) suggested that tasks were activities carried out through language according to procedures for communication requiring the encoding and acting on of information. A similar information-processing approach was followed by Nunan (1989, 1993), who defined tasks as classroom work requiring learners to comprehend, manipulate, produce, or interact in meaning focused use of the TL.

A synthesis of the various definitions of task has been proposed by Skehan (1998, p. 95), who considers tasks to be activities in which:

1. meaning is primary;
2. there is a communication problem of some type to solve;
3. the activity has some relationship to real-world activities;
4. task completion is usually required; and
5. task performance can be assessed in terms of the outcome.

It should be noted that these definitions generally do not regard solitary activities as task performance, although with the rise of computer-assisted language learning, learner-computer interaction to complete online tasks is becoming quite common and necessitates reexamination of what constitutes a "task."

Classification. Building on the research of Prabhu (1987) and others, in 1993, Pica and her associates classified tasks on the basis of who holds and conveys information, who requests and who gives feedback on the information, the direction of the information flow, the precision of the information required, and the number of possible task solutions. On this basis, five types of communicative tasks were identified:

1. the information gap task, where one participant holds information that must be given to others;
2. the jigsaw task, which is a multiway information gap task, requiring all participants to give and receive information;
3. the problem-solving task, which is a multiway information gap task requiring the participants to agree on a single task solution;

4. the decision-making task, which is similar to the problem-solving task and requires the participants to agree on a decision, and

5. an opinion exchange, which often does not require a task solution.

Nunan (1989, 1993), however, classified tasks on the basis of their communicative function, and identified two task types, real-world or pedagogical. Real-world tasks consisted of essential communicative activities that learners needed to function in their new country, and pedagogic tasks were designed to promote the language acquisition process, although they might have no connection to the language functions required by the learners in their daily lives. Skehan (1998) has maintained this distinction in his discussion of task types, considering that pedagogic, structure-oriented tasks that require production of particular grammar forms are perhaps "unnatural" and may be less relevant to the learners' needs and processing requirements than real-world communication-driven tasks (pp. 123–124), for which the requirement for language production is more "natural" and is conducted in an unforced way. This consideration has been raised by other researchers as well (Breen, 1987; Long & Crookes, 1992; Long & Robinson, 1998). In fact, Breen (1987, p. 42) firmly states that "tasks must accommodate objectives which can been seen by learners as directly in harmony with their own perceived and stated learning needs."

As discussed previously, although the distinction between task content serving pedagogic purposes and communication-driven task content related to the learners' real-world needs for life within in the host country may be useful in the ESL situation, this chapter stresses the suitability of structure-based tasks for the EFL situation, in which learners' needs regarding the target language are quite different, and involve the development of formal knowledge and rules regarding English grammar and accuracy in the use of specific structures on which they will be tested.

Features. The type of task features that promote learner interaction has also been examined (see reviews in R. Ellis, 1997; Long, 1991; Skehan, 1998), and the presence of four task features has been suggested to maximize use of the target language:

1. the requirement for a single task solution;
2. the requirement for task participants to agree on the solution;
3. the requirement for all participants to exchange information; and
4. opportunities for participants to plan their language use (referring to thinking through or rehearsing language, often by writing it down).

Tasks should therefore incorporate as many of these features as possible.

CHARACTERISTICS OF THE EFL SETTING

Before two types of structure-based tasks designed to teach grammar within the EFL setting are described, it is useful to consider some characteristics of the EFL environment.

To start, we must acknowledge that, numerically, much of the English language instruction in the world is not ESL based but occurs overseas in the EFL situation, mainly with teachers who are not native speakers of English themselves. Well over a decade ago it was estimated that more than half of the world's population is bi- or multilingual, with one third speaking English as a first or second language or learning it as a foreign language (Crystal, 1985). As I have noted (Fotos, 1998, pp. 303–304), certain features tend to characterize many EFL environments. For example, in many countries the educational system is controlled by a central agency that determines the curriculum to be taught and the textbooks to be used. When EFL teaching commences, usually in the first year of middle school, the goal is learner mastery of specific vocabulary items, translation skills, and grammatical structures that will be tested during rigorous examinations determining entry into high schools. In high school the teaching of EFL is usually test driven, preparing learners for university entrance examinations.

Given these circumstances, it is clear why grammar instruction on mastery of specific patterns, lexical items, and translation dominates the secondary level EFL curriculum. Indeed, in some countries it is possible to buy English examination preparatory material containing lists of vocabulary, phrases and idioms, required grammar structures, and practice sentences for translation, and universities often publish their previous entrance examinations as a study guide for future test takers.

Educational agencies in these countries recognize that learners are unable to use the English language communicatively despite their years of study because of this exclusively grammatical focus. As a result, both middle school and high school curricula have undergone significant reform in countries such as Japan and Korea and now contain an "oral communication" emphasis.

This change in emphasis is producing test reform, with some nations already encouraging use of a TOEFL-type listening section on the English portion of university entrance examinations. However, whether these revisions will be successful in promoting communicative ability remains to be determined. Although the central agency guidelines stress communicative competence, the means to achieve this have not been specified. Consequently, in practice, many "oral communicative" classes are not essentially different from classes lacking a communicative emphasis.

An additional factor mitigating against purely communicative methodology is the large class size at many secondary and tertiary institutions, making teacher supervision of pair/group work very difficult. Thus, learner use of a first language to perform communicative activities meant to be done in the target language is a constant problem. Furthermore, seats and desks are often attached to the floor, making it difficult to arrange the learners in groups.

A more serious problem is the fact that task performance, with its noise, shifting of chairs, and so forth may not be regarded as a "serious" educational activity by traditionally minded educators (Fotos, 1994) or by the learners themselves, who are quite unused to a group participation pattern during study of a required subject. Indeed, the emphasis on the benefits of task performance is culturally linked to Western instructional methodology and deserves reexamination in the light of non-Western cultures' perceptions of what constitutes acceptable pedagogic activities and classroom participation patterns.

Communicative Approaches in EFL Grammar Teaching

Given the traditional pedagogy characterizing many EFL classrooms, the large class size, the culturally based expectations of teachers and learners as to what constitutes acceptable pedagogy, the frequent constraints on what is taught, and the need to teach to examinations, it is obvious that implicit grammar instruction, where learners are exposed to a target grammatical form through modified communicative input, is not sufficient for the EFL situation. Not only are there few, if any, opportunities for use of the target language outside the classroom, but even within many EFL classrooms, target language use may be surprisingly low, especially during translation activities (Kaneko, 1993). However, if implicit approaches are incorporated into a three-step grammar lesson format, allowing for formal instruction and feedback on errors, they offer considerable promise.

Whereas in the ESL situation, an implicit approach is recommended to position grammar instruction within communicative pedagogy, in the EFL context it provides a way to introduce meaning-focused language use into the traditional grammar classroom (Fotos, 1998) through performance of communicative tasks. In this case, task performance is seen as enhancing formal instruction, not replacing it.

TWO TYPES OF INTERACTIVE, STRUCTURE–BASED TASKS

This section presents two types of structure-based tasks providing a communicative dimension to formal grammar lessons. However, these tasks are different from production-based activities designed to promote accuracy. Like pattern practice tasks, the grammar tasks are aimed at assisting learners to notice grammar forms, but this is achieved through communicative activities rather than fill-in-the-blank or sentence production activities. Whereas some researchers have recommended the use of tasks for accuracy development (e.g., Ur, 1988), the structure-based interactive tasks presented here may not require production of the form but are rather designed to increase learner awareness of how the target structure is used in context. The tasks are nonetheless communicative because the participants are engaged in meaning-focused interaction.

Structure-Based Tasks With an Implicit Focus on Grammar

The first type of task consists of purely communicative tasks designed so that learners must use the target structure to complete the activity. As an example, two researchers (Loschky & Bley-Vroman, 1990, 1993) in the ESL setting developed a "spot the difference" task targeting locative pronouns. The learners were asked to compare two similar pictures and explain how they differed. To complete the task, they had to use different locative pronouns. In this case, the researchers noted, the learners recognized what they needed to know and even asked their teacher how to say various locatives. Although the task had a communicative emphasis, the learners were able to become aware of the target structure and were able to produce it correctly.

Two Implicit Structure-Based Tasks

Inspired by the idea of implicit tasks as a way to teach grammar, my colleagues and I developed similar tasks for our Japanese first-year university EFL learners. In the following description, the tasks were performed by an intact class of 40 learners during their regular 90-minute weekly English lesson. Since the desks and chairs were bolted to the floor, the learners worked in pairs rather than small groups. To complete the tasks, the learners had to comprehend the form and use it correctly, but no explicit reference was made to the target grammar structures in the task.

The two grammar forms were comparatives (*big–bigger; expensive–more expensive*) and prepositions of location (*in, at, on,* etc.) (see Fotos, Poel, & Homan, 1994, for the final versions of these tasks). To serve as pre/posttests measuring accuracy in recognition of correct use of the forms, 10-sentence grammaticality judgment tests based on the task material were prepared. The learners completed the pretest before task performance and did the posttest immediately afterward.

The task on comparisons was not an information gap task but required planned language and a task solution. Here learners were asked to compare two cities, telling each other about features of cities with which they were familiar (e.g., *Sapporo is cold; Naha is warm*) and writing their partner's information on task sheets. The learners were then requested to combine their information and write sentences comparing the two cities on the various features (e.g., *Sapporo is colder than Naha*). To complete the task, they had to use comparative forms, but there was no mention of the grammar point in the task or on the pre/posttest. The tests took 10 minutes, and the task performance time was 30 minutes.

The second task was a drawing activity targeting locative prepositions. The task was a two-way information gap with opportunities for planned language but no requirement for a task solution. The teacher first gave the learners directions for drawing several geometric shapes inside a picture frame on their task sheets (e.g., *Draw a triangle in the upper left corner of your picture frame*). After checking that their previous drawings were correct, each learner drew pictures, placing different shapes inside a frame. When the learners were finished, they gave their partners instructions on how to draw their pictures (e.g., *Draw a circle in the center of your picture* or *Draw a triangle below the squareand then draw a diamond in the triangle*). When the learners were finished, they compared their drawing with the originals held by their partners. Again, there was no explicit mention of the grammar points embedded in the task either before or after the activity. The tests took 10 minutes, and task performance time was 20 minutes.

Following both task performances and posttests, the learners received teacher-fronted instruction on the grammar points, rewrote incorrect sentences from their pre/posttests, did production exercises, and read stories containing multiple usages of the target forms.

In both cases, the implicit structure-based tasks provided communicative use of the target structures, and the subsequent instructional activities called learner attention to rule-based aspects of the forms. The final reading exercise provided further examples of use of the structures in meaningful contexts.

Structure-Based Tasks With an Explicit Focus on Grammar

The next task type has been called the "grammar consciousness raising task" (Fotos, 1993, 1994; Fotos & Ellis, 1991). Although it is communicative, the task content involves developing rules for use of a grammar form. The learners are required to solve grammar problems through meaning-focused interaction about the grammar structure, which is the task content.

This type of explicit structure-based task may not require immediate production of the grammar structure to complete the task solution but is designed to call the learners' attention to the target structure and raises their consciousness of it (Fotos, 1994; Fotos & Ellis, 1991). Once consciousness has been raised, task performance is followed by a formal lesson on the structure, production exercises, and communicative activities containing the target structure so that continued awareness is facilitated. Alternatively, instruction may precede task performance and serve as an Advance Organizer presenting the structure and describing the rules for its use so that learners can activate their previous knowledge of the form and integrate the new material with what they already know.

Regarding the design features of this task type, an explicit structure-based task generally requires learners to work in pairs/small groups and listen to their partners read examples of correct uses of a grammar structure—often as questions that must be answered by use of the structure—to create an information-gap activity, then to generate rules (the task solution) explaining the observed use of the structure. On completion of the task, each pair/small group presents its rules to the rest of the class, an activity that leads to a formal grammar lesson or production exercises, rewriting of incorrect sentences from the pre/posttests, and a reading with multiple embeddings of the target structure.

An Explicit Structure-Based Task.   Several years ago I developed a grammar task on the use of *If* + conditional forms (one version is in Fotos, 1995), a problematic structure but one with clear rules for usage. Again, the task presented here was performed by an intact class of 40 first-year Japanese university EFL learners working in pairs during their regular 90-minute weekly English class. The activity was an information-gap task designed to raise students' consciousness of the correct usage of present and future conditional forms using *if.* The grammar task combined the opportunity for meaning-focused use of the target language with study of the grammar form and the requirement to generate grammar rules for correct word order and verb tense use. A grammaticality pre/posttest again permitted assessment of gains in recognition of correct usage of the structure. Although there was no mention of the target form during the task performance, the learners had to understand and produce sentences using two types of if-conditionals; *if* + will and *if* + would (i.e., *If I study hard, I will pass the test* compared with *If I won the lottery, I would travel around the world*). This was done by requiring the learners to ask their partners six questions, three for each form, which their partners answered. The learners wrote down their partners' answers.

Again, the task presented here was performed by an intact class of 40 first-year Japanese university EFL learners working in pairs during their regular 90-minute weekly English class. The activity was an information-gap task designed to raise students' consciousness of the correct usage of present and future conditional forms using *if.* The grammar task combined the opportunity for meaning-focused use of the target language with study of the grammar form and the requirement to generate grammar rules for correct word order and verb tense use. A grammaticality pre/posttest again permitted assessment of gains in recognition of correct usage of the structure. Although there was no mention of the target form during the task performance, the learners had to understand and produce sentences using two types of *if*-conditionals *if* + will and *if* + would (i.e., *If I run fast, I will win the race* compared with *If I won a million dollars, I would travel around the world*). This was done by requiring the learners to ask their partners six questions, three for each form, which their partners answered. The learners wrote down their partners' answers.

One type of question involved possible events in the future, such as, *"What will you do if you have homework today?"* The second type involved events that were not likely to happen, such as *"What would you do if you saw a spaceship?"*

After the learners had each asked and answered three questions for each form, they were requested to unscramble words forming two rules for making correct sentences for likely and unlikely events, directing them to use the *past tense* + would for unlikely events and the *present tense* + will for likely events.

As usual, the task activity and posttest were followed by a teacher-fronted lesson on the use of *If* + *conditional*, including production exercises and the correction of incorrect sentences from the two grammaticality judgment tests. The learners were then given a reading containing many communicative uses of the structure.

Empirical Support for This Task Type

As mentioned in the Introduction to this volume and in earlier sections of this chapter, psycholinguistic theory suggests that once consciousness has been raised, many learners are able to notice the structures in subsequent meaning-focused activities (Schmidt, 1990). In my formal investigations of explicit structure-based tasks (Fotos 1993, 1994), an intact class of first-year Japanese university EFL learners worked in groups of four during their weekly 90-minute English class and studied three grammar structures (adverb placement, indirect object placement, and relative clause use) only through performance of explicit structure-based tasks. After completing grammaticality judgment and sentence-writing pretests, they had to read and listen to sentences containing target structures, and then develop rules for their usage. The pretests were then given as posttests following task performance. Furthermore, since this was a research project designed to measure whether task performance resulted in accuracy gains, high levels of interaction, and promoted subsequent noticing of the structures, there was no orientation to the task content before performance, or discussion of the grammar rule afterward.

One and two weeks after task performance, the learners were given reading passages and dictation exercises containing the target structures and were asked to underline anything that they noticed. Whereas the control groups, who had not performed the tasks, did not notice the structures at all, nearly 50% of the task performers underlined the structures in the passages. However, both control and grammar task performers noticed nongrammatical material equally. Thus, I speculated that explicit structure-based task performance has the potential to raise the learners' consciousness of problematic grammar points so that they remained aware of them in communicative input given later (Fotos, 1993).

I also suggested (Fotos, 1994) that it would be possible to use structure-based grammar tasks as a substitute for formal grammar lessons if two conditions were met. First, task performance should be at least as effective at promoting gains in explicit knowledge of the grammar feature as traditional grammar lessons, while maintaining the communicative benefits of task performance. Second, performance of the task should produce amounts of target language task talk comparable to that produced by performance of meaning-focused communicative tasks, because it is through the provision of such comprehensible input and the need to produce comprehensible output that language acquisition has been suggested to take place (Ellis, R., 1997; Pica, 1997).

To determine task effectiveness in developing understanding of the target structure, I compared pre/posttest gains in use of the target structures made by task performance with the gains achieved from traditional, teacher-fronted grammar lessons (see the full report in Fotos, 1994). Dealing with adverb placement, indirect object placement, and relative clause usage, these tasks were found to be equivalent to traditional grammar lessons in promoting significant gains in accuracy and were also similar in the amount of task talk produced to performance of nongrammatical communicative tasks.

Therefore, on the basis of these positive research results, explicit structure-based tasks were suggested to be a useful communicative activity for EFL grammar instruction because they promoted proficiency gains and produced meaningful interaction.

The next section considers the optimal combination of task features for producing learner interaction in the target language, a major problem in the EFL situation because use of the target language can often be avoided because of the shared mother tongue.

Task Features Promoting Learner Output

Building on Vygotskyan theory (Vygotsky, 1978) regarding the creation of knowledge through interaction with others, an interesting consideration has been raised in research on learner output during task performance (Kowal & Swain, 1994; Swain & Lapkin, 1995, 1998) and on subsequent corrective feedback (Aljaafreh & Lantolf, 1994). It was suggested that if learners can discuss the language they are producing during task performance, such task talk will not only increase their consciousness of the relationship of forms and grammar rules to meaning, thereby improving accuracy, but will also enable them to gain some control over their learning. During performance of the explicit structure-based tasks described above, the learners discussed their own understanding of the target structures and, through negotiated interaction, it was suggested that they developed awareness of the target grammar feature (Fotos, 1993, 1994).

A follow-up study (Fotos, 1997[1]) examined audiotapes of all learner groups during performance of the three explicit structure-based tasks to investigate the amount and types of task talk produced by different combinations of task features (an information gap, an agreed-on solution, and planned language). The following interaction categories (adapted from Long, 1983, and Pica & Doughty, 1985) were used. Negotiations were coded by the author into the following categories and were then recoded by a second trained researcher to determine interrater reliability. Agreement was 89%.

1. Clarification requests, which were made by the listener when she had not understood. Example: *I don't understand. Please teach me.*
2. Confirmation checks, which were made by the listener when she thought she had understood but wanted to be sure. In this case, information was held by the speaker, who wanted confirmation that the information was accurate. Example: *Sentence two not correct, yes?*
3. Comprehension checks, which were made by the speaker to make certain that the listeners had understood. Example: *Object is before verb, you understand?*
4. Questions regarding correctness or incorrectness of task card sentences. Example: *Which one correct?*
5. Repetitions and requests for repetitions. Example: *Say again!*

The number of negotiations in each category were counted and analyzed according to the features of the task.

As Swain and her associates have noted repeatedly (Kowal & Swain, 1994; Swain, 1985; Swain & Lapkin, 1995, 1998), for grammatical accuracy to develop, it is necessary for learners to both become aware of form-meaning relationships and receive feedback on their output using the forms to create meaning. Clearly, those task features that promote the

---

[1]A version of this article was published previously as a working paper for the Institute of the Humanities, Senshu University, In *Annual Bulletin of the Humanities*, p. 25.

most interaction, particularly interaction requiring learners to adjust their output, are desirable. The multiway information gap task requiring an agreed-on task solution was found to significantly produce the most words and the greatest number of all types of negotiations, including clarification requests (Fotos, 1997), a particularly valuable form of negotiated interaction suggested to facilitate improved learner output (Kowal & Swain, 1994; Swain & Lapkin, 1995). An additional important function for modified learner output has been suggested: it's recycling as new input for the learner herself (this is called "autoinput" by Schmidt & Frota, 1986).

The requirement for a task solution in the target language meant that learners were required to use the language for at least part of the time, avoiding the possibility that they could solve the task entirely in their first language, which is a significant problem for most purely communicative tasks. Furthermore, when the learners used their shared first language, a preliminary study examining first language use as a learning strategy in the EFL classroom (Fotos, 2000) suggests that the learners' shared first language is primarily used for framing and calling attention to important target language information, repeating or paraphrasing confusing target language utterances, and indicating that a repair would follow to a target language utterance. Consequently, it is necessary to consider whether use of the learners' first language during target language study is necessarily negative, and this is an important area for future research.

Summary

In this section I have recommended use of two types of structure-based communicative tasks to support formal grammar instruction by supplying communicative usages of the instructed form for learners to notice and by providing opportunities for learners to receive input and produce output containing the structures. In addition, tasks with a grammar structure as task content assist learners to develop their formal knowledge of the structures. I have particularly recommended the development of these tasks for the EFL situation, where access to communicative input is extremely limited and where grammar-based syllabuses are the norm. These tasks are also recommended for ESL situations where the learners expect and require formal grammar instruction. And, as mentioned, an additional point favoring structure-based tasks over purely communicative tasks with nongrammatical content is that the grammar-based tasks circumvent the problems of being viewed as frivolous activities lacking a clear tie-in with the course syllabus.

The next section gives recommendations for the creation of course/program-specific structure-based tasks.

CREATING COURSE/PROGRAM-SPECIFIC STRUCTURE–BASED TASKS

Syllabus Design

The steps in the creation of a syllabus based on course-specific tasks were discussed in earlier works by Crookes and Gass (1993a, 1993b) and Nunan (1989). In a chapter in the first work, Nunan (1993, p. 57) clearly outlines the steps for developing a syllabus, whether for a traditional structure-based approach or a more communicative orientation.

The first step is a needs analysis to determine what language forms and functions the learners require. This step begins with assessment of the learners' proficiency, then moves to grouping of learners according to ability. The next step is selection of the instructional content. For structural approaches, this entails the choice and sequencing of grammar forms, vocabulary, and so forth based on the requirements of the learner. Communicative approaches use real-world needs to identify necessary language functions learners require for communicative activities outside the classroom. However, both types of syllabus require the design of tasks to meet their target objectives. The final stage of the syllabus consists of assessment activities, which are proficiency based in structural approach programs and involve the attainment of communicative goals in communicative programs.

Grammar Task Design

Once the syllabus is created and target grammar structures have been identified and sequenced, the teacher can develop tasks, particularly multiway information gap tasks requiring an agreed-on solution—task features shown to promote interaction. The tasks can be implicit grammar tasks—entirely communicative, with no grammatical content but requiring use of the target structure to perform the task—or they can have the grammar point as the task content, requiring the students to consider or generate sentences using the grammar point, and then develop rules for its use.

Regarding selection of the structure, it is useful to keep in mind that recent research (Ellis, N., 1995; Robinson, 1996) suggests that grammar structures with a few simple rules benefit from instruction followed by communicative usage of the instructed form. Thus, implicit structure-based tasks following instruction on the grammar rule structure can facilitate learner acquisition of the point. For structures with complex rule systems, formal instruction has again been found to facilitate acquisition, particularly if done early in the lesson but must be followed by communicative examples of structure used in context. However, other research (discussed in Skehan, 1998) suggests that explicit instruction alone will not enable learners to process complicated structures, and recommends extensive meaning-focused use of the target form so that learners can become aware of its features in context. From this perspective, as well, implicit structure-based tasks are useful to provide communicative use of instructed forms.

CONCLUSION

In the EFL setting, where access to communicative input containing target grammatical structures is extremely limited, it is necessary to have some type of formal instruction—whether through a teacher-fronted grammar lesson, or through performance of more meaning-focused activities that nonetheless call attention to specific forms in communicative content—to develop learner awareness of the grammatical features. This chapter has noted the durability of the structural syllabus and formal instruction within the EFL situation and presents evidence suggesting that such instruction can be facilitated through structure-based communicative task performance.

The structure-based tasks described here not only promoted meaning-focused learner output and facilitated comprehension of input but also required attention to and accuracy in use of the target structures. Many EFL learners have studied the formal properties of the English language, so it has also been suggested that task performance should be preceded by a general explanation of the target structure to activate previously developed knowledge and facilitate the establishment of form-meaning relationships, which would then be followed by a review to increase learner awareness of the structure. Provision of subsequent communicative input containing the target structure is recommended to facilitate continued awareness of its use in context. Such three-part grammar lessons combine the strengths of structural and communicative approaches to grammar teaching.

REFERENCES

Aljaafreh, A., & Lantolf, J. (1994). Negative feedback as regulation and second language learning in the Zone of Proximal Development. *Modern Language Journal, 78,* 465–483.

Ausubel, D., Novak, J., & Hanesian, H. (1978). *Educational psychology* (2nd ed.). New York: Holt, Rinehart & Winston.

Breen, M. (1987). Learner contribution to task design. In C. Candlin & D. Murphy (Eds.), *Language learning tasks.* Englewood Cliffs, NJ: Prentice Hall.

Cadierno, T. (1995). Formal instruction from a processing perspective: An investigation into the Spanish past tense. *Modern Language Journal, 79,* 179–193.

Carroll, S., & Swain, M. (1993). Explicit and implicit negative feedback: An empirical study of the learning of linguistic generalizations. *Studies in Second Language Acquisition, 15,* 357–386.

Crookes, G., & Gass, S. (Eds.). (1993a). *Tasks and language learning: Integrating theory and practice.* Clevedon, UK: Multilingual Matters.

Crookes, G., & Gass, S. (Eds.). (1993b). *Tasks in a pedagogical context: Integrating theory and practice.* Clevedon, UK: Multilingual Matters.

Crystal, D. (1985). How many millions?—the statistics of English. *English Today, 1,* 7–9.

Dickins, P., & Woods, E. (1988). Some criteria for the development of communicative language tasks. *TESOL Quarterly, 22,* 623–646.

Ellis, N. (1995). Consciousness in second language acquisition: A review of field studies and laboratory experiments. *Language Awareness, 4,* 123–146.

Ellis, R. (1994). *The study of second language acquisition.* Oxford: Oxford University Press.

Ellis, R. (1995). Interpretation tasks for grammar teaching. *TESOL Quarterly, 29,* 87–106.

Ellis, R. (1997). *Second language research and language teaching.* Oxford: Oxford University Press.

Ellis, R. (1998). Teaching and research: Options in grammar teaching. *TESOL Quarterly, 32,* 39–59.

Fotos, S. (1993). Consciousness raising and noticing through focus on form: Grammar task performance versus formal instruction. *Applied Linguistics, 14,* 385–407.

Fotos, S. (1994). Integrating grammar instruction and communicative language use through grammar consciousness-raising tasks. *TESOL Quarterly, 28,* 323–351.

Fotos, S. (1995). Problem-solving tasks for teaching if-conditionals. In M. Pennington (Ed.), *New ways in teaching grammar* (pp. 83–87). Alexandria, VA: TESOL.

Fotos, S. (1997). Communicative task performance and second language acquisition. Do task features determine learner output? *Revista Canaria de Estudios Engleses, 34,* 51–68.

Fotos, S. (1998). Shifting the focus from forms to form in the EFL classroom. *ELT Journal, 52,* 301–307.

Fotos, S. (2000). Codeswitching by Japan's unrecognized bilinguals: L1 use as learning strategy in university EFL students. In M. Noguchi & S. Fotos (Eds.), *Studies in Japanese bilingualism.* Clevedon, UK: Multilingual Matters.

Fotos, S., & Ellis, R. (1991). Communicating about grammar: A task-based approach. *TESOL Quarterly, 25,* 605–628.

Fotos, S., Poel, C., & Homan, R. (1994). *Grammar in Mind: Communicative English for Fluency and Accuracy.* Tokyo: Logos International.

Kaneko, T. (1993). L1 use in foreign language classrooms. *Temple University Japan Research Studies in TESOL, 1,* 69–79.

Kowal, M., & Swain, M. (1994). Using collaborative language production tasks to promote students' language awareness. *Language Awareness, 3,* 73–94.

Lightbown, P. (1992). What have we here? Some observations on the influence of instruction on L2 learning. In R. Philipson, E. Kellerman, L. Selinker, M. Sharwood Smith, & M. Swain (Eds.), *Foreign language pedagogy research: A commemorative volume for Claus Faerch* (pp. 197–212). Clevedon, UK: Multilingual Matters.

Lightbown, P., & Spada, N. (1990). Focus on form and corrective feedback in communicative language teaching: Effects on second language learning. *Studies in Second Language Acquisition, 12,* 429–448.

Long, M. (1983). Native speaker/non-native speaker conversation and the negotiation of comprehensible input. *Applied Linguistics, 4,* 126–141.

Long, M. (1991). Focus on form: A design feature in language teaching methodology. In K. de Bot, D. Coste, R. Ginsberg, & C. Kramsch (Eds.), *Foreign language research in cross-cultural perspective* (pp. 39–52). Amsterdam: John Benjamins.

Long, M., & Crookes, G. (1992). Three approaches to task-based syllabus design. *TESOL Quarterly, 26,* 27–56.

Long, M. & Robinson, P. (1998). Focus on form: Theory, research, practice. In C. Doughty, & J. Williams (Eds). *Focus on form in classroom second language acquisition.* New York: Cambridge University Press.

Loschky, L., & Bley-Vroman, R. (1990). Creating structure-based communication tasks for second language development. *University of Hawaii Working Papers in ESL, 9,* 161–212.

Loschky, L., & Bley-Vroman, R. (1993). Grammar and task-based methodology. In G. Crookes & S. Gass (Eds.), *Tasks and language learning: Integrating theory and practice* (pp. 123–167). Clevedon, UK: Multilingual Matters.

Nunan, D. (1989). *Designing tasks for the communicative classroom.* Cambridge, UK: Cambridge University Press.

Nunan, D. (1993). Task-based syllabus design: Selecting, grading and sequencing tasks. In G. Crookes & S. Gass (Eds.), *Tasks in integrating theory and practice* (pp. 55–68). Clevedon, UK: Multilingual Matters.

Pica, T. (1997). Interlanguage adjustments as an outcome of NS-NSS negotiated interaction. *Language Learning, 38,* 45–57.

Pica, T,. & Doughty, C. (1985). Input and interaction in the communicative language classroom: A comparison of teacher-fronted and group activities. In S. Gass & C. Madden (Eds.), *Input and second language acquisition* (pp. 115–132). Rowley, MA: Newbury House.

Pica, T., Holliday, L., Lewis, N., & Morgenthaler, L. (1989). Comprehensible output as an oucome on linguistic demands on the learner. *Studies in Second Language Acquisition, 11,* 63–90.

Prabhu, N. (1987). *Second language pedagogy.* Oxford: Oxford University Press.

Rulon, K., & McCreary, J. (1986). Negotiation of content: Teacher-fronted and small group interaction. In R. Day (Ed.), *Talking to learn: Conversation in second language acquisition* (pp. 182–199). Rowley, MA: Newbury House.

Robinson, P. (1996). Learning simple and complex second language rules under implicit, incidental, rule-search and instructed conditions. *Studies in Second Language Acquisition, 18,* 27–68.

Schmidt, R. (1990). The role of consciousness in second language learning. *Applied Linguistics, 11,* 129–158.

Schmidt, R., & Frota, S. (1986). Developing basic conversational ability in a second language: A case study of an adult learner of Portuguese. In R. Day (Ed.), *Talking to learn: Conversation in second language acquisition.* Rowley, MA: Newbury House.

Sharwood Smith, M. (1993). Input enhancement in instructed SLA: Theoretical bases. *Studies in Second Language Acquisition, 15,* 165–179.

Skehan, P. (1996). A framework for the implementation of task-based instruction. *Applied Linguistics, 17,* 38–62.

Skehan, P. (1998). *A cognitive approach to language learning.* Oxford: Oxford University Press.

Swain, M. (1985). Communicative competence: Some roles of comprehensible input and comprehensible output in its development. In S. Gass & C. Madden (Eds.), *Input and second language acquisition* (pp. 235–253). Rowley, MA: Newbury House.

Swain, M., & Lapkin, S. (1995). Problems in output and the cognitive processes they generate: A step towards second language learning. *Applied Linguistics, 11,* 371–391.

Swain, M., & Lapkin, S. (1998). Interaction and second language learning: Two adolescent French immersion students working together. *Modern Language Journal, 82,* 320–337.

Trahey, M., & White, L. (1993). Positive evidence and preemption in the second language classroom. *Studies in Second Language Acquisition, 15,* 181–204.

Ur, P. (1988). *Grammar practice activities: A practical guide for teachers.* Cambridge, UK: Cambridge University Press.

Vygotsky, L. (1978). *Mind in society: The development of higher psychological processes.* Cambridge, MA: Harvard University Press.

White, L. (1991). Adverb placement in second language acquisition: Some effects of positive and negative evidence in the classroom. *Second Language Research, 7,* 133–161.

White, L., Spada, N., Lightbown, P., & Ranta, L. (1991). Input enhancement and L2 question formation. *Applied Linguistics, 12,* 416–432.

Wilkins, D. (1976). *Notional syllabuses: A taxonomy and its relevance to foreign language curriculum development.* Cambridge, UK: Cambridge University Press.

9

Methodological Options in Grammar Teaching Materials

Rod Ellis
University of Auckland, New Zealand

INTRODUCTION

Teachers have a large number of published grammar practice books from which to select. Key questions are as follows: What methodology for teaching grammar do these books employ? What is the empirical/theoretical basis for the chosen methodology?[1] The first question can be answered by undertaking a careful analysis of the methodological features of a selection of the available books. The second can be answered by examining the explicit comments of the authors of the books (e.g., in the introductory sections) or by inferring the guiding principles from the types of activities employed. In this chapter I address both questions.

There have been relatively few attempts to conduct a methodological analysis of the instructional options incorporated into grammar practice books. Fortune (1998), in a survey review of six widely used grammar books for English as a foreign language (EFL), identifies a number of primary features. He refers to the gang of three: (1) isolated, uncontextualized sentences; (2) sentence completion involving the adaptation of an unmarked

---

[1]There are, of course, other important questions concerning grammar teaching—in particular, what grammar points should be taught? However, my concern in this chapter is entirely with the methodology of grammar teaching, not with its content.

lexical item (often a verb) presented in brackets; and (3) gap filling. He then discusses a number of significant developments in pedagogy, in particular consciousness-raising activities directed at "noticing" how specific grammatical structures are used and understanding how the structures work. Fortune's features provide a basis for carrying out a methodological analysis. It will be elaborated on in the following section.

There have been rather more attempts to address the question how grammar should be taught, both from an empirical and a theoretical standpoint. For example, a number of recent studies have investigated the effectiveness of "implicit" as opposed to "explicit" grammar teaching (e.g., DeKeyser, 1995; Robinson, 1996) and also, more relevant to my concerns here, of production-based as opposed to input-based grammar teaching (e.g., Salaberry, 1997; VanPatten & Cadierno, 1993). There is, of course, no shortage of theorizing about grammar teaching on the basis of models of second language (L2) acquisition (e.g., Ellis, N., 1993; Krashen, 1982; Long, 1998).

The main purpose of this chapter is to develop a framework that can be used to describe and design materials for teaching grammar. I proceed as follows. First, I examine the instructional options typically selected by authors of some popular grammar teaching books. This provides a picture of how grammar teaching is currently conceptualized. Second, I review theoretical and empirical research that has addressed a number of options that have been neglected in grammar teaching. Third, I consider some materials for teaching grammar that incorporate these options.

AN ANALYSIS OF METHODOLOGICAL OPTIONS IN GRAMMAR PRACTICE BOOKS

Elsewhere I have outlined a system of options for teaching grammar based on a psycholinguistic model of language acquisition (see, e.g., Ellis, R., 1997, chap. 3). Here I would like to try to develop a parallel system of options based on a sampling of grammar practice teaching materials. These options differ from the psycholinguistic options in that they are *methodological* in nature, reflecting the practice of grammar teaching as this is represented in published textbooks. As might be expected, the two sets of options do not match exactly, although, as we will see, there are some noteworthy correspondences.

The methodological options described in following sections were derived from inspecting a number of English as a second language (ESL)/EFL grammar practice books (see Table 9.1 for a list). I looked at one unit from each book, choosing the unit dealing with the present

TABLE 9.1
Analysis of Methodological Features in Six Grammar Practice Books

Feature	Grammar Books[a]						Totals
	1	2	3	4	5	6	
Explicit description							
Supplied	•	•	•		•	•	5
Discover				•			2
Data							
Source							
Authentic							0
Contrived			•			•	2
Text size							
Discrete sentences							0
Continuous			•			•	2
Medium							
Oral						•	1
Written			•			•	2
Operations							
Production							
Controlled	•	•	•	•	•	•	6
Free	•		•	•		•	4
Reception							
Controlled	•					•	2
Automatic						•	1
Judgments							
Judge only							
Correct	•					•	2
Total features per book	5	2	6	3	2	11	

[a]Key: 1. Badalamenti and Henner-Stanchina (1993); 2. Eastwood (1992); 3. Elbaum (1996); 4. Jones (1992); 5. Murphy (1994); 6. Schoenberg (1994).

continuous tense as this grammar point figured in all the books.[2] I read through each unit making a note of the options that were used. I then attempted to codify the options (to build a system) by classifying them into general categories with subdivisions. The system that I arrived at is shown in Figure 9.1. The terms used in this system are intended to be entirely descriptive (i.e., not evaluative). For example, the terms *authentic* or *contrived* are not intended to convey either positive or negative views about their value in grammar teaching.

---

[2]There was no unit dealing with the present continuous tense in Jones (1992). However, as my aim was to include a representative sample of current grammar practice books, I felt it important to include Jones' book, as it represented a more "functional" approach to grammar teaching than the other books. I selected the unit dealing with past continuous and present perfect continuous.

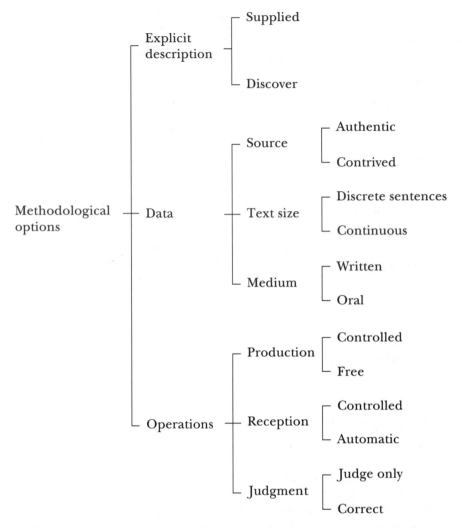

FIG. 9.1   A system of methodological options employed in grammar practice books.

Three sets of options were identified related to general aspects of the materials: *explicit description*, *data*, and *operations*. These aspects may or may not all be present in any one grammar practice book. As we will see, all the books I examined used options relating to explicit description and operations, but only some included a data option. It is also possible to envisage a grammar practice book that does not include any explicit description (i.e., one based on audiolingual principles). The only obligatory options, it would seem, are those concerning operations as these relate to the *practice* function of the books. A grammar *reference* book, in contrast, would obligatorily provide explicit descriptions but probably not offer any operations for the reader to perform.

Explicit description refers to whether the materials either provide learners with an explanation of the grammar point (i.e., *supplied*) or whether they require learners to develop their own explanation (*discover*). Other more detailed methodological options relating to this general distinction can be identified but are not included in Figure 9.1. For example, in the case of explicit descriptions that are supplied, a distinction might be drawn between "verbal" and "diagrammatic" descriptions.

The data options involve the provision of text containing exemplars of the target structure. To count as "data" this text must be independent of any text associated with operations. For example, complete dialogues illustrating the target structure constitute "data," but gapped dialogues requiring students to fill in the missing words were classified under "operations." Data options were subdivided in terms of *source, text size,* and *medium.* Source refers to whether the data provided consisted of *authentic* materials (i.e., texts for which there was a real-life and not just a pedagogic context) or *contrived* materials (i.e., the author of the grammar practice book had devised the sentences him or herself to illustrate the grammar point). Text size concerns whether the text comprising the data consists of *discrete sentences* (one of Fortune's gang of three) or is *continuous.* Finally, the text comprising the data can be written or oral. There is the potential for these options to combine in different ways. For example, the data could consist of text that was authentic, discrete sentences, and oral or contrived, continuous and written. As we will see, the actual combinations evident in the materials were very restricted.

The operations evident in the materials were classified according to whether they involved *production* (i.e., the students were required to produce sentences containing the target structure), *reception* (i.e., the students were required to perform some activity to demonstrate they had understood sentences containing the target structure), or *judgment* (i.e., the students were required to identify whether sentences containing the target structure were grammatical or ungrammatical). Each of these options is further broken down. Production can be *controlled* or *free.* This distinction reflects a continuum rather than a dichotomy. That is, production activities can be more or less controlled/free. Controlled activities provide students with a text of some sort (usually discrete sentences) and require them to operate on it in a way that involves producing the target form. Free activities give the students the opportunity to construct their own sentences using the target structure. Again, both the controlled and free options could be broken down further. There are many different types of controlled grammar activities (e.g., substitution, gap-filling, sentence completion, transformation, insertion, jumbled sentences), although a potentially important distinction within free production activities concerns whether the text produced is representational or more personal in function. Reception can be *controlled* (i.e., students are able to control the speed at which they have to process the sentences containing the target structure) or *automatic* (i.e., students are required to process the sentences in real time). Finally, judgment tasks can involve *judgment only* (i.e., simply stating whether a sentence is or is not grammatical) or *correct* (i.e., trying to correct the sentences judged to be ungrammatical).

What options, then, are utilized by the authors of the textbooks I sampled? Are there some options that appear to be underutilized? What does the author's choice of options suggest about their underlying philosophy of grammar teaching? To answer these questions, one unit of the six grammar practice books (dealing with the present continuous tense) was analyzed using the system of options shown in Figure 9.1. No attempt was made to determine the frequency with which each author used the different options. Instead, I sought to simply ascertain whether a particular option was evident at any point in a unit. The results of the analysis are shown in Table 9.1.

It is clear that two features are predominant: explicit description supplied and controlled production. Only one of the grammar practice books (Jones, 1992) failed to provide any grammatical explanation; all the books provided opportunities for controlled production practice. In this respect then, the grammar practice books of today are probably not so different from those of previous decades. Grammar teaching is still characterized as (1) explaining/describing grammar points and (2) providing opportunities for controlled production practice. However, most of the books also cater for free production practice. Usually, this takes the form of contextualized grammar activities (sometimes rather misleadingly labeled "communicative"), but occasionally there are also information-gap activities.

It is also revealing to note which features are not common in these books. Only two of the books, Jones (1992) and Schoenberg (1994), provide any opportunity for students to discover how a grammar point works for themselves. In fact, even these two books provide very few grammar discovery tasks and the actual tasks themselves are very restricted, offering little guidance to the student. Also rather rare are data options. Of course, most of the other books do provide examples of usage as part of the explicit description and all the books provide examples in the context of the production activities. However, only Elbaum (1996) and Schoenberg (1994) offer the learners independent data illustrating the use of the present continuous tense. In both cases the data are contrived rather than authentic and involve continuous text. In Schoenberg, the data are provided in both an oral and a written form. This is the only book to be accompanied with an audiocassette. Finally, there is conspicuous paucity of receptive practice activities or activities involving grammatical judgments. Students have little opportunity to practice processing these structures in oral or written texts without some form of accompanying production activity.

The books also vary in the number of different features they incorporate. Two of the books, Eastwood (1992) and Murphy (1994), both bestsellers, are most limited in this respect; they make use of only 2 features—supplied explicit description and controlled production practice. Such materials have the virtue of simplicity but they offer a rather impoverished view of grammar teaching. In contrast, Schoenberg (1994) manifests 11 different methodological features. This book provides a rich and varied approach to grammar teaching. One of the "costs," however, is that each unit is rather long, the one on the present continuous tense running to 22 pages (compared with 2 pages in Eastwood or Murphy).

The predominant "theory" of grammar teaching that emerges from this analysis is a very traditional one. Grammar constitutes a "content" that can be transmitted to students via explicit descriptions and a "skill" that is developed through controlled practice—an amalgamation of the beliefs underlying the grammar translation and audiolingual methods. However, there are also signs that this predominant philosophy is being rethought by some authors. In particular, the need to encourage learners to discover grammar rules for themselves, to provide them with data where they can "notice" how grammatical features are used, and to teach grammar through input-processing rather than through production practice are evident in some of the materials. In the sections that follow we will examine the theoretical rationale for such options and also consider some of the empirical research that has investigated them.

DISCOVERING ABOUT GRAMMAR

The first neglected option I would like to consider is discovering about grammar—enabling the students to build their own minigrammars by helping them investigate how specific points of grammar work. In effect, this requires students to function in much the same way as field linguists[3] do when they set about constructing descriptions of languages (see Bloomfield, 1933). There are two key theoretical issues that relate to this option: the role of explicit knowledge in second language (L2) acquisition and the value of discovery as a general method of learning.

---

[3]This is not a new idea. Jesperson (1904) advocated what he called "Inventional Grammar," which was created by students themselves as they gained insight into the grammar of the language they were studying.

Current theories of L2 acquisition distinguish implicit and explicit knowledge. Implicit knowledge is knowledge of grammar. It refers to that knowlcdgc that is intuitivc and automatic (i.e., it can be rapidly accessed for use in unplanned language use). For example, native speakers of English "know" that a nonsence form like *flacate* is a verb that does not permit dative alternation (i.e., cannot be used in sentences such as **Mary flacated John the cake*). However, they would be unable to tell you why (i.e., their knowledge of the underlying rule is entirely implicit).[4] Probably the bulk of a native speaker's grammatical competence is comprised of implicit knowledge. Explicit knowledge is knowledge about grammar. It refers to knowledge that is conscious and can be accessed only slowly. It is typically used in what I have elsewhere termed "secondary processes" of language use (e.g., monitoring output derived initially from implicit knowledge or translating sentences constructed in the learner's first language; see R. Ellis [1984]). Explicit knowledge is, therefore, analyzed. However, it exists independently of learners' ability to verbalize it and thus cannot be equated with metalanguage. Native speakers draw on explicit knowledge in certain contexts, especially those that call for a careful style. This distinction between implicit and explicit knowledge is widely recognized in both cognitive psychology (e.g., Paradis, 1994; Reber, 1989) and in SLA (e.g., Bialystok, 1991; Schmidt, 1990). As Schmidt (1994) points out, it is separate from and should not be confused with the distinction between implicit and explicit learning. That is, whether a person is able to learn a language without consciousness, a matter of controversy, needs to be considered independently of the kind of knowledge they develop.

It would seem reasonable that writers of grammar practice materials should make clear what kind of grammatical knowledge they are aiming at. In fact, though, they rarely do so. Eastwood (1992), for example, says in the introduction that "special attention is given to those points which are often a problem for learners" (p. 8) but does not explain what he means by "problem." Does he mean a problem in understanding (i.e., explicit knowledge) or a problem in using a grammatical structure in unplanned language use (i.e., implicit knowledge)? Probably the latter, but there is no way of being sure. Murphy (1994) is a little clearer. He tells us the book "concentrates on those structures which intermediate students want to use but which often cause difficulty" (p. viii). Presumably, then, Murphy has implicit knowledge in mind. This would seem to be also the case with the other books listed in Table 9.1.

---

[4]Roughly speaking, the rule is that if the verb is two syllables or longer, as in the case of verbs of Latin origin, they do not permit dative alternation, but if the verb is one syllable and of Anglo-Saxon origin it does.

There is, however, a major problem in trying to teach implicit knowledge. This is that learners have been shown to acquire grammatical structures in a particular order and also to learn each structure very gradually, manifesting sequences of acquisition that include transitional structures (see R. Ellis, 1994a, chap. 3, for an account of the natural order and sequence of acquisition). This has led to what Pienemann (1986) calls the teachability hypothesis, which predicts that "instruction can only promote language acquisition if the interlanguage is close to the point when the structure to be taught is acquired in the natural setting" (p. 37). In other words, learners have their own "inbuilt syllabus" (Corder, 1967), which they follow no matter what order grammatical structures are taught in. Mostly, writers of grammar practice books simply ignore this problem. That is, they present and practice grammatical structures in accordance with notions of difficulty that have been passed down from one generation of writers to another without bothering about whether these notions have any psycholinguistic basis. Where writers do recognize the problem of teaching learners grammatical structures for unplanned language use (i.e., implicit knowledge), the solution is to ensure that "students practice new structures in a variety of contexts to help them internalize and master them" (Schoenberg, 1994, p. xii) and, in particular, to ensure that there are plenty of opportunities to use the structure in communicative activities (see Larsen-Freeman's introduction to Badalamenti & Henner-Stanchina, 1993). This faith in production practice seems to reflect an unacknowledged adherence to behaviorist theories of language learning, now discredited. In fact, the available evidence is clear; grammar practice, even when it is "communicative," does not allow learners to sidestep the natural processes of grammar learning (see R. Ellis, 1988, for a review of studies that have investigated the effects of grammar practice). In short, then, teaching implicit knowledge through production practice is unlikely to work unless it so happens that the instruction coincides with the learner's state of readiness—a condition that is virtually impossible to meet.[5]

One solution to this problem is to make explicit knowledge rather than implicit knowledge of grammar the target of the teaching materials. This is what I have proposed in a series of publications (e.g., Ellis, R., 1993, 1994b, 1997). This solution is based on three assumptions. The first is that the constraints that govern the teaching of implicit knowledge do not apply to

---

[5]The impracticality of basing grammar syllabuses on the natural order and sequence of acquisition derives primarily from the fact that grammar structures cannot be taught as "accumulated entities" (Rutherford, 1987) but rather need to be integrated into highly complex interlanguage systems. This involves not just the "addition" of new features but also the "restructuring" of existing knowledge (McLaughlin, 1990), a process that is highly complex and necessarily gradual.

the teaching of explicit knowledge. That is, the notions of order and sequence do not apply where explicit knowledge is concerned. In this respect, I would argue that explicit knowledge of grammar is not dissimilar to explicit knowledge of dates in history; it can be learned in any order, and one piece of information can be added to another incrementally. The second is that L2 learners (at least adolescent and adult learners) are capable of mastering quite sophisticated explicit knowledge. In this respect, I differ from Krashen (1982), who believes that learners are able to learn only simple and portable rules like the third person -s rule, and follow instead Green and Hecht (1992), who have demonstrated empirically that the learners in their study (high school and university level German learners of English) could demonstrate a good understanding of complex rules. The third assumption is that explicit knowledge assists the processes involved in the use and acquisition of implicit knowledge. I have argued that this occurs because explicit knowledge serves to (1) monitor language use and, thereby, to improve accuracy in output; (2) facilitate noticing of new forms and new form-function mappings in the input; and (3) make possible "noticing the gap" (i.e., comparing what is noticed in the input with what learners are producing themselves). In other words, teachers may be able to facilitate the development of implicit knowledge indirectly by helping learners develop explicit knowledge. The fourth assumption is that grammar teaching, directed at explicit knowledge, should not seek to have an immediate effect on learners' ability to use a grammatical structure accurately in communication. Instead, it should accept that any effect is likely to be delayed.

If it is accepted that explicit knowledge constitutes a valid instructional goal, the next question concerns how such knowledge can best be taught. There are two basic options here. It can be taught directly or indirectly (see Ellis, R., 1997). Direct instruction takes the form of explicit descriptions/ explanations of grammar points given to the learners. As we have seen, this is the preferred approach in the grammar practice books analyzed in Table 9.1. Indirect instruction involves helping learners discover grammatical rules for themselves. It implies a problem-solving approach in which students are given data illustrating a specific grammatical structure, which they are then helped to analyze in order to extract the underlying rule. As we have seen, this approach was rare in the grammar practice books we examined.[6]

A discovery-based approach to teaching explicit knowledge has much to recommend it. First, it is potentially more motivating than simply being

---

[6]There are some books that adopt a discovery-based approach to grammar, notably Bolitho and Tomlinson's *Discover Grammar* (1995), designed for trainee teachers of a second/foreign language who need to develop an explicit knowledge of grammar.

told a grammatical rule and, for this reason, students may be more likely to remember what they learn. Second, it can encourage students to form and test hypotheses about the grammar of the L2, processes that are believed to be central to ultimate acquisition (Corder, 1967). Third, it can lead to powerful insights about the grammar of a language that cannot be found in any published descriptions. As Hawkins (1984) points out, there is a great deal that linguists do not know about the grammar of a language and an exploratory approach can lead students to insights not to be found in any published description. Related to this point, a discovery-based approach enables learners to recognize that grammar is conventional rather than logical. As Faerch (1985) puts it, "students have to learn that grammar and vocabulary do not always operate on the basis of what they consider to be normal, relative to their knowledge of other languages (primarily L1 [first language]), nor on the basis of what appears to be logical" (p. 190). In contrast, a direct approach may foster the false belief in learners that grammar is inherently logical. Fourth, and perhaps most important, discovery grammar tasks have a learning-training function. They help to develop the skills learners need to investigate language autonomously—to become field linguists. Armed with these skills, students can carry out their own analyses of how the L2 grammar works, an activity that studies of the good language learner (e.g., Naiman, Frolich, Stern, & Todesco, 1978) suggest may be important for successful language learning. Finally, if students carry out the discovery tasks by talking in the L2, they are in fact "communicating;" grammar can serve as a content for talk. For some learners at least, talking about grammar may be more meaningful than talking about the kinds of general topics often found in communicative language courses.

Of course, to justify an indirect approach it is necessary to demonstrate that it is at least as effective as a direct approach in developing accurate explicit knowledge of L2 grammar in students. This is what Fotos set out to investigate. Fotos and Ellis (1991) reported a study designed to investigate the relative effectiveness of direct and indirect explicit grammar instruction. They found that both options resulted in statistically significant gains in understanding the rule for dative alternation in two groups of college-level Japanese students. In one group, direct explicit instruction resulted in higher scores on a grammaticality judgment test[7] but in the other indirect explicit instruction proved equally effective. In a more elaborate follow-up

---

[7]The explanation that Fotos and Ellis (1991) offer for the superiority of the direct instruction with one of the groups they studied was that the instructor did not ensure that the discovery grammar task was carried out properly. This, of course, may reflect an inherent limitation of such tasks—namely, that they require considerable expertise and care on the part of the instructor to ensure that they work.

study, Fotos (1994) found indirect instruction worked as well as direct instruction in teaching explicit knowledge of three different structures (adverb-placement, dative alternation, and relative clauses). Fotos (1993) also demonstrated that the explicit knowledge that the learners gained from the discovery tasks helped to promote noticing of the target structures in subsequent message-oriented input. Caution must be exercised in generalizing from these studies as they investigated only one type of learner (Japanese university-level students taking general English classes), but they suggest that at least in some teaching contexts indirect teaching of explicit knowledge can work as well as direct.

NOTICING GRAMMATICAL FEATURES

The data options were also poorly represented in the grammar practice books analyzed in Table 9.1. That is, there were relatively few activities exposing students to what Sharwood Smith (1993) has called "enhanced input" and requiring them to pay attention to the specific grammatical structure(s) targeted in this input. The exception was Schoenberg (1994), which typically begins each section with a dialogue specially written to contain many examples of the target structure (e.g., present continuous tense). The students are asked "to listen and read" this text and then to answer some surface comprehension questions of a general nature.

A computational model of L2 acquisition, of the kind advocated by Krashen (1985) or R. Ellis (1994b), views acquisition as originating in input.[8] Learners acquire new grammatical structures when they encounter them in input, take them in, and incorporate them into their existing interlanguage system. Such a model lends theoretical support to activities that expose learners to input rich in specific grammatical structures. However, exposure alone may not be enough for acquisition to take place. Learners may also need to pay conscious attention (i.e., to notice) the grammatical structures in the input (Schmidt, 1990, 1994). Noticing may be the necessary condition for input to become intake. There are a number of ways in which such noticing can be brought about. One is by requesting students to identify the examples of the target structure in the data (e.g., "Underline all the verbs in the present continuous tense"). Another is to highlight the examples in some way, for instance, by italicizing them. A question of

---

[8]In some versions of the computational model of L2 acquisition, output also has a role to play (see, e.g., Swain, 1995, and Skehan, 1998). However, even in these versions, output works primarily in terms of either securing quality input or creating the psycholinguistic conditions that promote input.

some importance, then, is which type of input data is most effective in promoting noticing and acquisition.

In fact, there have been relatively few studies examining what effect different ways of enriching input has on noticing and acquisition. Jourdenais, Ota, Stauffer, Boyson, and Doughty (1995) found that learners exposed to texts in which the preterit and imperfect verb forms in Spanish were typographically highlighted in texts were more likely to subsequently use these past tense forms than learners who read texts where the same verbs forms were not highlighted. Trahey and White (1993) and Trahey (1996) showed that input that is enriched but not enhanced (i.e., no attempt was made to focus learners' attention on the target feature) resulted in the learners acquiring a new rule for adverb positioning in English but not for eliminating a nontarget rule that was part of the learners' current interlanguage. Leeman, Arteagotia, Fridman, and Doughty (1995) found that instruction consisting of highlighting Spanish preterit and imperfect verb forms in written input, telling the students to pay special attention to them, and correcting learner errors led to students supplying the target forms more frequently in comparison to students who received no such instruction. However, it is not possible in this study to distinguish what effect each of these different options had. Two other studies have reported that enriched input has little effect on acquisition. White (1995) failed to find any effect for either enriched input or explicit instruction on Japanese and francophone learners' ability to master reflexive binding in English, although this may have been because of problems with the test used in this study. Alanen (1995) also found that enriched input had little effect on beginner learners' acquisition of Finnish locative expressions and consonant gradation, although he did note that input containing typographically enhanced forms led to the learners using a greater a variety of suffix forms, albeit ungrammatical. The amount of enriched input in this study was very small.

It is likely that we will see further research directed at identifying the kinds of enriched input that work best for noticing and acquisition. Ideally, such studies should be theoretically based (i.e., there should be some principled selection of the input features that are chosen for investigation). Also, there is a need to find ways of measuring the effects on noticing and acquisition separately. Research investigating the data options shown in Table 9.1 is desirable. Various claims have been made for using authentic data in language teaching materials (see, e.g., Harmer, 1983, p. 150) but, to my knowledge, there has been no research testing whether such data enhances acquisition. Indeed, there are strong arguments to be found in both SLA (e.g., Krashen, 1981) and language pedagogy (e.g., Tickoo, 1993) in support of simplified texts. Also, a number of studies have found that simplified input aids comprehension (Parker & Chaudron, 1987) and some (e.g., Ellis, R., 1995) that it also facilitates acquisition. There is also widespread support in language pedagogy for the use of continuous text as opposed to discrete sentences, but research investigating this belief is completely absent. Neither has there been any research examining the relative advantages of presenting data in oral or written form. Oral data require learners to process the target structure "online" (i.e., as the input is received); in contrast, written data typically allow learners the opportunity to process the data more slowly and deliberately.[9] This difference may be important. The development of implicit knowledge may require opportunities for online processing of input. In contrast, controlled processing may be more likely to result in explicit knowledge. It is possible, therefore, that oral data are more likely to promote real interlanguage change than written data. Such an argument suggests that teaching grammar through listening may prove especially effective, but, like the other options, it has not been empirically tested.[10]

Several studies have compared two instructional options—enriched input and direct explicit instruction—on acquisition. These studies show a clear advantage for direct explicit instruction. Alanen (1995), for example, found that the group of learners receiving explicit instruction outperformed the groups receiving different kinds of enriched input. Robinson (1996) also found that learners given explicit instruction in both an easy grammatical rule (adverbial preposing as in *Into the house ran John*) and a difficult rule (pseudoclefting as in *Where Mary and John live is Chicago*) outperformed learners who just received input (referred to as the implicit condition by Robinson) on a grammaticality judgment test. Studies by DeKeyser (1995) and N. Ellis (1993) have also found in favor of explicit instruction. However, the method of testing in these studies (usually a grammaticality judgment test) favored the explicit group. It is possible that enriched input will work better than explicit instruction if acquisition is measured by means of a test that requires online processing of the target structures.

Also, from a materials development point of view, it may make little sense to juxtapose data options and explicit instruction options in this way, as they can be easily combined, both contributing to the development of awareness in learners. Explicit instruction based on discovery tasks of the kind discussed above involve both data options and explicit rule formation.

---

[9]Of course, it would is possible to induce rapid, less controlled processing of written data if the learners are required to read the texts at speed, as in faster reading exercises.

[10]A body of research that could be interpreted as lending support to teaching grammar through listening is that conducted by Asher and his associates (see Asher, 1982) comparing Total Physical Response (TPR) and other language teaching methods (e.g., grammar translation and audiolingualism). TPR is a method that teaches grammatical structures through oral commands. Asher's research regularly found that this method proved superior to other methods for beginner-level learners. However, Asher did not compare the relative advantages of using oral or written commands, as in TPR the commands are primarily oral.

Students are presented with structured data, which they analyze to extract the underlying rule for the target structure. The relationship between the two options, then, is as follows:

data (analyzing) → explicit rule

An alternative arrangement might be to begin by providing an explicit rule and then to follow up with noticing activities, where students are asked to identify the target structure in data:

explicit rule → data (noticing)

A more complicated sequence might consist of:

data (analyzing) → explicit rule → data (noticing)

as in Fotos (1994). Materials illustrating this type of sequence are discussed in a later section.

INPUT–PROCESSING INSTRUCTION

Closely connected to the data options associated with noticing are the reception-based options referred to under Operations in Table 9.1. Although it is technically feasible to envisage an approach to grammar teaching based solely on exposing learners to data rich in the targeted structures (sometimes referred to as input-flooding), a more likely approach is one that combines data options with some kind of task designed to promote input processing.

VanPatten (1996) defines input-processing instruction as "a type of grammar instruction whose purpose is to affect the ways in which learners attend to input data" (p. 2). He emphasizes that "it does not mean that any old input activity is viable" (p. 8) but involves attempts to alter the way learners actually process input. In other words, VanPatten pays attention to form in the input. Such training is intended to help students move from the default strategies that they typically employ and that give rise to the transitional constructions found in interlanguage. For example, learners typically operate a "first-noun strategy" according to which they assign the role of subject or agent to the first noun in an input string. Such a strategy leads to incorrect processing of strings in which the first noun phrase is not the agent, as for example in passive sentences in English:

The committee was given a prize by Marcia.

As part of input-processing instruction, students can be told to pay careful attention to the first noun to see whether it really is functioning as agent/subject and to look for linguistic clues (such as passive verb forms) to help them decide. Another example involves morphological marking of verbs. L2 learners frequently ignore these, relying instead on adverbial markers of time and aspect. In such a case, strategy training consists of pointing out to students the necessity of attending to tense/aspect markers in sentences that do not contain an adverbial. Such training, then, is designed to overcome the natural processes of simplification found in L2 acquisition.

Input processing also involves eliciting nonverbal (or, perhaps, minimally verbal) responses from learners that show whether they have been successful in processing the target structure in the input. This can be achieved in a variety of ways: performing an action (as in TPR), matching sentences with pictures, indicating whether statements are true or false, filling in the gaps in a written text by listening to an oral version of the text, choosing the correct L1 translation of an L2 sentence, agreeing/disagreeing with statements, and so forth. The kinds of input-processing responses required by such tasks depend on the learners having comprehended the input, but they involve more than just comprehension; they entail processing the specific linguistic forms they have noticed for meaning. In this respect, input-processing instruction differs from general listening/reading instruction, which encourages learners to make extensive use of contextual information and background knowledge (i.e., to engage in top-down processing). Input-processing instruction induces learners to attend to linguistic form (i.e., it forces bottom-up processing).

Both VanPatten (1996) and myself (Ellis, R., 1995) have suggested guidelines for developing input-processing teaching materials. VanPatten suggests the following principles:

1. Teach only one thing at a time.
2. Keep meaning in focus.
3. Learners must do something with the input.
4. Use both oral and written input.
5. Move from sentences to connected discourse.
6. Keep the psycholinguistic processing strategies in mind.

I have suggested that the activities in input-processing instruction might be usefully sequenced to require first attention to meaning (i.e., learners are invited to comprehend the message content of the input), then noticing the target form and the meaning it conveys in the input, and finally noticing the gap (i.e., spotting the kinds of typical errors that learners make when using the target structure). These guidelines are reflected in the materials discussed in the following section.

A number of studies (e.g., DeKeyser & Sokalski, 1996; Salaberry, 1996; Tanaka, 1996; VanPatten & Cadierno, 1993; VanPatten & Oikennon, 1996; VanPatten & Sanz, 1995) have investigated the effectiveness of input-processing instruction, usually in terms of a comparison with production-based instruction. In R. Ellis (1999), I have summarized the results and proposed the following conclusions. Input processing instruction in conjunction with explicit instruction leads to gains in learners' ability to comprehend the target structures. Furthermore, it works better in this respect than production-based instruction. Input-processing instruction also results in gains in learners' ability to produce the target structures, but in this respect it is not superior to production-based instruction. However, the gains in production that result from input-processing instruction appear to be more durable than those obtained from production-based instruction. That is, improvement in learners' ability to produce the target structures accurately tends to disappear in the case of production-based instruction but to persist in the case of input-processing instruction. However, research has failed to demonstrate that input-processing instruction results in learners' ability to immediately use the target structures in unplanned language use Thus, it remains to be seen, then, whether input-processing instruction affects interlanguage development (implicit knowledge) or whether it just serves to raise awareness (noticing and understanding). This is a key issue that needs to be studied further.

In general, the theoretical rationale and the results of research to date are sufficiently supportive of input-processing instruction for writers to incorporate tasks requiring reception-based operations in their materials. Input-processing operations, of course, can be combined with other options, including explicit instruction and production-practice. In the next section we discuss some materials that illustrate how this might be achieved.

SOME ILLUSTRATIVE TEACHING MATERIALS

The main thesis of this chapter is that materials writers have typically neglected a number of methodological options that SLA theory and research suggest may be effective in promoting L2 acquisition. What, then, might materials that incorporate these neglected options look like? We will briefly consider some examples from Rutherford (1987) and Ellis and Gaies (1998).

Rutherford suggests two kinds of instruments for raising learners' consciousness about grammar: (1) those involving learner judgment or discrimination and (2) those posing a task to be performed or a problem to be solved. The examples below are taken from Rutherford (1987, pp. 160–167). The first type includes both conventional grammaticality judgment tasks, as in this example directed at helping learners recognize that English needs a formal subject:

(A) Decide whether each sentence is correct or incorrect. Identify the errors and correct them.

   1. In Lake Maracaibo was discovered the oil.

   2. After a few minutes the guests arrived.

   3. In my country does not appear to exist any constraint on women's rights.

This type also includes semantic discrimination tasks that explore learners' ability to process particular grammatical constructions, such as complex noun phrases, as in this example:

(B) Which of the statements can be inferred from the text provided?

   The passing of the bill has given rise to further bitterness among the various linguistic communities in the province.

   1. The various linguistic communities are bitter.

   2. Bitterness caused the bill to be passed.

   3. The province is bitter at the linguistic community.

Task completion/problem-solving tasks also involve judgment on the part of the learner, but, in addition, they require learners to act on their intuitions (i.e., they involve a degree of production as well as reflection). Here is an example of a task that requires learners to use dummy *it* and the appropriate verb complementizer (e.g., *Many Canadians find it important to learn English*).

(C) Rewrite each of the sentences below incorporating the sentence in brackets into the main sentence.

   1. Many French Canadians find [They learn English] important.

   2. Quebec makes [Quebec preserves its French-speaking identity] a rule.

   3. Quebec takes [French is to be given priority over English] for granted.

It should be noted that in such a production activity the aim is not so much to practice the target structure as to develop the learners' understanding of it. As Rutherford's examples make clear, production tasks can serve a consciousness-raising function.

Like Rutherford's activities, the materials in Ellis and Gaies (1998) are remedial in nature; that is, they focus on grammatical problems that L2 learners are known to experience. The materials have already been described in chap. 1. Figure 9.2 provides an example of a complete unit. The activities are sequenced as suggested in R. Ellis (1995)—they begin with general comprehension of the text, then prompt noticing (and rule discovery), and finally address noticing the gap. There is also an opportunity for students to experiment with using the target structure in their own sentences. Table 9.2 provides a list of the methodological options used in this unit.

CONCLUSION

The design of grammar teaching materials needs to draw on the accumulated experience of teachers. By analyzing the methodological options in a number of popular grammar practice books, I have attempted to show that

TABLE 9.2
Analysis of methodological features in Ellis and Gaies (1998)

Feature	Included
Explicit description	
Supplied	•
Discover	•
Data	
Source	
Authentic	•
Contrived	•
Text size	
Discrete sentences	
Continuous	•
Medium	
Oral	•
Written	•
Operations	
Production	
Controlled	
Free	•
Reception	
Controlled	
Automatic	•
Judgments	
Judge only	•
Correct	•
Total features	10

4

Holiday Postcards

Where do you like to go on holiday?
What do you like to do?

ERROR BOX

✗ Every day I am sitting by the pool.

✗ At the moment I drink a glass of wine.

LISTENING TO COMPREHEND 🎧

Brad and Gloria are on holiday. Listen to them read their postcards.

1. Where is Brad?
   a. at a jazz festival
   b. on an island
   c. in California

2. Where is Gloria?
   a. in Paris
   b. in London
   c. by the sea

WORD BOX
*nightlife
*jealous
*rush
*seafood

LISTENING TO NOTICE 🎧

Listen again. Fill in the blanks with a form of the verb in parentheses ( ).

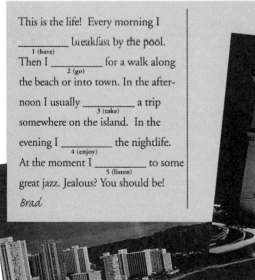

This is the life! Every morning I
_____ breakfast by the pool.
    1 (have)
Then I _____ for a walk along
         2 (go)
the beach or into town. In the afternoon I usually _____ a trip
                3 (take)
somewhere on the island. In the
evening I _____ the nightlife.
          4 (enjoy)
At the moment I _____ to some
                 5 (listen)
great jazz. Jealous? You should be!
Brad

Remember George Rush from
London? Well, surprise, surprise, he
_____ at the same hotel for a
  6 (stay)
few days. We _____ a great
              7 (have)
time. He _____ me all the best
         8 (show)
places in Paris. Well, I must rush now.
We _____ out to this new
    9 (go)
seafood restaurant right now. I
_____ you always.
  10 (love)
Gloria

Bra
21
Lo

FIG. 9.2 Holiday postcards.

UNDERSTANDING THE GRAMMAR POINT

1. Look at the postcards again.
   a. Circle all the verbs in the simple present tense.   I have
   b. Underline all the verbs in the present continuous tense.   I am listening.

2. Find these adverbials in the postcards.
   - every morning
   - in the afternoon
   - at the moment
   - usually
   - for a few days
   - in the evening
   - always
   - now

3. Write the adverbials in the correct column.

Simple Present	Present Continuous
every morning	
usually	

CHECKING

Can you correct the errors in this holiday postcard?

Dear Daniel,

   At the moment I am sitting in a little restaurant in Copacabana. It is late and
the sun ~~just begins~~ *is just beginning* to set. I am watch some teenagers. They playing volleyball on
the beach. A middle-aged man is jogging past my table. Every day I am coming to
the same restaurant. I am eating a light meal — just a salad or some fish — and
drinking a glass of wine. Sometimes I chat with the waiter. He is telling me about
his young boy and I tell him about you. Life is almost perfect, except, of course,
you are not here!

                         Love always,
                         Laura

LANGUAGE NOTE
Use some of the adverbials (every morning, always, now) and the present continuous or simple present tenses.

TRYING IT

Imagine you are on holiday. Write a postcard to a friend.
Tell your friend what you are doing at the moment and what
you do every day. Try to make the person wish he or she was with you!

....
....
....

4

The editors would like to thank Pearson Education for permission to reprint this figure.

there is a clear tradition evident in such materials. This emphasizes two predominant methodological features: the provision of descriptions of grammatical points and controlled production exercises.

Tradition, however, also needs to be challenged. One way of doing so is by drawing on SLA theory and research. Over the past 25 years this has been directed primarily at describing and explaining how learners acquire the grammar of an L2 and has led to a number of insights and possibilities that can be incorporated into teaching materials. In particular, SLA suggests that grammar practice materials might include discovery-type grammar tasks for raising learners' consciousness about grammar, data in the form of structured input to induce noticing of target structures and input-processing tasks. I have given examples of materials that include these options. I have tried to show in this chapter how SLA can guide the development of teaching materials.

Of course, I do not wish to claim that because such materials have the support of SLA theory and research they are more valid than materials based on teachers' accumulated experience. This would be not only presumptuous but also wrong. For a start, SLA researchers and theorists are not in total agreement as to what constitutes the optimal conditions for grammar acquisition.[11] Also, countless learners have successfully learned from traditional grammar teaching materials. Therefore, it would be very mistaken to argue that all such materials should include grammar discovery, noticing, and input-processing tasks. Rather, as I have argued elsewhere (see Ellis, R., 1997), SLA should be seen as one source of "provisional specifications" (Stenhouse, 1975) that teachers need to experiment with through their own day-to-day teaching and through "insider research" (Widdowson, 1990). Teaching materials have an important mediating role in this process. They constitute a means of operationalizing research or theory-based specifications about teaching. In this respect, grammar practice materials can serve as an important source of innovation in language teaching.

ACKNOWLEDGMENT

I would like to thank Michael Rost for his very helpful comments on this chapter.

REFERENCES

Alanen, R. (1995). Input enhancement and rule presentation in second language acquisition. In R. Schmidt (Ed.), *Attention and awareness in foreign language learning* (pp. 259–302). Honolulu: University of Hawaii Press.

---

[11]DeKeyser and Sokalski (1996), for example, argue on the basis of skill-learning theory that production and receptive activities are beneficial, contributing respectively to learners' ability to comprehend and produce the target structures.

Asher, J. (1982). *Learning another language through actions: The complete teacher's guidebook.* Los Gatos, CA: Sky Oaks.

Badalamenti, V., & Henner-Stanchina, C. (1993). *Grammar dimensions: Form, meaning and use: Book one.* Boston: Heinle & Heinle.

Bialystok, E. (1991). Achieving proficiency in a second language: a Processing description. In R. Phillipson, E. Kellerman, L. Selinker, M. Sharwood Smith, & M. Swain (Eds.), *Foreign/second language pedagogy research.* Clevedon, UK: Multilingual Matters.

Bloomfield, L. (1933). *Language.* New York: Holt, Rinehart and Winston.

Bolitho, R., & Tomlinson, B. (1995). *Discover English.* London: George Allen and Unwin.

Corder, S. P. (1967). The significance of learners' errors. *International review of applied linguistics, 5,* 161–169.

DeKeyser, R. (1995). Learning second language grammar rules: An experiment with a miniature linguistic system. *Studies in second language acquisition, 17,* 379–410.

DeKeyser, R., & Sokalski, K (1996). The differential role of comprehension and production practice. *Language Learning, 46,* 613–642.

Eastwood, J. (1992). *Oxford practice grammar.* Oxford: Oxford University Press.

Elbaum, S. (1996). Grammar in context book 1 (2nd ed.). Boston: Heinle & Heinle.

Ellis, N. (1993). Rules and instances in foreign language learning: Interactions of explicit and implicit knowledge. *European Journal of Cognitive Psychology, 5,* 289–318.

Ellis, N. (Ed.). (1994). *Implicit and explicit learning of languages.* London: Academic Press.

Ellis, R. (1984). *Classroom second language development.* Oxford: Pergamon.

Ellis, R. (1988). The role of practice in second language learning. *Teanga, 8,* 1–28.

Ellis, R. (1993). The structural syllabus and second language acquisition. *TESOL Quarterly, 27,* 91–113.

Ellis, R. (1994a). *The study of second language acquisition.* Oxford: Oxford University Press.

Ellis, R. (1994b). An instructed theory of second language acquisition. In N. Ellis (Ed.), *Implicit and explicit learning of languages* (pp. 79–114). London: Academic Press.

Ellis, R. (1995). Interpretation tasks for grammar teaching. *TESOL Quarterly, 29,* 87–105.

Ellis, R. (1997). SLA research and language pedagogy. Oxford: Oxford University Press.

Ellis, R. (1999). Input-based approaches to teaching grammar: A review of classroom-oriented research. *Annual Review of Applied Linguistics, 19,* 64–80.

Ellis, R., & Gaies, S. (1998). *Impact grammar.* Hong Kong: Longman Addison Wesley.

Faerch, C. (1985). Meta talk in FL classroom discourse. *Studies in second language acquisition, 7,* 184–199.

Fortune, A. (1998). Survey review: Grammar practice books. *ELT Journal, 52,* 67–79.

Fotos, S. (1993). Consciousness and noticing through focus on form: Grammar tasks performance versus formal instruction. *Applied Linguistics, 14,* 385–407.

Fotos, S., (1994). Integrating grammar instruction and communicative language use through grammar consciousness-raising tasks. *TESOL Quarterly, 28,* 323–351.

Fotos, S., & Ellis, R. (1991). Communicating about grammar: A task-based approach. *TESOL Quarterly, 25,* 605–628.

Green, P., & Hecht, K. (1992). Implicit and explicit grammar: An empirical study. *Applied Linguistics, 13,* 168–184.

Harmer, J. (1983). *The practice of English language teaching.* London: Longman.

Hawkins, E. (1984). *Awareness of language: An introduction.* Cambridge, UK: Cambridge University Press.

Jesperson, J. (1904). *How to teach a foreign language.* London: George Allen and Unwin.

Jones, L. (1992). *Communicative grammar practice.* Cambridge, UK: Cambridge University Press.

Jourdenais, R. J., Ota, M., Stauffer, S., Boyson, B., & Doughty, C. (1995). Does textual enhancement promote noticing? A think-aloud protocol analysis. In R. Schmidt (Ed.), *Attention and awareness in foreign language learning* (pp. 183–216). Honolulu: University of Hawaii Press.

Krashen, S. (1981). *Second language acquisition and second language learning.* Oxford: Pergamon.

Krashen, S. (1982). *Principles and practice in second language acquisition.* Oxford: Pergamon.

Krashen, S. (1985). *The Input Hypothesis.* London: Longman.

Leeman, J., Arteagotia, I., Fridman, B., & Doughty, C. (1995). Integrating attention to form in content-based Spanish instruction. In R. Schmidt (Ed.), *Attention and awareness in foreign language learning* (pp. 217–258). Honolulu: University of Hawaii Press.

Long, M. (1998). Focus on form in task-based language teaching. *University of Hawaii Working Papers in ESL, 16,* 35–49.

McLaughlin, B. (1990). Restructuring. *Applied Linguistics, 11,* 113–128.

Naiman, N., Frohlich, M., Stern, H., & Todesco, A. (1978). *The good language learner.* Toronto: Ontario Institute for Studies in Education.

Murphy, R. (1994). English in use: A self-study reference and practice book for intermediate students (2nd ed.). Cambridge, UK: Cambridge University Press.

Paradis, M. (1994). Neurolinguistic aspects of implicit and explicit memory: Implications for bilingualism and SLA. In N. Ellis (Ed.), *Implicit and explicit learning of languages* (pp. 393–420). London: Academic Press.

Parker, K., & Chaudron, C. (1987). The effects of linguistic simplifications and elaborative modifications on L2 comprehension. *University of Hawaii Working Papers in ESL, 6,* 106–133.

Pienemann, M. (1985). Learnability and syllabus construction. In K. Hyltenstam & M. Pienemann (Eds.), *Modelling and assessing second language acquisition.* Clevedon, UK: Multilingual Matters.

Reber, A. (1989). Implicit learning and tacit knowledge. *Journal of Experimental Psychology: General, 118,* 219–235.

Robinson, P. (1996). Learning simple and complex rules under implicit, incidental rule-search conditions, and instructed conditions. *Studies in Second Language Acquisition, 18,* 27–67.

Rutherford, W. (1987). *Second language grammar: Learning and teaching.* London: Longman.

Salaberry, M. (1997). The role of input and output practice in second language acquisition. *Canadian Modern Language Review, 53,* 422–451.

Schmidt, R. (1990). The role of consciousness in second language learning. *Applied Linguistics, 11,* 129–158.

Schmidt, R. (1994). Deconstructing consciousness in search of useful definitions for applied linguistics. In J. Hulstijn & R. Schmidt (Eds.), *Consciousness in second language learning. AILA Review, 11,* 11–26.

Schoenberg, I. (1994). *Focus on grammar.* Reading, MA: Longman Addison Wesley.

Sharwood Smith, M. (1993). Input enhancement in instructed SLA. *Studies in Second Language Acquisition, 15,* 165–179.

Skehan, P. (1998). *A cognitive approach to language learning.* Oxford: Oxford University Press.

Stenhouse, L. (1975). *An introduction to curriculum research and development.* London: Heinemann.

Swain, M. (1995). Three functions of output in second language learning. In G. Cook & B. Seidhofer (Eds.), *For H. G. Widdowson: Principles and practice in the study of language.* Oxford: Oxford University Press.

Tanaka, Y. (1996). *The comprehension and acquisition of relative clauses by Japanese high school students through formal instruction.* Unpublished Ed.D. dissertation, Temple University Japan, Tokyo.

Tickoo, M. (1993). *Simplification: Theory and application.* Singapore: SEAMEO Regional Language Centre.

Trahey, M. (1996). Positive evidence in second language acquisition: Some long-term effects. *Second Language Research, 12,* 111–139.

Trahey, M., & White, L. (1993). Positive evidence and preemption in the second language classroom. *Studies in Second Language Acquisition, 15,* 181–204.

VanPatten, B. (1996). *Input processing and grammar instruction in second language acquisition.* Norwood, NJ: Ablex.

VanPatten, B., & Cadierno, T. (1993). SLA as input processing: A role for instruction. *Modern Language Journal, 77,* 45–57.

VanPatten, B., & Oikennon, S. (1996). Explanation versus structured input in processing instruction. *Studies in second language acquisition, 18,* 495–510.

VanPatten, B., & Sanz, C. (1995). From input to output: Processing instruction and communicative tasks. In F. R. Eckman, D. Highland, P. Lee, & R. Weber. (Eds.), *Second language acquisition theory and pedagogy* (pp. 112–140). Mahwah NJ: Erlbaum.

White, L. (1995). Input, triggers, and second language acquisition. Can binding be taught? In F. R. Eckman, D. Highland, P. Lee, R. Weber (Eds.), *Second language acquisition theory and pedagogy.* Mahwah, NJ: Erlbaum.

Widdowson, H. (1990). *Aspects of language teaching.* Oxford: Oxford University Press.

Teaching Grammar in Writing Classes: Tenses and Cohesion

Eli Hinkel
Seattle University, Washington

INTRODUCTION

Grammar instruction in many English as a second language (ESL) and English as a foreign language (EFL) classrooms includes deductive teaching and learning, when the teacher presents grammar rules followed by various forms of practice. Student practice can take the form of cloze exercises, a translation of an English text into the learners' native language, or oral training (read alouds, dialogues, or small-group activities) (Ellis, this volume). In most cases, such exercises draw the learners' attention to verb forms in sentence-level contexts that are created by textbook authors, teachers, or students themselves. This learning practice largely addresses the skills associated with identification of time adverbials and the manipulation of verbal inflections and tense-related forms of auxiliaries. Other approaches to grammar teaching focus on contextualized uses of grammatical structures to promote applications of grammar knowledge to particular situations when students are involved in meaningful or meaning-related communications (e.g., games, problem-solving activities, and role-plays).

In part, because a good deal of linguistic research separates the analysis of rhetorical discourse conventions (such as topic sentences, sentence transitions, and rhetorical development) and the grammatical structures of language, the teaching of writing and the teaching of grammar tend to occupy somewhat distinct domains in second language (L2) pedagogy as well. This separation of grammar teaching from L2 writing instruction may also come from the expectation that if learners acquire L2 grammar through exposure to and interaction with L2, they may also apply their grammar knowledge and skills to writing. On the other hand, L2 writing instruction often has the goal of developing learners' rhetorical, organization, and text-based skills (Leki, 1995; Raimes, 1995; Reid, 1993) and addresses their grammar skills as largely secondary. In particular, Grabe & Kaplan (1996, p. 29) point out that "L2 writing research strongly follows English L1 [first language] writing research," which does not include syntactic and linguistic analyses. The authors further point out that in L2 writing pedagogy and, in general, in L2 writing research, the benefits of adhering to L1 writing research are not always clear.

Research has demonstrated that in evaluations of nonnative speaker (NNS) writing, grammatical accuracy plays an important role. The presence of grammar errors has a negative impact on the native speaker (NS) perceptions of the quality of L2 writing (Johns, 1997; Johnson & Roen, 1989). Some studies report that to attain advanced proficiency in L2 writing, learners need to attend to grammar in their writing, and that L2 pedagogy genuinely concerned about learner proficiency in writing needs to include the teaching of relevant L2 grammar (Hammerly, 1991). Specifically, Fathman and Whalley (1990) found that attention to and feedback on grammar in the writing of NNSs significantly improves grammatical accuracy and the overall quality of writing. Ellis (1997) pointed out that many L2 linguistic features, such as verb inflections and uses of tenses, are so complex that they are often difficult to learn in the process of communication. He also noted that because of the complexity of these L2 grammar features, they need to become instructional foci within a syllabus that also promotes communication.

The contextualized uses of English tenses have been noted as one of the more difficult aspects of L2 grammar because inappropriate uses of tenses may obscure the meaning of text in writing (Hinkel, 1992, 1997). Vaughn (1991) pointed out that in holistic assessment of essays, incorrectly used tenses occupy a prominent place among the factors that lead to low ratings of L2 writing. She also commented that, in general, raters believe that errors in phrase-level grammar (tenses, morphology, and word form) are more detrimental to the overall quality of text than, for example, flawed clause structure. Based on the study of Hamp-Lyons (1991), who reviewed the rating scales and evaluation guides of L2 writing developed by the British Council and used with the Michigan English Language Assessment Battery, tense errors are often seen as rather grievous.

Many writing and composition textbooks for ESL students published in the United States include units that specifically address the teaching of tenses (Holten & Marasco, 1998; Leki, 1995; Ruetten, 1997). However, because such texts usually see their goals as developing learners' writing fluency and rhetorical skills, they often rely only on lists of adverbial time markers and brief guides to the teaching of tenses. In their detailed text-book for NNS graduate students, Swales and Feak (1994) indicate that in academic writing, the uses of past and present tenses need to be explicitly taught because in the context of academic writing, the occurrence of particular tenses is highly conventionalized. For example, in abstracts, data descriptions, summaries, purpose statements, and generalizations the present tense is usually expected, and the use of the past tense is discouraged. On the other hand, in descriptions of particular experiments, study findings, case studies, or past-time events uses of the past tense may be requisite (Hinkel, 1997). Overall, however, although the teaching of tenses is the staple of all grammar teaching books in EFL and ESL pedagogy, it is not always directly connected to tense uses in actual writing and writing instruction.

Because the teaching of L2 tenses is often carried out under the umbrella of the grammar curriculum, learners often do not establish an effective connection between the knowledge gained in grammar classes and their writing. In most cases, the teaching of grammar has not changed a great deal despite the research published in applied linguistics and text analysis (Ellis, chapters 2 and 9). Traditional approaches to grammar pedagogy largely consist of training in the inflectional forms of English verb tenses with the teacher's explanations of when particular forms of tenses are used, followed by cloze exercises in sentence-long contexts. The sentences for the practice of tense uses and contexts are usually supplied by the material writer and include explicit contextual markers and adverbs (e.g., *yesterday, five years ago, next summer*) that require learners to identify the time frame for the sentence and use a particular verb form, congruent with the time markers, such as:

> *The traffic situation* —————— *(get) worse every year.*

> *Martha's birthday* —————— *(be) Friday, so we'd better buy her a gift.*
> (Thewlis, 1997, pp. 212, 238, respectively)

Although many L2 learners become quite skilled in identifying the adverbs supplied in practically all exercise sentences, they often do not associate their explicit and/or implicit knowledge of tense uses attained in grammar classes with other language production tasks, such as writing (Hinkel, 1997). For example, the following excerpt in (1) was written by a nonnative speaker who had received seven years of ESL training in the United States and was one year away from graduating from a university:

> (1) In my culture, young people *have* to learn how to respect older people. We *had* to listen to whatever they say and we *don't* have the right to talk back even when we *know* what the older person said *was* wrong. We *were* considered to be rude if we *talk* back. All we *needed* to do *was* to sit there and listen to them.

In this paragraph, the tenses shift from the present to the past and then back to the present seemingly at random without a discernable cause or time markers to explain the changes in the frame of the narrative. Even within this short excerpt, the shifting tenses create a text that lacks cohesion and seems temporally disjointed.

Similarly, in the following example the tense shifts can actually obscure the meaning in a paper on the socioeconomic influence on demographics, written by a graduating senior:

> (2) Early marriage *is* very common in Russia. With the collapse of communism, young couples *got* married in their twenties, and this *is* time when they *are* still in universities. The assumption *was* that parents always *help* their children after marriage. It *is* common for a young married couple to live at their parents' house after they *got* married, or if parents *are* wealthy enough, they *buy* an apartment for their children.

In this excerpt it may be difficult to tell whether the NNS author discusses the situation as it existed just before "the collapse of communism" or as it exists now, following the political change. In the case of the former, the writer's use of the past tense is justified, but the use of the present tense is erroneous. On the other hand, if she describes the current situation, then the shifts to the past tense seem to be unwarranted.

ESL and EFL teachers and researchers have long noted that in NNS writing, the use of appropriate tenses often appears to be a pervasive problem that can result in confusing text and narrative structure (Guiora, 1983; Riddle, 1986). However, McCarthy (1991) and Lewis (1986) argue that the uses and meaning of English tenses in writing are conventionalized to a great extent. Specifically, they point out that the uses of tenses in written text are not so much determined by the objective time in which the events take place, but more so by the discourse framework shared by the reader and the writer within the given context. It appears, however, that even advanced learners (as the authors of the two excerpts already given) are not always able to identify the contextual frame that calls for the use of a particular tense and may undervalue the importance of the meanings that the shifting tenses can impart to written text.

In the teaching of tense uses in written text, a variety of approaches can be used, ranging from analyses of sentences to examinations of larger excerpts from texts. As Celce-Murcia (chap. 7, this volume) points out, rudiments of discourse analysis can be employed for teaching various grammar structures and developing teaching materials and examples based on authentic language use in both spoken and written English. A similar pedagogical technique can be beneficial in the teaching of the conventionalized tense structures in expository and academic writing.

This chapter presents an approach to the teaching of tenses that centers on analyses of authentic texts to help learners develop familiarity with the notion of a contextual frame and its conventions in L2 writing. The method for teaching English tenses and cohesive time frames presented here helps to establish a direct connection between contextualized instruction and the production of L2 writing and, hence, the concurrent development of both L2 fluency and accuracy. The suggested teaching method, based on grammar discovery tasks (Ellis, 1997; also chaps. 2 and 9, this volume), allows learners to examine how tenses are used in time frames in real language and increase their implicit and explicit knowledge of grammar. In addition, because these discovery tasks rely on authentic language, the teacher can create his or her materials to suit diverse proficiency levels of students and/or instructional goals. Based on text analysis, the pedagogical goal of learners' noticing the context in which particular uses of tenses occur is to enhance learner awareness and understanding of how cohesive text can be situated and maintained in a temporal contextual frame.

Although tense use in newspaper articles and academic writing has differences, there are pedagogically useful similarities, for example, the tense use in spot news resembles that in humanities and social sciences, and the temporal frames in scientific reporting are similar to those in technical and natural science disciplines (geology, meteorology, and biology) (Biber, 1988, 1995). The advantage of employing newspaper articles in the teaching of tenses and time frames is that usually discourse in newspapers is lexically, syntactically, and conceptually less complex than that in academic prose. All of the following examples were extracted from local and student papers. Both types of publications represent sources of authentic written discourse, accessible in EFL and ESL settings alike. Because newspaper reports of events, scientific findings, business analyses, and reviews of books and movies are easy to obtain (for example, from the Internet), they may represent an almost inexhaustible supply of materials that can be made relevant and interesting for students. Although it is unlikely that examples of all the tenses can be found in most newspaper texts, examples of the past and present tenses abound, and these tenses are common in academic writing (Biber, 1988; Swales, 1990).

IDENTIFYING COMMON TIME FRAMES
IN AUTHENTIC WRITING

Many practicing EFL/ESL teachers know that adverbial markers (or time adverbs) are usually employed to establish the time frame in written discourse. The time frame in a text does not necessarily refer to objective time. For example, the past tense can be used to refer to events that take place both in the present and the past, but only the past time of the event is relevant to the discourse frame:

(3) Nearly 71 percent of women [college students] *were* at least somewhat concerned about financing their college education, compared with 58.5 percent of men. . . . About 38 percent of women *reported* they frequently "*felt* overwhelmed," compared with 7.3 percent of men. *(Seattle Times,* January 25, 1999)

In this example, it is important to note that the use of the past tense verb markers does not imply that the information in the text is not applicable to the present time. Rather, the written discourse convention requires that the tense use is consistent throughout the contextual frame. It is not known whether the differences between men and women apply to the present time because the text is framed for the past time; hence, the past tense of the verbs is used.

Learners are commonly taught that in most cases, the tenses within the contextual frame rarely shift until another adverbial marker is employed to warrant the shift and reframe the discourse flow. In teaching, a good analogy may be to compare these markers to movie flashbacks when the story line switches from the present to the past (or leaps several years forward). Examples for changing time frames are common in written discourse and can serve as points of departure for text analysis and models for composition.

In written discourse, time frames are usually marked by means of past-time adverbials or past tense verbal inflections. For example, in the following excerpt, time adverbials clearly delineate the past time frame and the frame shifts from the past to the present:

(4) *Last Monday,* Café Paradiso *closed* shop forever—soon to be replaced by Café Vita, a local Seattle coffee chain. . . . Café Paradiso *was* the place where you *went* for coffee on that first awkward college first date. Café Paradiso *was* the place where you *took* your out-of-town friends when they *wanted* to see a "real Seattle coffeehouse." . . . Café Paradiso *was* the place where you *tried* your first cigarette or *got* hooked on caffeine. . . . *Now* only the sign *remains.* *(The Spectator,* December 3, 1998)

In this excerpt, the past time marker *[l]ast Monday* determines the use of the past tense in the first sentence. Then the story moves to more remote, general past, until the present time marker *[n]ow* shifts the time frame and the tense to the present. Both the past and the present tenses need to remain consistent throughout the framed portions of the discourse.

However, it appears that in authentic texts the time frame markers are not always overt but can also be implicit. In such cases, the tenses can shift between the past and the present as the discourse necessitates. For example, in the excerpt below the time frames move between the past and the present, mostly without explicit adverbial markers:

> (5) A national panel of scientists *yesterday warned* of the hazards of teenage employment, saying that young people who *work* more than 20 hours a week, regardless of their economic background, *are* less likely to finish high school. . . . The panel also *warned* that work *can* be dangerous: Young people *are* injured at work at twice the rate of adults, and 100,000 *show up* in hospital emergency rooms *each year* for job-related injuries they *receive.* A committee of the National Research Council and the Institute of Medicine *portrayed* a generation of young people eager to enter the work force . . . . The panel, which *reviewed* years of research from leading scientists in the field, *acknowledged* that work *can* have positive effects, from teaching punctuality to money management and how to work effectively with other people. . . . One study cited by researchers *found* that for every additional hour worked, they *saw* an . . . increase in the likelihood that a child *would* drop out of school. *(Seattle Times,* November 12, 1998)

The portion of discourse exemplified in Example 5 illustrates that in writing, reporting verbs (in main clauses) are often used in the past tense to refer to the past event of presenting information to the reader. The past time marker *yesterday* refers to the past event of information reporting and, thus, all reporting verbs in this context are used in the past tense. The change in the frame from the act of reporting, expressed in the past tense *(warned, portrayed, reviewed, acknowledged,* and *found)* to the reported information, conveyed in the present tense, can also allow the teacher to bring students" attention to the variety of reporting verbs and their usefulness in academic, and business writing, as well as narration and exposition.

Based on her corpus analysis of academic texts in several disciplines (such as economics, law, and linguistics), Tadros (1994) found that reporting verbs are very common in academic writing, when writers need to demonstrate their knowledge of material and convey propositions expressed in subordinate clauses. Following almost all reporting verbs (e.g., *argue, believe, claim, consider, define, discuss, develop, find, notice, point out, realize, recognize),* the past tense generally shifts to the present in *that*-clauses, as, for example, in the first sentence in this paragraph. Because these verbs are very frequent in academic texts and because they often account for tense shifts within sentences, it may be beneficial to familiarize students with their uses and discourse functions. For example, Leech and Svartvik (1994) point out that in reported statements, modal verbs *(must, could, might,* and *should)* do not take the past tense (although *must* can be reported as *had to).* They also note when "the idea expressed in the reported statement" (p. 134) applies to both the past and the present, the use of the past tense depends on the context (as in Example 4). Swan (1995, p. 482) also comments that with reporting verbs the choice of the present or the past tense in the reported statement depends specifically on whether reporters "agree" with the information in the reported statement and/or consider it to be applicable to both the past and the present. Hence, since the reporter of the information in Example 4 seems to believe it to be generally applicable to the current time, the use of the present tense in reported statements accurately reflects this view.

Although in Example 4 all verbs carry the past tense following the time-marker *last Monday* until the frame is changed to the present by means of the adverb *now*, in Example 5, the information that is reported and included in the subordinate clause can be narrated in the present tense (as with the verbs *work*, *are*, and *can*). In this case, the reported information refers to events that are *generally* (or occasionally) applicable to the situation discussed in the context. Because adverbs of frequency *(often, usually, generally, sometimes)* are ordinarily used with verbs that express general truths, habits, and routines (Byrd, 1992), they are typically used in the simple present tense.

To test whether the information can be narrated in the present tense, students may find it helpful to insert a "litmus" frequency adverb into a sentence (or several adjacent sentences) to see whether the meaning of the discourse excerpt can be retained. Such adverbs can be *usually, generally, almost always, often, frequently, sometimes, occasionally,* or *rarely*, depending on the context. Students usually find this litmus test easy to apply in identifying the time frame when writing information reports or editing. For example,

(6) A national panel of scientists yesterday *warned* of the hazards of teenage employment, saying that young people who *[usually/frequently/normally] work* more than 20 hours a week, regardless of their economic background, *are [generally/typically/occasionally]* less likely to finish high school . . . . The panel also *warned* that work can be dangerous: Young people *are [frequently/usually]* injured at work at twice the rate of adults . . . .

A simple rule of thumb that can be applied to such structures is that if the inserted adverb of frequency does not conflict with the overall meaning of the clause, then the simple present tense can be used following the past tense reporting verb. Conversely, if the adverb does not seem to be congruent with the sentence meaning, the present tense cannot be used. For example, in Example 7, an insertion of frequency adverbs, such as *usually, generally,* or *frequently* results in an obscure structure with conflicting temporal meanings that even intermediate-level learners can readily identify.

(7) *On Friday night,* police and fire dispatchers throughout the area *reported* that scores of accidents *[usually/generally] occurred* on King County roads and that traffic on the I-5 *slowed* to a crawl.

It is important to note that the verb tense does not always shift in *that*-clauses following reporting verbs (as in Example 7). However, maintaining the past tense in *that*-clauses may change the meaning of a text to imply that the reported information has somehow changed and does not apply to present (or general) situations discussed in the text (Swales & Feak, 1994). To exemplify this change in the text meaning, a productive exercise can be to ask students to switch the verb tenses from the present to the past and see whether they can identify how the meaning of the entire discourse excerpt alters. In most cases, intermediate and advanced language learners can easily detect the changes in the text meanings when asked to replace the verbs in the present tense with those in the past.

DISCOURSE CONVENTIONS AND TENSE COHESION IN AUTHENTIC WRITING

Lewis (1986) observed that in written discourse, actions and events are not necessarily presented in their objective time. Rather, they represent manifestations of textual discourse reality and contextualized time frames. As McCarthy (1991) notes, the uses of tenses in writing are highly conventionalized and, in particular, academic discourse can follow rules of convention more rigidly than other types of writing (such as fiction, newspaper editorials, or letters). The conventionalization of tense uses in writing needs to be exemplified and discussed to illustrate that in writing, tenses are not always used to reflect the time of events objectively (and factually accurately). In fact, their contextual meanings can convey factually inaccurate implications and may even appear to be counterintuitive.

In many languages other than English, little distinction is made between the real time of events and the use of tenses in discourse (Hinkel, 1997). Although they can be the same, often they are not. For example, the sentence *Two years ago, I applied to some universities in the U.S. because I want to study here* describes a real past-time event *(applied)* framed by the adverbial *two years ago*. On the other hand, the use of the present tense verb *want* appears to be incongruous with the conventions of the English-language academic discourse that requires the time frame and tense use to remain consistent until a different time marker is encountered and, thus, the contextual frame is established. The use of the present tense with the verb *want* shifts the time frame to a situation that is generally (or currently) true. However, the use of the present with *want* does not refer to the past time, as the written discourse convention dictates. Simply correcting the tense from the present to the past may create an implication that the student no longer desires to study in the United States (or that it is not known if he or she does). In this case, the resulting sentence *Two years ago, I applied to some universities in the U.S. because I wanted to study here* may appear to be factually inaccurate and even untruthful to the student.

An important feature of written academic discourse in English is that within the past time frame, events and actions expressed by the verbs are expected to be used in the past tense because for the purposes of writing, it may be irrelevant whether the event and/or the action is current at the present time. In a piece of writing framed for the past (or future) tense, the use of verb tenses needs to be consistent throughout the framed context to provide for textual cohesion, even if the event or the action is currently relevant and not completed in the objective time (Hinkel, 1997). In the sentence, *I applied to some universities in the U.S. because I want to study here,* the use of the present tense is not appropriate even if the individual still desires to study in the United States at the present time because the discourse frame of the past time restricts the relevance of events and actions only to the past.

In the following example of authentic language use, the tenses are employed to reflect written discourse conventions, possibly at the expense of factual accuracy.

> (8) When the Essential Baking Co. *reached* its 10-year goal for growth just 18 months after it *was* founded *in 1994,* general manager . . . Teal *knew* that a move to a bigger facility *was* in order. But the business *prided* itself on being a part of the community, and a move *would* be challenging. . . . *(Pacific Northwest, Supplement to Seattle Times,* December 20, 1998)

This text is framed for the contextualized past tense by means of the past time marker *in 1994.* The tense of the first verb in a piece of discourse *(reached)* can also be used to frame a discourse excerpt for a particular time. However, in an objective analysis of the isolated clause *the business prided itself on being a part of the community,* the use of the past tense with the verb *prided* may imply that at the present time, the business no longer prides itself on being a part of the community (the use of the past tense may also imply the completedness of an action or event). It is important to emphasize that written discourse conventions, much more than spoken, have the goal of developing textual and contextual cohesion by means of a conventionalized tense structure throughout a discourse frame. For this reason, a piece of writing does not always adhere to the factual reality of events and situations, and in advanced writing in English, the issues of text cohesion take precedence. In this case, the choices of appropriate tenses may be limited by the conventions of written discourse, combined with the meanings of pastness or completion.

The verbs that learners often have difficulty situating in contextual time frames usually belong in several large classes. They are commonly associated with durative *(work, study, live, attend, wait, expect)*, emotive *(love, like, suffer, hurt)*, and mental activities *(think, believe, know, understand)*; modal meanings of ability and obligation *(can, may, should, need to, and have to)* (Hinkel, 1995); as well as pseudo-modals *(want to, hope to, plan to, and expect to)*. For example, *When my uncle gave me the money, he knew that I can succeed in America.* To help learners produce cohesive pieces of writing, the teacher may specially bring their attention to such verbs and the contexts in which they occur, such as personal narratives, short stories, and accounts of newsworthy developments or historical events.

FLUID TIME FRAMES AND COHESION IN AUTHENTIC WRITING

When learners write, they often encounter contexts in which time frames (and hence, uses of tenses) need to change frequently. For example, expanded answers to exam questions, lab reports, and business or engineering projects may necessitate changes of tenses in relatively short texts. Regardless of text length, however, written discourse conventions require cohesion that, among many other important considerations, includes appropriate (or conventionalized) uses of tenses (Halliday & Hasan, 1976; McCarthy, 1991; Swales, 1990).

Example 9 presents two time frames and the attendant tense shift in a very short context of two adjacent sentences.

(9) *Last year,* Americans *consumed* an estimated 3.4 billion gallons of bottled water—12.7 gallons per person. That *is* expected to increase *in 1998* by nearly 10 percent. *(Seattle Times,* November 5, 1998)

In this short text, adverbials explicitly mark a change in the time frame, even if it occurs only within a context of two sentences. The cohesion conventions in written discourse often require that tense shifts be anchored to the textual time frames.

Example 10 presents a longer piece of writing with multiple tense shifts, some of which are marked explicitly by means of time markers, and others implicitly by using regularities of English grammar. A text excerpt such as this reveals many systematic features of English syntax. Although the pertinent information can be found in many traditional EFL/ESL grammar texts, an example text analysis appropriate for an intermediate to advanced level class is also presented below. For example, texts such as the following can also serve as a basis for constructing teacher- or student-generated materials for practicing contextualized tense meanings and implications. (Suggestions for materials development are presented later in this chapter.)

(10) *A year ago*, scientists from around the world *decided* the Great Smokies census *was* a job worth doing. *This week* the same 100 researchers *have been meeting* outside the park to map out a strategy. The research *is* expected to start *in March*. If they *succeed* in the Smokies, scientists *hope* to use strategies developed there to poke around every park and schoolyard in the nation. The simple spider illustrates how mammoth the Smokies job *will be*. Fred Coyle, a Western Carolina University researcher, *got* an *early start* looking for spiders in the park. *Over three years*, he *has collected* 180,000 spiders. He *found* 456 species—38 of them never identified before. It *will take* Coyle and a dozen graduate students *five more years* . . . to finish the study. *(Seattle Times,* December 18, 1998)

In this excerpt, the initial time frame, *[a] year ago*, is established for the past tense in the first sentence. In the second, however, the adverbial marker *[t]his week* shifts the tense to the present perfect. The perfective aspect of present tense verbs often occurs in time frames marked by adverbials that include *(in, over, during) this* +, *the past* +, and *the last* + (time marker), as in *this year, in the past decade*, and *during the last month* (see Celce-Murcia, this volume, for additional information). In addition, the progressive aspect of verbs is commonly employed to show that the action expressed by the verb is continuing at the moment of speech—and in this case, at the time when the text is published (see Byrd, 1992, and Ruetten, 1997, for techniques in the teaching of progressive tenses). The use of the present simple tense *(is expected)* with future time markers *(in March)* is also very common in English (e.g., *I leave for Chicago tomorrow* or *The store closes in an hour*). The clause *[i]f they succeed* is used in the present tense because clauses of time and condition (marked by *if, whether,* or *when*) rarely take the future tense in written discourse (although they sometimes do in speaking). For example, in writing, **If the sales will improve, we will have to hire additional staff* would be considered ungrammatical, and in such clauses, the use of the present tense is appropriate.

However, the future time marker *in March* determines the use of the future tense in *The simple spider illustrates how mammoth the Smokies job will be*. A reference to Fred Coyle's background is made by the past time marker *an early start* that explains the use of the past tense *got*. The perfective aspect in the verb phrase *has collected* is framed by the adverbial *over three years*—because the implication of the present perfect tense use is that the result of his three-year work is available at the present or that his work on the project is not quite finished. The past tense in *found* can be also changed to *has found*, and both tenses would be appropriate in this context. The future marker *in five more years* clearly marks the verb *will take* for the future tense.

SUGGESTIONS FOR USING AUTHENTIC TEXTS IN THE CLASSROOM

In general terms, bringing the learners' attention to particular contextualized tense uses and discourse frames represents a key factor in bringing the discourse conventions and regularities to the level of effective production in writing. Schmidt (1995) points out that "noticing" and paying attention to the focal points of language and its linguistic features greatly enhances students' performance with complex syntactic structures and vocabulary. The suggestions for information gathering and communicative activities in the following discussion have the goal of advancing students' overall language proficiency with a particular focus on writing. Specifically, they concentrate on promoting students' discourse-level skills and lead to knowledge-building and the production of written texts that adhere to the conventions of writing in English.

Depending on the students' proficiency level, an occasional advanced vocabulary item may be replaced or simply omitted (e.g., in a compound noun phrase or attributive adjective and adverb phrase). Complex names of relatively unknown individuals (as in . . . *Teal* in Example 8 above) or unfamiliar geographical locations (e.g., *the Great Smokies)* can be replaced with generic synonyms (such as *John Smith* or *the Great Mountain Range* in Example 10). However, the advanced vocabulary items in original texts gradually can be retained to promote the learners' exposure to real-life and idiomatic language use. If needed, long text excerpts can be shortened by omitting whole sentences or portions of sentences (as in Examples 3, 4, and 9) without loss of the lesson content when authentic time markers and tense shifts are maintained. Once students are familiar with this type of frame analysis, they, perhaps with the guidance of the teacher, can examine their own writing for tense cohesion.

Several suggestions for teacher- or student-generated materials and practice are presented below. All of these activities and projects have been used in teaching for several years and can provide various benefits for learners because they represent integrated and fluency-based venues for exposure to real-life language and fluency development.

Suggestion 1: Recognizing and Anticipating Adverbials of Time

Students can be asked to mark adverbials of time, shifts in time frames, and tense-related inflections and/or verb phrases in selected texts. If students work in small groups, each group can be assigned a different text to work with, and when their search for adverbials and verb inflections is completed, groups can present their findings to one another. Anticipating the appropriate tense markers in contexts framed for a particular time frame can be productive and interesting for learners at the intermediate (and/or high intermediate) level of proficiency. For example, an authentic text with explicit time markers but omitted verbal inflections can be used effectively. Because students at intermediate levels of proficiency may have a limited vocabulary range, authentic texts for this exercise can be found among advertisements from newspapers and magazines with sufficient amounts of text, juvenile periodicals and books, book cover copies, or brief news reports from adapted or authentic news media and the Internet.

To make this exercise enjoyable, groups of students can compete for accuracy to see which group can complete the task with the greatest number of correct tense inflections in a specified amount of time.

Suggestion 2: Reporting Verbs and *That*-Clauses

Students can be assigned to read a text (a story, a chapter from a textbook, or a news article) and recast the information in writing. If possible, the story or the article should include several personages who "speak" or provide information (as in Example 4). These are very common in most U.S. newspapers and can be found in the science, business, automotive, travel, and entertainment sections. Alternatively, the teacher can read a short story to the class or show a movie clip with a dialogue to describe, as well as a portion of a videotaped TV program or a news report (easily obtained in many ESL and/or EFL settings) that they need to recast in writing and focus on information provided by various speakers.

A project for practicing reporting verbs can also center around short skits or student-developed role-plays that groups present to the entire class (or other small groups). An additional benefit of this technique lies in the fact that it works to promote diverse language skills in context.

Suggestion 3: Authentic Language and
Information Reports: Interviews

In ESL settings, students can be assigned to interview two to four individuals or obtain information from employees in school or university administrative offices, a library, a car rental agency, a museum, cellular phone or computer stores, or car dealerships. Their interview questions can become the first step in their writing practice. It is often advisable that the teacher approve of the questions before the actual interview. Following the interview, as the next step the students can write a report about their findings and indicate what they learned during the interviews. This writing project requires students to create texts that contain various time frames (and tense uses) within the conventions of English written discourse.

Students usually learn a great deal from such exposures because they foster contact with real language speakers outside the classroom. Although interviews can be carried out individually or in pairs, the actual writing can be done by students individually. The information collected during the interviews can become a springboard for another writing assignment (see the next section).

Suggestion 4: Information Synthesis

For high-intermediate or advanced students, synthesizing information obtained during interviews can become an excellent venue for a more sophisticated writing practice. Groups of two or three students can be asked to pool together (but certainly not merely rewrite or retype) the information for a broader, synthesis-like summary of their findings. This assignment often extends beyond the practice with reporting verbs because it requires learners to produce a longer piece of writing and report the information from several outside sources.

Suggestion 5: Text Cohesion in Past Time Frames

Students can be assigned reading logs or written book reports. Biographies and autobiographies of interesting people, such as sports figures, movie stars, popular singers, political figures, and scientists, are usually available for diverse audiences and language proficiency levels. They range from those published for school-age readers to highly advanced personality analyses for educated adults.

As an interim-length project, students can write their own autobiographies or histories of their families.

CONCLUSION

Grammar instruction based on authentic or simplified discourse can provide fruitful opportunities for teaching tenses, clause structure, articles, and prepositions in context. The contextualized teaching of grammar can expose learners to ways in which language is used in real life and heighten their awareness of its conventions and complexities. When working with discourse analysis in the classroom, presenting authentic texts and explaining how real-life written texts are constructed can heighten learner awareness and provide for an understanding of written discourse conventions. On the other hand, presentations of models and explanations may not be sufficient to improve the quality of writing production. For this reason, it is important to supplement the explanations with ample practice to allow learners to produce writing. Although theoretical models have identified language input as an essential component for second language learners, the crucial place of output in production has not received sufficient attention in research and literature. It would be difficult to develop communicative competence in speaking or writing based on input alone because to engage in a meaningful interaction or writing, one has to be understood, as well as be able to understand. As has been noted, the use of tenses and temporal cohesion occupy a prominent place in how written text is understood or evaluated.

Schmidt (1995) observed that through exposure to models and examples, learners can become aware of regularities in input and thus accurately judge the grammaticality of structures they have never before encountered. He also pointed out, however, that whether grammatical rules are presented inductively or deductively does not seem to have a great deal of impact on the learners' grammaticality judgments of structures. He commented that paying attention to particular aspects of input that one sets out to learn enhances learning. Hence, looking for clues in the input and becoming aware of discourse markers when producing writing also promotes effective learning; even if at various levels of proficiency, learners are unable to make accurate generalizations about a particular system or rules.

One of the reasons that many practicing EFL and ESL teachers often become disenchanted with grammar book learning is that pedagogical grammar rules are frequently simplistic and do not account for the large number of cases or examples that learners come across in real life. Another reason is that many students can "learn" grammar rules as they are presented in grammar textbooks but fail to apply them when it comes to output. Although the reasons for these learner behaviors are complex, it appears that instruction may help learners focus on particular features of language and organize learner attention (Ellis, 1994). In light of the research conducted in second language learning and acquisition, it appears that although overt instruction in grammar does not necessarily lead to direct improvement in language learning, it can serve as an indirect cognitive means of increasing learners' exposure to language and their ability to notice discourse and language features. From this perspective, classroom analyses of time frames and the attendant tense uses can also add to learners' awareness of language structures and systems and benefit the development of second language writing proficiency and fluency.

REFERENCES

Biber, D. (1988). *Variation across speech and writing.* Cambridge, UK: Cambridge University Press.

Biber, D. (1995). *Dimensions of register variation.* Cambridge, UK: Cambridge University Press.

Byrd, P. (1992). *Applied English grammar.* Boston: Heinle & Heinle.

Ellis, R. (1994). *The study of second language acquisition.* Oxford: Oxford University Press.

Ellis, R. (1997). *SLA research and language teaching.* Oxford: Oxford University Press.

Fathman, A., & Whalley, E. (1990). Teacher response to student writing: Focus on form versus content. In B. Kroll (Ed.), *Second language writing* (pp. 178–190). Cambridge, UK: Cambridge University Press.

Grabe, W., & Kaplan, R. B. (1989). Writing in a second language: Contrastive rhetoric. In D. Johnson & D. Roen (Eds.), *Richness in writing* (pp. 263–283). New York: Longman.

Grabe, W. & Kaplan, R. B. (1996). *Theory and practice of writing.* London: Longman.

Guiora, A. (1983). The dialectic of language acquisition. *Language Learning, 33,* 3–12.

Halliday, M. A. K., & Hasan, R. (1976). *Cohesion in English.* London: Longman.

Hammerly, H. (1991). *Fluency and accuracy.* Clevedon, UK: Multilingual Matters.

Hamp-Lyons, L. (1991). Scoring procedures for ESL contexts. In L. Hamp-Lyons (Ed.), *Assessing second language writing* (pp. 241–277). Norwood, NJ: Ablex.

Hinkel, E. (1992). L2 tense and time reference. *TESOL Quarterly, 26,* 556–572.

Hinkel, E. (1995). The use of modal verbs as a reflection of cultural values. *TESOL Quarterly, 29,* 325–343.

Hinkel, E. (1997). The past tense and temporal verb meanings in a contextual frame. *TESOL Quarterly, 31,* 289–314.

Holten, C., & Marasco, J. (1998). *Looking ahead: Mastering academic writing.* Boston: Heinle & Heinle.

Johns, A. (1997). *Text, role, and context: Developing academic literacies.* Cambridge, UK: Cambridge University Press.

Johnson, D., & Roen, D. (1989). *Richness in writing.* New York: Longman.

Lewis, M. (1986). *The English verb.* Hove, UK: Language Teaching Publications.

Leech, G., & Svartvik, J. (1994). *A communicative grammar of English* (2nd ed.). New York: Longman.

Leki, I. (1995). *Academic writing* (2nd ed.). New York: St. Martin's Press.

McCarthy, M. (1991). *Discourse analysis for language teachers.* Cambridge, UK: Cambridge University Press.

Raimes, A. (1995). Out of the woods: Emerging traditions in the teaching of writing. In S. Silberstein (Ed.), *State of the art TESOL essays* (pp. 237–260). Alexandria, VA: TESOL.

Reid, J. (1993). *Teaching ESL writing.* Englewood Cliffs, NJ: Prentice Hall.

Riddle, E. (1986). Meaning and discourse function of the past tense in English. *TESOL Quarterly, 20,* 267–286.

Ruetten, M. (1997). *Developing composition skills* (2nd ed.). Boston: Heinle & Heinle.

Schmidt, R. (1995). Can there be learning without attention? In R. Schmidt (Ed.), *Attention and awareness in foreign language learning* (pp. 9–64). Honolulu: University of Hawaii Press.

Swales, J. (1990). *Genre analysis.* Cambridge, UK: Cambridge University Press.

Swales, J., & Feak, C. (1994). *Academic writing for graduate students.* Ann Arbor: University of Michigan Press.

Swan, M. (1995). *Practical English usage.* Oxford: Oxford University Press.

Tadros, A. (1994). Predictive categories in expository text. In M. Coulthard (Ed.), *Advanced in written text analysis* (pp. 69–82). New York: Routledge.

Thewlis, S. (1997). *Grammar dimensions: Form, meaning, and use* (2nd ed.). Boston: Heinle & Heinle.

Vaughn, C. (1991). Holistic assessment: What goes on in the raters' minds? In L. Hamp-Lyons (Ed.), *Assessing second language writing* (pp. 111–126). Norwood, NJ: Ablex.

Research on Grammar Structures

Empirical research in applied linguistics and investigations into how language is used and seen by its speakers has much to contribute to second and foreign language pedagogy. Although traditional grammar texts have continued to rely on grammar rules and artificial examples (Ellis, this volume, chaps. 2 and 9), studies of when and how specific features of grammar are employed can help teachers develop new insights into language learning and heighten their awareness of grammar features. Part III of the book presents two examples of grammar teaching based on practical findings and recommendations of research.

In the first chapter, "Relative Clause Reduction in Technical Research Articles," Peter Master investigates when and how reduced relative clauses are employed in advanced academic writing. He finds that although such clauses are optional, and sentences can be grammatical without the reduction, in advanced writing the frequency of the reduced clause use actually exceeds that of full clauses. Although many English as a second/foreign language grammar texts at the high-intermediate and advanced levels of student proficiency contain presentations of how to reduce relative clauses, few attempt to explain when relative clauses can and should be reduced. Master's chapter, based on research of a large corpus of academic articles in nine disciplines, such as biology, chemistry, humanities, psychology, and engineering, determines the syntactic and contextual environments in which reduced relative clauses occur and defines the parameters in which relative clause reduction is prevalent. He begins with a definition of reduced relative clauses and provides numerous examples, as they occur in real academic writing. Master specifies that, for instance, writing in computer science and engineering contains the lowest proportion of reduced relative clauses, whereas that in humanities contains the highest. This finding can allow teachers in academic English as a second/ foreign language programs to better prepare their students for future academic writing tasks and design curricula based on the actual demands of their academic work.

In another example, Eli Hinkel's chapter on "Why English Passive Is Difficult to Teach (and Learn)" investigates the effects of noun animacy and verb transitivity on the learners' ability to determine grammaticality of English active and passive constructions. She discusses the lexical features of English nouns and verbs that make the English passive constructions difficult to learn for speakers of such languages as Chinese, Japanese, Korean, and Spanish. Hinkel finds that the native and nonnative speakers' evaluations of noun animacy are often similar, but the amount of similarity declines in contexts as small as attributive adjectives and prepositional phrases. She further determines that verb transitivity, combined with noun animacy, may create obstacles in the learners' ability to evaluate the grammaticality of English passive and active constructions. According to her findings, even advanced learners may not be able to recognize the syntactic environments in which passive constructions are grammatical or ungrammatical in English and, hence, the uses of passive need to be explicitly taught. Because the concepts of animacy and transitivity are rarely discussed in second and foreign language grammar texts, teachers need to become aware of the role these features play when learners' work with passive voice meanings and uses. Hinkel's chapter includes suggestions for teaching active and passive voice. Activities are described to promote learner recognition of the diminished role of noun animacy in English compared to that in other languages.

11

Relative Clause Reduction in Technical Research Articles

Peter Master
San Jose State University, California

Technical prose is characteristically brief and concise (Davis, 1977). It makes liberal use of linguistic economizing devices such as noun compounds (e.g., Dubois, 1982; Horsella & Pérez, 1991), which compress a great deal of information into very few words (e.g., *aircraft gas turbine temperature control amplifiers*), and is usually devoid of verbiage not essential for the comprehension of the text. Such excess, usually referred to as wordiness, Brogan (1973, p. xi) calls "semantic noise." Semantic noise arises from a variety of sources, including redundant terms (e.g., *human utterances* vs. *utterances*), unnecessary phrases (e.g., *with the use/aid of a thermometer* vs. *with a thermometer*), circumlocutions (e.g., *is not the case* vs. *is false*), and what Brogan (1973, p. 152) calls "verb-muffling expressions" (e.g., *the conclusions that were drawn* vs. *the conclusions drawn*). The latter category includes relative clause reduction, the focus of this chapter.

Relative clause reduction is the deletion (and often concomitant syntactic alteration) of certain elements of a relative clause, the result of which does not change the meaning of the clause in any way.[1] There are two basic

---

[1]Relative clause reduction should not be confused with the reduction found in the simple registers described by Bruthiaux (1996), in which, he maintains, ". . . there is no a priori reason to suppose . . . that all simple language is underpinned by elaborated form from which simpler texts are derived through the deletion of redundant material" (p. 9). The deletion found in such registers, he says, ". . . contrasts with *contextual* (Gunter, 1963) or *contracted* (Mathews, 1981) deletion, in which a missing element can be recovered uniquely from a preceding clause or turn. This is a syntax-based strategy whose contribution to textual cohesion is unquestioned" (p. 190).

types of reduction operations: Those that simply delete an element of the relative clause and those that combine deletion with the syntactic alteration of an element. Deletion of an element either:

1. removes the relative pronoun alone, e.g., *the man **whom** I met* can be reduced to *the man I met*, or

2. removes *be* along with the relative pronoun, for example, (a) *the money **that was** stolen from the bank* can be reduced to *the money stolen from the bank*; (b) *the man **who is** sitting on the bench* can be reduced to *the man sitting on the bench*; (c) *the material **that is** in the tanker* can be reduced to *the material in the tanker*; (d) *the people **who were** present* can be reduced to *the people present*; and (e) *Saturn, **which is** a gas giant* can be reduced to *Saturn, a gas giant*.

Deletion plus syntactic alteration either:

1. replaces the relative pronoun plus *be* with the *-ing* form of the verb, e.g., *the planets **that orbit** the sun* can be reduced to *the planets **orbiting** the sun*, or

2. replaces the relative pronoun and the verb *have* with the preposition *with*, e.g., *the planet **that has** the highest surface temperature* can be reduced to *the planet **with** the highest surface temperature*.

There are also two basic syntactic categories of reduction based on the element of the subordinate clause that is relativized: predicate form (P-form)[2] and subject form (S-form). P-form reduction, the simplest type, deletes the relative pronoun, for example *the man **whom** I met* is reduced to *the man I met*.

S-form reduction has several forms. The simplest is the deletion of the relative pronoun plus *be*, for instance,

1. *the money **that was** stolen from the bank* can be reduced to *the money/stolen from the bank*,

2. *the man **who is** sleeping on the bench* can be reduced to *the man sleeping on the bench*,

3. *the flowers **that are** on the table* can be reduced to *the flowers on the table*,

4. *the people **who were** present* can be reduced to *the people present*, and

5. *Saturn, **which is** a gas giant* can be reduced to *Saturn, a gas giant*.

---

[2]Celce-Murcia and Larsen-Freeman (1983), and many others, distinguish between subject-form and object-form relative clauses. I follow Master (1996) in using P-form to describe object-form relative clauses because it is not only the direct object (which this distinction implies) but also the indirect object, the object of the preposition, and the predicate complement that can be relativized.

The more complicated types require deletion plus syntactic alteration, for example, (a) *the planets **that orbit** the sun* can be reduced to *the planets **orbiting** the sun,* or (b) *the planet **that has** the highest surface temperature* can be reduced to *the planet **with** the highest surface temperature.*

Although as a general principle wordiness is curtailed in formal technical prose, there are some instances when a writer chooses not to reduce a relative clause even when it is grammatically possible. The purpose of this chapter is to determine under what circumstances (if any) writers of technical journal articles are likely to reduce a relative clause and, conversely, under what circumstances they are likely not to do so. In this way, students learning to write technical research articles would have a more principled pedagogical explanation of when to choose between economy (reduction) and explicitness (nonreduction) in using relative clauses.

HOW REDUCTION CAME ABOUT

According to some sources, the reduced form of the relative clause preceded the fully syntacticized relative clause in English. Bickerton (1995) cites Bever and Langendoen (1971), who point out that there was a time "a few hundred years ago, when even English allowed such sentences without any kind of relative clause marker" (p. 36). Givon (1984) believes that relativization arose as a result of parataxis (i.e., placing elements next to each other), which later became syntacticized. He provides the following "possibility" as an example (p. 223):

Parataxis: *The man, I saw him yesterday, he came in again today.*

Syntactization: *The man I saw yesterday came in again today.* (Note the absence of the relative pronoun *whom* in the example.)

Since paratactic structures of this kind are not possible in Latin, the use of the reduced form was long disparaged in English. However, Hall (1964), noting that subordination by parataxis is optional with clauses that modify nouns with zero relative object (e.g., the role of *him* in Givon's example), disagreed with those "classicizing grammarians" who describe the reduced structure "as being 'elliptical' and somehow less acceptable than those with subordinators" (p. 219). He argues that "clauses without subordinators [i.e., reduced forms] are completely normal and acceptable on all levels of usage" and that in some languages, e.g., neo-Melanesian, the paratactic construction is not optional but required.

In explaining why the fully syntacticized (i.e., nonreduced) relative clause came about in English, Bickerton (1995) suggests,

People have a hard time with unmarked relative clauses; language does not. Indeed, it may even prefer them. . . . Overt relative-clause markers are just things that people generally tack on to their languages, sooner or later, and they become obligatory in certain contexts, precisely because they are useful for communication. Language tolerates them, but they are, if you like, purpose-built: natural enough, but certainly no more natural than their absence—perhaps even less so. Why languages should need tense markers but not relative-clause markers is something that is quite impossible to explain in terms of social, cultural, or communicative "benefits." (p. 37)

WHAT COUNTS AS A REDUCED ADJECTIVE CLAUSE

There is a question as to whether some of the types of reduction described above constitute an adjectival participial clause rather than relative clause reduction. Quirk, Greenbaum, Leech, and Svartvik (1972) categorize both VERB$_{ing}$ (e.g., *the man writing the obituary*) and VERB$_{en}$ (e.g., *an obituary written by my friend*) structures following a noun as postmodification by nonfinite clauses and describe merely the "correspondence between restrictive relative and nonfinite clauses" (p. 876). Celce-Murcia and Larsen-Freeman (1983) note that "[d]espite the structural differences, we do not want to deny a functional and semantic similarity between adjectival participial clauses and relative clauses" (p. 452).

McCawley (1988), on the other hand, includes both deletion and deletion + syntactic alteration processes as relative clause reduction, even when constituents have to change category (e.g., *who lives* → *living, which have* → *with*). His conception of category "does not preclude change of category in the course of a derivation, and treats transformationally inserted items on a par with other items in the application of category notions" (p. 196). He cites as an example the equivalence of relative pronoun + *have* and *with* in a postnominal modifier.

1. a man *who has* a scar on his face
2. a man *with* a scar on his face
3. a plan *which has* no prospects for success
4. a plan *with* no prospects for success

McCawley also notes that in the other deletion + syntactic alteration reduction, relative pronoun + *be* → VERB$_{ing}$ is not solely a deletion from a progressive form (e.g., *the man who is sitting on the bench* → *the man sitting on the bench),* because it also applies with a verb such as *own*, which cannot normally be progressive (e.g., **Many persons are owning land in this city)* but which is acceptable as a postmodified NP, for example, *many persons owning land in this city* (pp. 381–382).

A number of sources consider appositive clauses to be reduced nonrestrictive relative clauses (Mathews, 1981, p. 229, cited in Meyer, 1992, p. 54). However, Meyer points out that appositions systematically correspond to reduced relative clauses "only if a copular relation exists between the two units in the apposition" (p. 55) and provides the following example (p. 55):

1. There is also, in the larva, a tissue known as mucocartilage, **which is** an elastic material serving more as an antagonist to the muscles than for their attachment.

2. There is also, in the larva, a tissue known as mucocartliage, an elastic material serving more as an antagonist to the muscles than for their attachment.

Quirk, Greenbaum, Leech, and Svartvik (1985) also note that a defining appositive "may be seen as a reduced relative clause" (p. 1313).

WHEN REDUCTION MAY BE APPLIED

Relative clause reduction can only be applied when the meaning is not affected. Chafe (1970) describes both S-form and P-form reduction as a "postsemantic" process (p. 298) and thus considers reduction as an option, not a syntactic requirement.

Restrictive S-form relative clause reduction is allowed only when the relative clause contains a finite form of *be* followed by a present participle (VERB$_{ing}$), a past participle (VERB$_{en}$), a preposition, or a small group of predicate adjectives. It is normally blocked when the word following *be* is an attributive adjective or an NP (unless the clause constitutes an appositive clause). However, most nonrestrictive S-form relative clauses can be reduced only if a postmodifying phrase is also present (e.g., *the graph, *shown/shown on page 7;* Master, 1986).

The present participle (VERB$_{ing}$) in S-form reduction has no tense, so it generally indicates the all-time sense of the present tense as used in reporting facts, for example, *The rings surrounding Saturn contain small particles of ice.* For this reason, the reduction is not possible if the statement describes a single event with a punctual verb, for example, * *The scientist discovering DNA was Friedrich Meischer* (Master, 1986, pp. 54–55). Huckin and Olsen (1983) claimed that good writers "avoid applying the rule [of relative pronoun + *be* → VERB$_{ing}$] more often than not" (p. 400) and that its use "depends mainly on how much emphasis or focus the writer wants to give the relative clause: a full relative clause tends to command more attention than an *-ing* type of relative clause" (p. 400). However, Huckin, Curtin, and Graham (1986) modified this view to state that S-form VERB$_{ing}$ reduction (also known as "whiz-deletion," i.e., relative pronoun *[who/which]* + *is* deletion) is "the standard choice of good writers in most circumstances" (p. 185). Exceptions occur only when "(1) the word that follows the whiz needs emphasis, or (2) the whiz-words help create better sentence rhythm, or (3) the whiz-words are needed to avoid ambiguity, particularly following desiderative verbs [such as *want*]" (p. 185). They are careful to note that "contextual factors (textual, rhetorical, other) play a major role in deciding what constitutes emphasis and what constitutes ambiguity" (p. 185).

Restrictive S-form relative clauses containing predicate adjectives are often reduced if the adjective ends with *-ble* (e.g., *capable, possible, responsible, visible*), that is, *the person who is responsible → the person responsible* (Master, 1986, pp. 53–55). Several other adjectives also allow reduction, many ending with *-ant/-ent* (e.g., *appropriate, inherent, present, relevant, reminiscent*). S-form reduction can also occur with many adjectives + allied prepositions, e.g., *a lawyer who is eager to make money → a lawyer eager to make money* (McCawley, 1988, p. 379). Moreover, Swales (1981), in contrasting words that can occur as either premodifiers or postmodifiers, such as, *the underlined words* versus *the words underlined,* supports Bolinger's (1967) claim that postmodifiers are temporary or ephemeral compared to the more permanent premodifiers. Postmodifiers would include reduced restrictive S-form relative clauses since *the words underlined* is a reduced form of *the words which are/were underlined.* The function of such postmodifiers, Swales notes, is primarily to provide textual linkage and cohesion.

P-form relative clause reduction (e.g., *the person I met*) indicates an NP that is familiar, whereas nonreduction (e.g., *the person whom I met*) suggests one that is more distant (Bolinger, 1980). However, P-form reduction may be applied only to restrictive relative clauses and is blocked from applying to nonrestrictive ones (e.g., **the person, I met*).

Celce-Murcia and Larsen-Freeman (1983) also speculate as to when reduction can be applied. "While definite rules for when a relative clause may be reduced remain to be worked out, one can imagine that reduction might be favored in contexts where a number of relative clauses appear in sequence. . . . On the other hand, the reduction of a relative clause might be favored in those cases where an ambiguous surface structure would result (e.g., Carla painted the picture in the den)" (p. 381). They thus suggest, like Huckin et al. (1986), that reduction is a means of clarifying ambiguous or confusing sentences.

Vande Kopple (1998), citing Lehmann (1988, p. 193), suggests that when a relative clause is reduced "the components of a clause that allow reference to a specific state of affairs are lost and the state of affairs is 'typified' " (p. 181). Expanding on this definition, he states that "as a modifying phrase is reduced to a phrase, it becomes more and more thinglike and less processlike, the information it carries comes to be treated more as information to be assumed than as information to be asserted, and its information more and more resembles information that can fit into a slot in a taxonomy for later referral" (p. 181). In sum, the information in a reduced relative clause should be regarded as "firmly established, highly typical, and widely generalizable" (p. 191).

The circumstances under which reduction may be applied described above are all potential material for presentation and practice in the classroom, expecially if students have envinced problems with relative clause reduction, either in generating such sentences or in decoding them in written text. The most common "error" that students make is not to reduce relative clauses at all; indeed, it is quite possible that their instructors have warned them that reduction is too informal a process for formal academic writing.

OBJECTIVE OF THE PRESENT STUDY

The objective of the present study is to determine the number and nature of relative clause reductions in 18 technical research articles (written in English) and to consult experts for their opinions on those cases in which the option to reduce was not taken. This objective is framed in terms of the following research questions:

1. Does syntactic environment affect the decision to reduce relative clauses?
2. Does field of study affect the decision to reduce relative clauses?
3. How do expert technical writers account for the decision not to reduce a relative clause that could have been reduced?

For the purposes of this study, every type of relative clause was included. Although the ultimate objective is to help learners acquire the syntactic conventions of the genre of research reports, it is hoped that the results will help technical writers, particularly nonnative speakers of English, to understand the general pragmatics of when they should reduce relative clauses and when not.

METHOD

Faculty in nine university science and engineering departments (biology, chemistry, clinical psychology, computer science, engineering geology, mechanical engineering, mathematics, medicine, and physics) at a large university in the western United States were asked to identify a current respected journal in their fields. From these, the first two research articles (in most cases) that appeared in the journal were selected per field, resulting in a corpus of 18 research articles for analysis, comprising a total of 51,824 words. The authors, dates, and titles of these articles are as follows (full citations appear at the end of this chapter under Research Reports Analyzed):

Biology

Bio 1: Gahukar, R. T. (1990). Sampling techniques, spatial distribution and cultural control of millet spike worm, *Raghuva albipunctella* (Noctuidae: Lepidoptera). [1,791 words]

Bio 2: Howard, M. T., & Dixon, A. F. G. (1990). Forecasting of peak population density of the rose grain aphid *Metopolophium dirhodum* on wheat. [3,288 words]

Chemistry

Chem 1: Hall, H. K., Jr., & Padias, A. B. (1990). Zwitterion and diradical tetramethylenes as initiators of "charge-transfer" polymerizations. [3,589 words]

Chem 2: Miller, R. E. (1990). Vibrationally induced dynamics in hydrogen-bonded complexes. [4,251 words]

Clinical Psychology

Clin Psych 1: Bennett, P., & Carroll, D. (1990). Stress management approaches to the prevention of coronary heart disease. [4,296 words]

Clin Psych 2: Jack, R. L., & Williams, J. M. (1991). The role of attributions in self-poisoning. [4,323 words]

Computer Science

Comp Sci 1: Pease, D., Ghafoor, A., Ahmad, I., Andrews, D. L., Foudil-Bey, K., Karpinski, T. E., Mikki, M. A., & Zerrouki, M. (1991). PAWS: A performance evaluation tool for parallel computing systems. [3,217 words]

Comp Sci 2: Stunkel, C. B., Janssens, B., & Fuchs, W. K. (1991). Address tracing for parallel machines. [4,088 words]

Mechanical Engineering

Mech Eng 1: Angeles, J., & Ma, O. (1991). Performance evaluation of four-bar linkages

Mech Eng 2: Olsen, D. G., Erdman, A. G., and Riley, D. R. (1991). Topical analysis of single-degree-of-freedom planetary gear trains. [3,677 words]

Engineering Geology

Eng Geo 1: Collins, T. K. (1990). New faulting and the attenuation of fault displacement. [6,923 words]

Eng Geo 2: El-Hussain, I. W., & Carpenter, P. J. (1990). Reservoir induced seismicity near Heron and El Vado Reservoirs, Northern New Mexico. [3,143 words]

Mathematics

Math 1: Colombeau, J. F. (1990). Multiplication of distributions. [3,127 words]

Math 2: Ashbaugh, M. S., & Benguria, R. D. (1991). Proof of the Payne-Polya-Weinberger conjecture. [2,264 words]

Medicine

Med 1: Hansotia, P., & Broste, S. K. (1991). The effect of epilepsy or diabetes mellitus on the risk of automobile accidents. [3,004 words]

Med 2: Polten, A., Fluharty, A. L., Fluharty, C. B., Kappler, J., von Figura, K., & Gieselmann, V. (1991). Molecular basis of different forms of metachromatic leukodystrophy. [2,598 words]

Physics

Phys 1: Ponce de Leon, J. (1990). Model-independent description of intermediate-range forces in static spherical bodies. [2,787 words]

Phys 2: Dickson, R. S., & Weil, J. A. (1990). The magnetic properties of the oxygen-hole aluminum centres in crystalline SiO_2.IV. $[AlO_4/Na]^+$. [8,212 words]

Two articles from a discipline in the humanities (TESOL), comprising 12,464 words, were also analyzed for comparison:

TQ 1: Chapelle, C. (1990). The discourse of computer-assisted language learning: Toward a context for descriptive research. [6,714 words]

TQ 2: Carson, J. E., Carrell, P. L., Silberstein, S., Kroll, B., & Kuehn, P. (1990). The relationship between overall reading comprehension and comprehension of coreferential ties for second language readers of English. [5,750 words]

The research articles (RAs) were all selected from the same time period (1990–1991) to avoid the diachronic shifts discussed in Vande Kopple (1998). A total of 914 relative clauses[3] were identified in the technical RAs, 246 in the TESOL RAs.

For the analysis, each relative clause occurring in the data was coded for the following information: status (full/reduced), type (S-form/ P-form, restrictive/nonrestrictive), head noun (including syntactic role, level of subordination, and determiner preceding), and the number and type of syntactic structures separating the head noun and the relative clause.

All the relative clauses that could have been reduced but were not were analyzed by a technical writing expert and a mechanical engineer, both published authors who do a good deal of technical writing. These expert opinions were used to probe the limits of relative clause reduction.

RESULTS

The results of the study were derived from three separate analyses. The first two analyzed relative clause reduction in terms of (1) syntactic environment and (2) field of study and were directly dependent on the database. The last analysis considered all the relative clauses that could have been reduced but were not and was based on feedback from expert technical writers. An analysis of postmodifying clauses in the 130,000-word Nijmegen corpus (de Haan, 1989), which included both spoken and written text and may thus be considered a more general representation of reduced relative clause usage in English, was used for comparison where appropriate.

Relative Clause Reduction and Syntactic Environment

To determine if any particular syntactic element has an effect on the use of full or reduced forms of relative clauses in the corpus, the data were analyzed in terms of status (full/reduced), type (S-form/P-form, restrictive/ nonrestrictive), head noun (including syntactic role, level of subordination, and determiner preceding), and the number and type of syntactic structures separating the head noun from its relative clause. Any full relative clauses in each category that could have been reduced (i.e., were not

---

[3]Fox and Thompson (1990) analyzed 414 relative clauses in their study of the use of relative clauses in conversational English. Thus, the 914 clauses analyzed in this study should be sufficient to draw basic conclusions.

restricted from doing so by syntactic constraints but were not reduced for various reasons) are indicated in the "nonreduced" (sometimes shortened to "nonred") column in each table as a percentage of the full relative clauses. These are further discussed under Feedback From Expert Writers.

Status

The full/reduced status of the relative clauses is shown in Table 11.1 (parentheses show that the number or category is a subset of another category). Table 11.1 shows that 55% of the 914 relative clauses in the corpus were reduced. Ninety-one percent of the relative clauses were S-form, of which almost two thirds were reduced. Reduction is clearly the preferred status in the S-form category. Nine percent of the relative clauses were P-form, of which only 2% were reduced. As for nonreduction, just over 13% of the full relative clauses were not reduced when they could have been. S-form clauses, for which many more forms of reduction are possible, showed a slightly higher percentage of nonreduction than P-form clauses.

Table 11.1 also shows that 78% of the relative clauses were restrictive, of which almost 60% were reduced, whereas 22% were nonrestrictive, of which 39% were reduced (these percentages are not so different from those in the Nijmegen corpus, where the ratio was 69% restrictive, 31% nonrestrictive). Restrictive relative clauses were much more prevalent, as was also found in the Nijmegen corpus, and more likely to be reduced than nonrestrictive relative clauses. Despite the predominance of restrictive relative clauses, the rate of nonreduction was similar for all types.

TABLE 11.1
Status of the Relative Clauses

Relative Clause	Total	Reduced	Full	(Nonred)
Number	914	502	412	(55)
%	100.0	54.92	45.08	13.35
Type				
S-form	832	500	332	(47)
%	91.03	60.10	39.90	14.16
P-form	82	2	80	(8)
%	8.97	2.44	97.56	10.00
Restrictive	713	424	289	(38)
%	78.01	59.47	40.53	13.15
Nonrestrictive	201	78	123	(17)
%	21.99	38.81	61.19	13.82

Note. $n = 914$.

Syntactic Role of Head Noun

The syntactic role of the head noun of the relative clause is shown in Table 11.2, which shows that relative clauses modifying the subject of the main clause were more than twice as likely to be reduced than full. Relative clauses within object or predicate NPs were more likely to be full, whereas relative clauses within adverbial NPs were more likely to be reduced. The rate of nonreduction was similar for each role except VP Modifier (also known as "sentence relatives"). Relative clauses modifying VPs rather than NPs (e.g., *In this case, a single-carbon-carbon bond is broken to form a diradical,* **which** *can initiate the polymerization* [Chem 1]) are usually S-form clauses with no form of *be* present (the one exception shown in the table is an anomalous appositive) and therefore must be full.

The syntactic role of the head NP within its main or subordinate clause is shown in Table 11.3 (n = 902 because 12 relative clauses modified VPs rather than NPs). Table 11.3 shows that reduction was preferred except when the head noun was the main object or the main or clause predicate nominative. Nonreduction was generally higher for the subordinate clause NPs (i.e., clause subject, clause object, clause predicate NP), which tend to appear later in the sentence, than for the main clause NPs.

Level of Subordination of Head Noun

The level of subordination of the head noun indicates the degree to which the head noun of the relative clause was subordinated, as shown in the following examples. Level 1 indicates relativization of a main clause NP. Level 2 indicates relativization of an NP within a subordinated clause, Level 3 indicates relativization of an NP within a subordinated clause that occurs

TABLE 11.2
Syntactic Position of the Head NP in the Main Clause

Role	Total	Reduced	Full	(Nonreduced)
Subject	213	150	63	(10)
%	23.30	70.42	29.58	15.87
Object	201	92	109	(12)
%	22.00	45.77	54.23	11.01
Adverbial	353	198	155	(22)
%	38.62	56.09	43.91	14.19
Pred. NP	136	61	75	(11)
%	14.88	44.85	55.15	14.67
VP Modifier	11	1	10	(0)
%	1.20	9.09	90.9	0

Note. n = 914.

TABLE 11.3
Head NP Role within Main or Subordinate Clause

Role	Total	Reduced	Full	(Nonreduced)
Main subject	172	116	56	7
%	19.07	67.44	32.56	12.50
Clause subject	63	43	20	5
%	6.98	68.25	31.75	25.00
Main object	102	39	63	3
%	11.31	38.24	61.76	4.77
Clause object	88	47	41	7
%	9.76	53.41	46.59	17.07
Main pred. NP	54	16	38	7
%	5.99	29.63	70.37	18.42
Clause pred. NP	27	12	15	4
%	2.99	44.44	55.56	26.67
Object of prep.	396	228	168	22
%	43.90	57.58	42.42	13.10

Note. $n = 902$.

within a subordinated clause, and so on. Examples from the corpus of subordination Levels 1–4 follow. The relative clause and its head noun are shown in italic; the subordinator (clause marker, including nonfinite *to* and *-ing*) is shown in boldface.

Level 1

The developmental stage at which wheat is attacked appears to affect the amount of damage caused. [Bio 2]

Those interventions, and indeed *those previously discussed*, need to be evaluated in terms of both absolute outcome and cost-effectiveness. [Clin Psych 1]

Level 2

Therefore, only programs **that** use *the SPMD (single program, multiple data) programming model, which only uses static scheduling*, can be traced. [Comp Sci 2]

If there is existing published data from the Nevada Test Site *which could be used to analyse the phenomena of attenuation*, it would be helpful. [Eng Geo 1]

Level 3

Thus the authors conclude **that** such attributions lead to performance deficits **because** they draw subjects' attention away from task performance and from situational *cues which indicate that the new, possibly solvable problem is different from the original unsolvable one.* [Clin Psych 2]

It is possible **to** simplify the determination of displacement isomorphism, and also facilitate a straightforward topological analysis approach by defin**ing** *a new graph representation called the coincident joint graph.* [Mech Eng 2]

Level 4

In addition the choice of [20] is interesting **because** it allows us **to** compare the behavior of solutions (with different N), in two extreme cases, namely, [**appositive**] the case of *a solid constant-density sphere obtained for* $x = 0$ with the case of a gaseous sphere obtained for r = 1. [Phys 1]

An upper limit of ca. 4.6 A may be set for the distance between the sodium and the hole-bearing oxygen, **since** this would give hyperfine (T^1) principal values of about 0.015 45 and -0.007 72 mT, **which** are plainly inadequate **to** yield *the size of sodium hyperfine principal values observed.* [Phys 2]

Subordination levels for the relative clauses in the corpus are shown in Table 11.4.

Although the numbers are fairly small at the deeper levels, Table 11.4 suggests that reduction generally increased with increasing subordination level. Nonreduction at Levels 1 and 2 was commensurate with the nonreduction figures in other tables (i.e., 10–20%). Subordination at Levels 3 and 4 had only one instance of nonreduction each, which may account for the low percentage for Level 3 and the high percentage for Level 4.

Determiner Attached to Head Noun

Ninety-five percent (869) of the head nouns had determiners attached to them (i.e., were not clauses or pronouns), of which 96% were articles. The articles are divided according to the binary classification/identification schema described in Master (1990), with the additional division between

TABLE 11.4
Level of Subordination of Head Noun

Sub. Lev.	Total	Reduced	Full	Nonreduced
1	573	304	269	32
%	62.69	53.05	46.95	11.90
2	356	214	142	21
%	30.85	58.16	41.84	14.79
3	61	36	25	1
%	5.47	56.00	44.00	4.00
4	12	7	5	1
%	0.98	66.67	33.33	20.00

zero ($Ø1$) and null ($Ø2$) described in Master (1997). Classified head nouns thus include those preceded by $Ø1$ and *a(n)*, whereas identified head nouns include those preceded by $Ø2$ and *the*, as shown in Table 11.5. Table 11.5 shows that the identified head nouns were more likely to occur with reduced relative clauses, though the percentage of nonreduced relative clauses is again commensurate with the figures in other tables. In general, identified head nouns appeared more often with reduced relative clauses than did classified head nouns. The apparently anomalous $Ø2$ figure can be explained by the fact that $Ø2$ occurs for the most part with proper nouns, which always require nonrestrictive relative clauses. The rules for the reduction of nonrestrictive relative clauses are more stringent than those for restrictive relative clauses, so it is not surprising that the latter would occur more frequently with full relative clauses.

Syntactic Structures Separating Head Noun and Relative Clause

The number and types of structures separating the head noun and its relative clause are shown in Table 11.6. The table shows that phrase structures separating the head noun from the relative clause did not appear to inhibit reduction when it was possible. Indeed, according to the Nonreduced column, the opposite seems to be the case: The more structures that intervened, the more likely reduction was to take place.

TABLE 11.5
Determiners Associated with the Head Noun of the Relative Clauses

Division	Total	Reduced	Full	Nonreduced
Classified	473	225	248	(34)
%	54.43	47.57	52.43	13.71
$Ø1$	(288)	140	148	(22)
%	60.88	48.61	51.39	14.86
a	(167)	78	89	(10)
%	35.31	46.71	53.29	11.26
Other	(18)	7	11	(2)
%	3.81	38.89	61.11	18.18
Identified	396	258	138	(20)
%	45.57	65.15	34.85	14.49
the	(350)	239	111	(16)
%	88.38	68.29	31.71	14.41
$Ø2$	(25)	7	18	(2)
%	6.31	28.00	72.00	11.11
Other	(21)	12	9	(2)
%	5.30	57.14	48.86	22.22

TABLE 11.6
Phrase Structures (PS) Separating the Relative Clause From its Head Noun

Number/Type	Total	Reduced	Full	Nonreduced
None	751	423	328	(42)
%	82.17	56.32	43.68	12.80
One PS	(148)	75	73	(12)
%	90.80	50.68	49.32	16.44
PP	(97)	44	53	10
%	65.54	45.36	54.64	18.87
(of PP)	(60)	31	29	(1)
%	40.54	51.67	48.33	3.45
S-RC	(19)	11	8	1
%	12.84	57.89	42.11	12.50
VP	(7)	2	5	1
%	4.73	28.57	71.43	20.00
Other	(25)	18	7	0
%	16.89	72.00	28.00	0.00
Two PSs	(14)	2	12	(1)
%	8.59	14.29	85.71	8.33
Three PSs	(1)	1	0	(0)
%	0.61	100	0	0.00
All (1–3)	163	78	85	(13)
%	17.83	47.85	52.15	15.29

In relative clauses constructed with one intervening phrase structure between the head noun and the relative clause, the intervening PS is most likely to be a prepositional phrase (PP), and of these the largest number (41%) were *of*-phrases. Relative clauses with intervening *of*-phrases were almost always reduced if reduction was possible. Relative clauses constructed with two intervening phrase structures between the head noun and the relative clause were much more likely to be full than reduced; however, the type of relative clause utilized under such conditions was usually one that could not be reduced (e.g., S-form with no form of *be* before the verb). In the one case of three intervening phrase structures (a chain of three prepositional phrases), the relative clause was reduced.

Relative Clause Reduction and Field of Study

The relative clauses in the corpus were also analyzed according to field of study. Two research articles from the humanities *(TESOL Quarterly,* or TQ) are included for comparison, though they are not included in the Total column. Table 11.7 shows that the two fields with the lowest proportion of relative clauses per hundred words were computer science and engineering geology. These two fields (i.e., the four articles from two respected journals in these fields) never used either appositive or reduced relative clauses

TABLE 11.7

Types of Relative Clauses by Field

Field	Total	Bio.	Chem.	Cl. Psy.	C. Sci.	Eng.	G. Math	M. Eng.	Med.	Phys.	TQ
No. of words	68,693	5,079	7,840	8,619	7,307	10,066	5,391	7,786	5,606	10,999	12,464
RCs	914	63	120	117	47	52	78	133	109	195	(246)
RCs/100 words	1.33	1.24	1.53	1.36	0.64	0.52	1.45	1.71	1.94	1.77	1.97
Type											
S-form	832	49	104	109	40	47	66	125	104	188	216
%	91.03	77.78	86.67	93.16	85.11	90.38	84.62	93.98	95.41	96.41	87.80
P-form	82	14	16	8	7	5	12	8	5	7	30
%	8.97	22.22	13.33	6.84	14.89	9.62	15.38	6.02	4.59	3.59	12.20
R	713	55	90	95	35	44	54	100	91	149	209
%	78.01	87.30	75.00	81.20	76.60	82.69	69.23	75.19	83.49	76.41	84.96
NR	201	8	30	22	12	8	24	33	18	46	37
%	21.99	12.70	25.00	18.80	23.40	17.31	30.77	24.81	16.51	23.59	15.04
Appositive	(29)	0	2	5	0	0	2	3	9	8	6
%	14.42	0	6.67	22.73	0	0	8.33	9.09	50.00	17.39	16.23
Full	412	29	46	50	47	52	43	52	45	48	85
%Total	45.08	46.03	38.33	42.74	100	100	55.13	39.10	41.28	24.62	34.55
Nonred	(55)	3	5	6	6	3	9	7	14	2	15
%Full	13.35	10.34	10.87	12.00	12.77	5.77	20.93	13.46	31.11	4.17	17.86
Red	502	34	74	67	0	0	35	81	64	147	161
%Total	54.92	53.97	61.67	57.26	0	0	44.87	60.90	58.72	75.38	65.45
Red/100 words	0.73	0.67	0.94	0.78	0	0	0.65	1.04	1.14	1.34	1.29
Reduction Type											
S-form	500	34	74	67	0	0	34	81	63	147	153
%	99.60	100	100	100	0	0	97.14	100	98.44	100	95.03
-ed	(306)	27	47	31	0	0	19	52	32	99	101
%	61.20	79.41	63.51	46.27	0	0	55.88	64.20	50.79	67.35	66.01
-ing	(125)	2	18	24	0	0	12	24	19	26	34
%	25.00	5.88	24.32	35.82	0	0	35.29	29.63	30.16	17.69	22.22
Adj.	(37)	4	7	8	0	0	1	1	3	13	10
%	7.40	11.77	9.46	11.94	0	0	2.94	1.23	4.76	8.84	6.54
Appositive	(29)	0	2	5	0	0	2	3	9	8	6
%	5.80	0	2.70	7.46	0	0	5.88	3.70	14.29	5.44	3.92
P-form	2	0	0	0	0	0	1	0	1	0	8
%	0.40	0	0	0	0	0	2.86	0	1.56	0	4.97

of any kind. However, the nonreduction figure was close to the average (14.08) in the computer science RAs (12.77), whereas it was very low in the engineering geology RAs (5.77), suggesting that the authors of the latter articles primarily used relative clauses that could not be reduced.

The TQ articles contained the highest proportion of relative clauses per hundred words (1.97), the highest proportion of reduced relative clauses per hundred words (1.29), and the greatest amount of P-form reduction (4.97). Thus, there appears to be a slight increase in relative clause reduction in the humanities RAs.

The most common kind of S-form reduction was *-ed* clauses, followed by *-ing* clauses, whereas adjectives and appositives accounted for a relatively small percentage. A comparison of reduced restrictive relative clauses alone showed 71.6% *-ed* versus 28.4% *-ing* in the technical RAs, 71.9% *-ed* versus 28.1% *-ing* in the humanities RAs, and 68.3% *-ed* versus 31.7% *-ing* in the Nijmegen corpus. Thus, there appears to be relatively little difference between general English, technical RAs, and humanities RAs regarding the use of these particular types of S-form of reduction.

The pedagogical application of these findings is considered in the Discussion section.

FEEDBACK FROM EXPERT WRITERS

Two expert technical writers were asked to comment on the 55 full relative clauses in the corpus that could have been syntactically reduced. As a result of their input, several conditions were identified under which reduction was usually blocked: all versus some, parallelism, unwieldy sentences, and potentially altered meaning.

All versus Some

A common instance in which relative clauses were not reduced when they could have been occurred when the head noun being modified did not represent all possible cases *(cf. The rings surrounding Saturn contain small particles of ice* vs. **The scientist discovering DNA was Friedrich Meischer).* The *all/some* distinction is usually the domain of nonrestrictive versus restrictive relative clauses; for example, *the books, which I ordered* (nonrestrictive) refers to all the books whereas *the books that I ordered* (restrictive) refers to a subset of books, the others having some other characteristic (e.g., *the books that were given to me).* However, in 17 of the 55 nonreduced relative clauses (30.91%), the uniqueness/particularity of the head noun was emphasized by the nonreduction of the relative clause:

- However, at least in *those **who are** homozygous for the arylsulfatase A pseudodeficiency allele*, enough arylsulfatase A is synthesized to prevent clinically apparent disease. [Med 2]
- A good example of detailed field measurement of *fault displacements **which are** needed to analyse attenuation* is found in the article by Muruoka and Kamata (1983). [Eng Geo 1]

Huckin et al. (1986) also found whiz-deletion to be blocked when emphasis was required, as noted earlier. Many of the examples also happened to be the last NP in the sentence.

Parallelism

A smaller category of nonreduced relative clauses included those in which the nonreduction fostered a clearer reading of a series of parallel structures:

- These captured references are typically *physical memory addresses,* **which are** *often desirable for cache simulation studies,* but *which are not as useful as* virtual *addresses for evaluating processor performance issues.* [Comp Sci 2]
- For an integrable real-valued function f defined on a bounded domain $\Omega \subset Rn$ the spherical decreasing rearrangement of f (also known as symmetric decreasing rearrangement [BLL, Ll, L2, HLP, pp. 276–278] or Schwarz symmetrization [Ba, p. 47, Ka, pp. 1516]; for more details, see [Ba, HLP, Ka]) is *a function, denoted f** **which is** *defined on the ball* $\Omega^* \subset Rn$ of volume $I\Omega I$ and with center at the origin, **which is** *invariant under rotations and nonincreasing with respect to distance from the origin,* and **which is** *equimeasurable with f,* i.e., the sets $\{xE\Omega lf(x) \geq t\}$ and $\{xE\Omega^* lf^*(x) \geq t\}$ have equal measures for all real t. [Math 2]
- These decisions have been based on *studies* **that were** *sometimes poorly controlled* and *that often gave conflicting results.* [Med 1]

Huckin et al. (1986) noted parallelism as a reason for reduction (i.e., applying whiz-deletion). These examples show that nonreduction can be used for the same purpose.

Unwieldy Sentences

In a few cases, reduction was blocked because of an unwieldy sentence (one of the experts described these examples as the authors trying to maintain control of a poorly initiated sentence). In these cases, reduction would have made the sentence even less intelligible.

- Moreover, *a unified method of performance evaluation for rigid-body guidance* is presented, **that is** *applicable to four-bar linkages of any type,* as long as the linkages have quadratic input-output or input-coupler functions. [Mech Eng 1]
- The displacement graph was defined to be the same as the rotation graph, but with each vertex also labeled with *the level of the revolute edge* **that is** *incident at it in the original graph.* [Mech Eng 2]

Nonreduction sometimes occurred with multiple embedding to keep the meaning clear:

- This result, taken together with *the weak transition seen on the high-frequency side of R7, **which is** also due to coupling to other optically inactive vibrational states,* suggests that the homogeneous line width associated with the dark state is much smaller than that of the H-F band responsible for the transition intensity. [Chem 2]

- The last reported finding that *repeaters—**who are** known to be at greater risk of further repetition—* showed less mood repair at Time 2 than did first-timers, whilst the attributional style of both groups remained stable and equally dysfunctional over time, suggests that the combination of high levels of mood disturbance and dysfunctional attributions may promote further self-poisoning. [Clin Psych 2]

In general, however, nonreduction was rarely motivated by unwieldiness. Huckin et al. (1986) did not mention unwieldiness, but they did find that whiz-deletion was sometimes used to improve sentence rhythm, as noted earlier.

Altered Meaning

There were a few cases in which reduction could have altered the meaning of the sentence:

- A good example of detailed field measurement of *fault displacements **which are** needed to analyse attenuation* is found in the article by Muraoka and Kamata (1983). [Eng Geo 1]

In this case, the "good example" is *measurement of fault displacements*, not *measurement of fault displacements needed to analyse attenuation*, which would have been implied by the reduction.In fact, this sentence should have been expressed as a nonrestrictive relative clause, in which case the reduction would not have been allowed.

- *All persons from the area **who were** not included in the epilepsy cohort* served as the comparison group for that cohort. [Med 1]

In this case, the reduction would have suggested "the area not included" rather than "the persons not included," though the pragmatics of the sentence, particularly the word *cohort*, would have allowed the correct linkage of the relative clause to the head noun *persons* rather than *area*.

- This is contrary to what one would expect of *students **who were** using the exercise as an exploratory activity.* [TQ 2]

In this case, what is "contrary to what one would expect" is *students*, not *using the exercise*, which would have been implied by the reduction. In general, nonreduction was seldom motivated by a potentially altered meaning. Huckin et al. (1986) also noted that whiz-deletion was blocked to avoid ambiguity, as mentioned earlier, and also found it to be relatively rare.

NEW INFORMATION

Feedback from the expert technical writers showed that NPs postmodified with a relative clause that came toward the end of the sentence were often not reduced. Material occurring at the end of a sentence generally constitutes new information, which suggests that new information is generally not reduced. In 34 of the 55 nonreduced relative clauses (61.80%), the nonreduced postmodified NP was the last NP in the sentence. This is most readily apparent in short extraposed sentences, in which P-form reduction was dispreferred.

- It is *this conjecture **which** we establish below.* [Math 2]
- This is *a key estimate **which** we call the basic gap inequality.* [Math 2]

Nonreduction of relative clauses modifying final NPs occurs in other P-form relative clauses:

- Figure 1 shows *a schematic diagram of the molecular beam apparatus **which** we have used for both types of experiments.* [Chem 2]
- Of the 60 overdose patients, 32 returned *the ASQ and mood scales **which** they had completed after a seven-day interval.* [Clin Psych 2]

It also occurs in S-form relative clauses:

- The temperature of 1°C was selected because it is *the temperature threshold **that is** used for predicting the development of winter wheat.* [Bio 2]
- The genuine difficulty is shifted to the final task of ascertaining whether the solutions thus obtained are indeed *"classical objects" **which are** capable of representing physical quantities.* [Math 1]
- The combination of wavefunction mixing and vibrational mode dependent line broadening can result in *a homogeneous line width **that is** dependent upon the rotational state.* [Chem 2]
- ARYLSULFATASE A is a lysosomal enzyme involved in the degradation of cerebroside sulfate, *a polar glycolipid **that is** found mainly as a component of the myelin sheaths of the nervous system.* [Med 2]

- In this approach, the program is split into units called *basic blocks,* **which are** *sets of machine-level instructions that always execute in sequence (in the absence of any interrupts).* [Comp Sci 2]

In one case, which one of the experts described as a "reversed sentence," new information came uncharacteristically at the beginning of the sentence, yet it was still nonreduced:

- *The results* **which** *we shall need for the arguments to follow* are the inequality (12) [equation] and the equivalent inequality (13) [equation]. [Math 2]

The nonreduction of relative clauses containing new information even when it comes earlier in the sentence also suggests that new information seems to mitigate against reduction.

In another case, new information that should have paralleled an earlier reduction remained nonreduced, again suggesting that new information is not usually reduced:

- This is based on the observation that the aphid burden built up and was high by D.S. 69 in *Watt and Wratten's experiments starting at D.S. 40,* but had not reached a significant size by D.S. 69 in their own and *Watt and Wratten's experiments* **that were** *started at D.S. 65.* [Bio 2]

Nonreduction also occurred with some fully parenthetical relative clauses, perhaps because new (but tangential) information is often provided in such clauses:

- In view of the fact that the HF is directly involved in the hydrogen bond, it is not surprising that the C-stretch (**which is** *remote from the hydrogen bond coordinate*) gives the longer VP lifetime. [Chem 2]

In most instances, nonreduced relative clauses appearing at the end of a sentence simply "sounded better" to the experts, though they could not articulate why this was the case.

DISCUSSION

The analysis shows that the reduction of relative clauses is common in technical RAs. Indeed, more than half (55%) of all the relative clauses in the corpus were reduced. It would thus be a pedagogical error to tell students that reduction is not appropriate in formal technical writing.

In terms of form and semantic category (as shown in Table 11.1), reduction occurred most frequently with S-form restrictive clauses by a substantial margin (the corpus showed a slightly higher use of restrictive relative clauses than the Nijmegen corpus, though restrictive relative clauses clearly predominate in both cases). This is not surprising given that there are seven types of S-form reduction and only one type of P-form reduction. However, because the percentage of nonreduced clauses (i.e., those in which the option to reduce was not taken) was fairly similar in S-form, P-form, restrictive, and nonrestrictive clauses, it would appear that reduction is generally not a consequence of the type of relative clause.

In terms of where in the main clause the head noun of the relative clause occurred (as shown in Table 11.2), NPs in the subject position tended to be reduced more often than NPs in any other position. Given information tends to come at the beginning of a sentence, new information at the end. In light of the finding that NPs representing new information tended to be nonreduced, the fact that subject NPs generally come at the beginning of a sentence and therefore usually represent given information would make them more likely to be reduced. Thus, syntactic position within the main clause does appear to affect whether a relative clause is reduced. From the pedagogical perspective, a qualified generalization could be made for students, or possibly be a subject for investigation in their own analyses of technical discourse: Relative clauses attached to subject NPs are often reduced, whereas those attached to other (later) NPs are less likely to be so.

In terms of the head noun role within the clause, either main or subordinate (as shown in Table 11.3), relative clauses modifying NPs that came earlier in the clause (i.e., main subject and clause subject) were the most likely to be reduced. PPs can modify any NP, so the Object of Prep. figure in Table 11.3 does not discriminate early- from late-occurring PPs. Further analysis showed that prepositional object NPs that occurred early in the sentence were also more likely to be reduced (main subject slot = 83% reduced) than those occurring later in the sentence (main object slot = 64% reduced, main adverbial slot = 56% reduced, main predicate NP slot = 54% reduced), which again supports the notion that new information is less likely to be reduced.

In terms of the level of subordination of the head noun (as shown in Table 11.4), reduction predominated at all three levels of subordination at about the same rate. Contrary to the expected finding that the deeper the level of subordination, the greater the likelihood of nonreduction (based on the assumption that the greater clarity and explicitness of nonreduction would be required as the sentence became more complex, and on Aarts and Schils 1995, finding that it was more difficult for nonnative speakers to relativize constituents in subordinate clauses than in main clauses, as predicted by Comrie, 1989, reduction was higher for the subordinated NPs than for the nonsubordinated NPs. This suggests that reduction may actually make a sentence easier to understand when relative clauses are multiply embedded, rather than making it less explicit, as it helps to align the focus. This is shown in the following example (the nonreduced elements, which were not present in the original, are included in curly brackets to show their effect):

> EPR spectra of $[A_{104}/Na]^+$ were taken at various temperatures between 35 and 163K to explore whether significant line width changes or site averaging {which are} *attributable to a motion of the Na^+ ion*, similar to that {which is} *observed for the iron centre [FeO$_4$/Na]^0(16) and germanium centres [GeO$_4$/Na]Ac* (R. S. Dickson et al., manuscript in preparation) are detectable. [Phys 2]

The reduction of the two italicized reduced relative clauses may help to decrease the reader's processing load, especially given the distance between the bare clause subject *(line width changes or site averaging)* and the clause predicate *(are detectable)*. Interestingly, 67% of the subordination at Level 3 occurred in the physics RAs, perhaps suggesting that physics may tolerate a higher degree of text density and consequent reduced accessibility (cf. Halliday, 1988, on the history of physics writing) than other fields. The pedagogical application of this finding would be to warn students not to reduce relative clauses that are too deeply embedded. This is unlikely to be a problem, however, because students are generally not inclined to embed to this extent.

In terms of the determiner attached to the head noun (as shown in Table 11.5), relative clauses whose head nouns were identified (i.e., definite) tended to be reduced more often than relative clauses whose head nouns were classified (i.e., indefinite). Identified NPs usually indicate given (or known) information, most commonly with the article *the*, whereas classified NPs typically indicate new information, most commonly with *Ø1* or *a(n)*. This finding again supports the suggestion that NPs reflecting new information tended to be nonreduced. Students can be advised that, when reduction is possible, relative clauses modifying NPs whose determiner is *the* (or another defining determiner) are more likely to be reduced, whereas relative clauses modifying NPs whose determiner is *a* or *Ø* (or another classifying determiner) are not.

In terms of the syntactic structures separating the head noun and its relative clause (as shown in Table 11.6), reduction (when an option, as shown in the Nonred column) appears to increase as the number of intervening structures increases. It was expected that clarity and explicitness would be required as the sentence became more complex, as was the case with level of subordination, but it seems again that reduction often makes a sentence easier to understand when phrase structures intervene between the head noun and the relative clause, as shown in the following example (the head noun is in boldface; the asterisk indicates the beginning of the relative clause and the deletion and syntactic alteration of *which approximates):*

> Between-treatment comparisons revealed *a significant addititive **effect** of cognitive therapy to relaxation training on both clinic and worksite readings *approximating 5 mmHg,* a statistically and clinically significant difference. [Clin Psych 1]

The occurrence of intervening structures in relative clause constructions is not that common, so it is generally good pedagogical practice to teach students that relative clauses usually directly follow the NP they are postmodifying. The use of intervening structures should probably be discouraged in producing written text, though their presence must be understood in decoding.

In terms of relative clause reduction by field (as shown in Table 11.7), computer science and engineering geology used no reduction whatsoever. This is a reminder that reduction is never an absolute requirement, that an editor (or an author, though the fact that four different authors in two different journals never reduced suggests that it may have been the policy of the editor or the journal rather than that of the authors, especially the computer science journal as noted earlier) may see reduced relative clauses as being too informal for a research article and simply not allow them. In the remaining 14 research articles, 90% of the relative clauses were S-form clauses, of which 70% were reduced. Within the subject-form reductions, nearly two thirds were of the past participle type (e.g., *the results **shown** in Table 1*), a quarter were of the present participle type (e.g., *the method producing the best results*), 7.4% were adjectives (e.g., *results similar to those found earlier*), and 6% were nominal appositive clauses (e.g., *the results, 100 parts per million*). The fact that reduced present participle (VERB$_{ing}$) clauses constituted 57% of the restrictive S-form relative clauses in the corpus supports Huckin et al.'s (1986) finding that whiz-deletion "is seen by good writers as a very useful device" (p. 185) although it challenges Huckin and Olsen's (1983) earlier claim that good writers "avoid applying the rule [of relative pronoun + *be* → VERB$_{ing}$] more often than not" (p. 400).

In the seven fields in which it occurred, reduction was applied somewhat more frequently in the physics, chemistry, and mechanical engineering RAs, but there is no discernible pattern in reduction according to field. Vande Kopple's (1998) diachronic study of relative clauses in spectroscopy RAs suggests that reduction is more common now than it was a century ago because the knowledge base is more secure and therefore generalizable. This is no doubt true for all fields. Thus, with the exception of the computer science and engineering geology RAs, in which some other philosophy may have been at work, a substantial level of reduction in all the fields represented is not surprising.

The notion that new information tends not to be reduced is supported by several of the conclusions found in the sources cited. For example,

Vande Kopple (1998) notes that full relative clauses "prevent giving the impression that the information should be regarded as typical or generalizable with confidence to other times, places, and experimental situations" (p. 181). Huckin and Olsen's (1983) observation that full relative clauses "command more attention" (p. 400) is also consonant with their signifying new information, which the English language does much to highlight (e.g., by the use of nonreferential *there* and *it* to delay the appearance of—and thus emphasize—new information). The all versus some distinction can be explained in the same way: A nonreduced relative clause makes the head noun particular and unique as opposed to typical and generalizable. It should be pointed out, however, that in P-form reduction the tense and modality lost in S-form reduction, thereby leading to timeless generality and typicality, is not lost in a P-form reduced relative clause, for example, *The periods of license revocation, suspension, and voluntary surrender were subtracted from the period *each subject was considered to be at risk* [Med 1]. It is therefore necessary to posit some other reason for the nonreduction of reducable P-form relative clauses, which I would argue is the likelihood that the head noun comprises new information, for example *Figure 1 shows a schematic diagram of the molecular beam apparatus which we have used for both types of experiments* [Chem 2].

Pedagogical Implications

This investigation of relative clause reduction in 20 published research articles in 10 fields suggests that relative clause reduction occurs frequently in technical RAs and that the mechanisms for reduction and when to use them are a valid object of study in technical writing classes, especially those for nonnative speakers of English (e.g., English for science and technology classes). The conclusion that reduction is less likely to be applied when information is new no doubt applies to more general texts as well as to technical RAs, though this remains to be studied.

Although many grammar textbooks for nonnative speakers of English, such as Ruetten (1997), Thewlis (1997), and Azar (1999), devote considerable space to describing the mechanism of relative clause reduction (Azar, for example, devotes seven pages to reduction rules and exercises, pp. 290–296), none provides an explanation of when reduction is appropriate and when it is not.

S-form reduction far outweighed any other type by a substantial margin. Therefore, it is probably safe to say that all S-form relative clauses modifying NPs that are thought to be typical or generalizable (and therefore associated with the simple present tense) rather than unique or uncertain should be reduced if possible to avoid wordiness (or "semantic noise," as Brogan put it). An exception would be when the head noun of the relative clause signifies new information, in which case it is usually positioned at or toward the end of the sentence. P-form reduction, on the other hand, was rarely applied in the technical RAs and it is probably safe to say that P-form relative clauses should almost never be reduced in this kind of writing unless they are deeply embedded. In the humanities articles, however, P-form reduction occurred 10 times more frequently, suggesting that this type of reduction is much more acceptable in the humanities and therefore should be taught to students writing in such fields.

One way that students might practice deciding when to reduce a relative clause and when not to is to provide them with a list of sentences containing nonreduced (but grammatically reducible) relative clauses and ask them to simply apply the mechanisms of reduction to them. Then, after presenting the generalization (either deductively or inductively) that relative clauses are generally not reduced when they signify new information, which typically comes at the end of the sentence, have the students go back to the same list of sentences and decide, using this information, whether they should have reduced the relative clauses or not. Figure 11.1 is a sample exercise based on authentic material that can be used for this purpose.

Directions: Reduce the underlined S-form relative clauses in the following sentences when appropriate.

1. The program is split into basic blocks, (a) *which are sets of machine-level instructions that always execute in sequence.* [Stunkel et al., 1991]

2. Molecules (b) *that display behavior of this type* are ofen said to be in the "large"-molecule limit. [Miller, 1990]

3. The temperature of 1°C was selected because it is the temperature threshold (c) *that is used in predicting the development of winter wheat.* [Howard et al., 1990]

4. This is contrary to what one would expect of students (d) *who were using the exercise as an exploratory activity.* [Carson et al., 1990]

5. Arylsulfatase A is a lysosomal enzyme (e) *which is involved in the degradation of cerebroside sulfate,* a polar glycolipid (f) *that is found mainly as a component of the myelin sheaths of the nervous system.* [Polten et al., 1991]

Answers: (a) no reduction; (b) *that display → displaying;* (c) no reduction; (d) no reduction; (e) *which is involved → involved;* (f) no reduction

---

FIG. 11.1   Sample exercise for reduction of relative clauses.

Even though relative clause reduction is an option, not a requirement, the study discussed in this chapter suggests that technical writers usually take the option for S-form relative clauses (as was also found by Huckin et al., 1986), especially when their head nouns signify given information. When carefully applied, reduction can be a useful means of helping the reader manage the information load in complex sentences. It thus behooves the technical writer to be aware of reduction techniques and when to use them.

ACKNOWLEDGMENTS

I am very grateful to Lois M. Rew and Burford Furman at San Jose State University for their expert commentary on the nonreduced relative clauses in the corpus and to Dwight Atkinson for his valuable comments on an earlier version of this paper.

REFERENCES

Aarts, F., & Schils, E. (1995). Relative clauses, the accessibility hierarchy and the contrastive analysis hypothesis. *IRAL, 33,* 47–63.

Azar, B. (1999). *Understanding and using English grammar* (3rd ed.). Upper Saddle River, NJ: Prentice Hall.

Bever, T. G., & Langendoen, D. I. (1971). The dynamic evolution of the language. *Linguistic Inquiry, 2,* 433–463.

Bickerton, D. (1995). *Language and human behavior.* Seattle: University of Washington Press.

Bolinger, D. (1967). Adjectives in English: Attribution and predication. *Lingua, 18,* 1–34.

Bolinger, D. (1980). *Language, the loaded weapon: The use and abuse of language today.* London: Longman.

Brogan, J. A. (1973). *Clear technical writing.* New York: McGraw-Hill.

Bruthiaux, P. (1996). *The discourse of classified advertising: Exploring the nature of linguistic simplicity.* Oxford: Oxford University Press.

Celce-Murcia, M., & Larsen-Freeman, D. (1983). *The grammar book.* Cambridge, MA: Newbury House.

Chafe, W. L. (1970). *Meaning and the stucture of language.* Chicago: University of Chicago Press.

Comrie, B. (1989). *Language universals and linguistic typology. Syntax and morphology* (2nd ed.). Oxford: Basil Blackwell.

Davis, R. M. (1977). Technical writing: Who needs it? *Engineering Education,* November 1977, *66,* 209–211.

de Haan, P. (1989). *Postmodifying clauses in the English noun phrase: A corpus-based study.* Amsterdam: Rodopi.

Dubois, B. L. (1982). The construction of noun phrases in biomedical journal articles. In J. Hoedt, L. Lundquist, H. Picht, & J. Qvistgaard (Eds.), *Pragmatics and LSP.* Copenhagen: Copenhagen School of Economics.

Fox, B. A., & Thompson, S. A. (1990). A discourse explanation of the grammar of relative clauses in English conversation. *Language, 66,* 297–316.

Givon, T. (1984). *Syntax.* Amsterdam: John Benjamins.

Hall, R. A., Jr. (1964). *Introductory linguistics*. Philadelphia: Chilton.

Halliday, M. A. K. (1988). On the language of physical science. In M. Ghadessy (Ed.), *Registers of written English: Situational factors and linguistic features* (pp. 162–178). London: Frances Pinter.

Horsella, M., & Pérez, F. (1991). Nominal compounds in chemical English literature: Toward an approach to test typology. *English for Specific Purposes 10*, 125–138.

Huckin, T., & Olsen, L. (1983). *English for science and technology: A handbook for nonnative speakers*. New York: McGraw-Hill.

Huckin, T., Curtin, E., & Graham, D. (1986). Prescriptive linguistics and plain English: The case of "whiz-deletions." *Visible Language, 20*, 174–187.

Lehmann, C. (1988). Towards a typology of clause linkage. In J. Haiman & S. A. Thompson (Eds.), *Clause combining in grammar and discourse* (pp. 181–225). Amsterdam: John Benjamins.

Master, P. (1986). *Science, medicine, and technology: English grammar and technical writing*. Englewood Cliffs, NJ: Prentice Hall.

Master, P. (1990). Teaching the English articles as a binary system. *TESOL Quarterly, 24*, 461–478.

Master, P. (1996). *Systems in English grammar*. Englewood Cliffs, NJ: Prentice Hall.

Master, P. (1997). The English article system: Acquisition, function, and pedagogy. *System, 25*, 215–232.

McCawley, J. D. (1988). *The syntactic phenomena of English* (Vol. 2). Chicago: University of Chicago Press.

Meyer, C. (1992). *Apposition in contemporary English*. Cambridge, UK: Cambridge University Press.

Quirk, R., Greenbaum, S., Leech, G., & Svartvik, J. (1972). *A grammar of contemporary English*. London: Longman.

Quirk, R., Greenbaum, S., Leech, G., & Svartvik, J. (1985). *A contemporary grammar of the English language*. London: Longman.

Ruetten, M. (1997). *Developing composition skills: Rhetoric and grammar*. Boston: Heinle & Heinle.

Swales, J. M. (1981). The function of one type of particle in a chemistry textbook. In L. Selinker, E. Tarone, & V. Hanzeli (Eds.), *English for academic and technical purposes* (pp. 40–52). Rowley, MA: Newbury House.

Thewlis, S. (1997). *Grammar dimensions: Form, meaning, and use* (2nd ed.), vol. 3. Boston: Heinle & Heinle.

Vande Kopple, W. J. (1998). Relative clauses in spectroscopic articles in the *Physical Review*, beginning and 1980: Some changes in patterns of modification and a connection to a possible shift in style. *Written Communication, 15*, 170–202.

RESEARCH REPORTS ANALYZED

Biology

Gahukar, R. T. (1990). Sampling techniques, spatial distribution and cultural control of millet spike worm, *Raghuva albipunctella* (Noctuidae: Lepidoptera). *Annals of Applied Biology, 117*, 45–50.

Howard, M. T., & Dixon, A. F. G. (1990). Forecasting of peak population density of the rose grain aphid *Metopolophium dirhodum* on wheat. *Annals of Applied Biology, 117*, 9–19.

Chemistry

Hall, H. K., Jr., & Padias, A. B. (1990). Zwitterion and diradical tetramethylenes as initiators of "charge-transfer" polymerizations. *Accounts of Chemical Research, 23*, 3–9.

Miller, R. E. (1990). Vibrationally induced dynamics in hydrogen-bonded complexes. *Accounts of Chemical Research, 23*, 10–16.

Clinical Psychology

Bennett, P., & Carroll, D. (1990). Stress management approaches to the prevention of coronary heart disease. *British Journal of Clinical Psychology, 29*, 1–12.
Jack, R. L., & Williams, J. M. (1991). The role of attributions in self-poisoning. *British Journal of Clinical Psychology, 30*, 25–35.

Computer Science

Pease, D., Ghafoor, A., Ahmad, I., Andrews, D. L., Foudil-Bey, K., Karpinski, T. E., Mikki, M. A., & Zerrouki, M. (1991). PAWS: A performance evaluation tool for parallel computing systems. *Computer (IEEE), 24*, 18–30.
Stunkel, C. B., Janssens, B., & Fuchs, W. K. (1991). Address tracing for parallel machines. *Computer (IEEE), 24*, 31–38.

Engineering (Mechanical)

Angeles, J., & Ma, O. (1991). Performance evaluation of four-bar linkages for rigid-body guidance based on generalized coupler curves. *Journal of Mechanical Design, 113*, 17–24.
Olsen, D. G., Erdman, A. G., & Riley, D. R. (1991). Topical analysis of single-degree-of-freedom planetary gear trains. *Journal of Mechanical Design, 113*, 10–16.

Engineering Geology

Collins, T. K. (1990). New faulting and the attenuation of fault displacement. *Bulletin of Engineering Geologists, 27*, 11–22.
El-Hussain, I. W., & Carpenter, P. J. (1990). Reservoir induced seismicity near Heron and El Vado reservoirs, Northern New Mexico. *Bulletin of Engineering Geologists, 27*, 51–59.

Mathematics

Ashbaugh, M. S., & Benguria, R. D. (1990). Proof of the Payne-Pólya-Weinberger conjecture. *Bulletin of the American Mathematical Society, 25*, 19–29.
Colombeau, J. F. (1990). Multiplication of distributions. *Bulletin of the American Mathematical Society, 23*, 251–268.

Medicine

Hansotia, P., & Broste, S. K. (1991). The effect of epilepsy or diabetes mellitus on the risk of automobile accidents. *New England Journal of Medicine, 324*, 22–26.
Polten, A., Fluharty, A. L., Fluharty, C. B., Kappler, J., von Figura, K., & Gieselmann, V. (1991). Molecular basis of different forms of metachromatic leukodystrophy. *New England Journal of Medicine, 324*, 18–22.

Physics

Dickson, R. S., & Weil, J. A. (1990). The magnetic properties of the oxygen-hole aluminum centres in crystalline $SiO_2.IV.[AlO_4/Na]^+$. *Canadian Journal of Physics, 68*, 630–642.
Ponce de Leon, J. (1990). Model-independent description of intermediate-range forces in static spherical bodies. *Canadian Journal of Physics, 68*, 574–578.

Humanities

Carson, J. E., Carrell, P. L., Silberstein, S., Kroll, B., & Kuehn, P. (1990). The relationship between overall reading comprehension and comprehension of coreferential ties for second language readers of English. *TESOL Quarterly, 24*, 267–292.

Chapelle, C. (1990). The discourse of computer-assisted language learning: Toward a context for descriptive research. *TESOL Quarterly, 24*, 199–225.

12

Why English Passive Is Difficult to Teach (and Learn)

Eli Hinkel
Seattle University, Washington

INTRODUCTION

As many English as a second language (ESL) and English as a foreign language (EFL) teachers know from experience, teaching the meanings, uses, and functions of the passive voice represents one of the thorniest problems in Second language (L2) grammar instruction, and speakers of many first languages (L1s) appear to have difficulty with passive constructions. However, the uses of passive structures are common in academic writing (Talmy, 1988), and advanced learners are often expected to produce written texts that utilize passive forms. Because learners often do not use passive verb phrases in correct forms, much of the L2 instruction associated with the passive voice includes the derivation of passive structures from active. For example, *The average American seeks independence. . . . Independence is sought by the average American* (Steer & Carlisi, 1998, p. 263).

The presentation of the passive verb form in simple tenses (present or past) is usually followed by the demonstration of passive verb forms in various tenses, such as progressive [*The letter is being written (by Mary)*] or perfect [*The book has been read (by John)*]. Most grammar textbooks provide exercise drills for various passive structures that often require learners to identify the tense and the voice of the verb in the context of a sentence or a short passage and produce the appropriate verb form.

A vast majority of grammar textbooks include a chapter on the meanings, forms, and uses of the passive voice, and most L2 learners at intermediate and higher levels of proficiency have studied the derivation of passive structures and worked through the exercises. Nonetheless, when it comes to L2 production in speaking or writing, many learners even at advanced levels often do not form passive constructions correctly and do not use passive voice in appropriate contexts. For example:

1. *I am sorry I did not come to class this morning. *I am suffered from a cold and feel terrible.*
2. *I'd like to schedule an appointment with you because I want to help my brother register for classes? ??My brother was picked up by me at the airport last night, and he is staying at a hotel near campus.*

In Example 1, the passive form of the verb is ungrammatical because *suffer* is an intransitive verb (i.e., it does not take a direct object), from which the passive cannot be derived. However, the questionable sentence in Example 2 seems somewhat inappropriate and stilted in the context of a relatively informal request for an appointment.

Although the teaching of L2 grammar almost always includes passive, investigations into L2 language learning have not been able to identify the features of the English passive that make it difficult for L2 learners to use appropriately. In one of the few studies devoted to the L2 use of passive, Master (1991) indicates that nonnative speakers (NNSs) need to be explicitly taught the use of active verbs with inanimate nouns because these verbs can become a formidable obstacle in L2 production. He explains that NNSs and, in particular, speakers of Asian languages often have difficulty with active verbs with inanimate subject nouns. For example, in *A thermometer measures the temperature* (p. 15), *the thermometer* is an inanimate noun that in English can be used with an active verb *measures*. Master points out that speakers of Japanese have difficulty with such sentences because, in their perception and due to L1 interference, animate subjects are needed in sentences with active verbs. He demonstrates that in English active or passive constructions, the notion of noun animacy does not appear to play an important role in sentences with inanimate and abstract nouns, which are frequently found as sentence subjects. He comments that the use of the active or passive voice in English sentences usually does not depend on the animacy of the subject noun, and the use of active verbs with inanimate subjects is a common phenomenon.

In L2 learning, other researchers have identified the constraints that the notion of lexical animacy imposes on the acquisition of various L2 syntactic and semantic features, such as the active or the passive voice. According to

Pfaff (1987), L2 developmental systems of adult learners of German appear to be sensitive to L1 and L2 lexical animacy. She points out that in sentences with the active voice, intermediate learners almost always introduce animate nouns, identified by gender/case markers in German as subjects, and inanimates are commonly used as objects. Similarly, Bates, MacWhinney, McNew, Davescovi, and Smith (1982) conducted an experiment to determine whether the notion of lexical animacy plays a role in how English-speaking learners of Italian and Italian-speaking learners of English identify syntactic and/or lexical features of nouns to comprehend L2 active and passive structures. Their findings indicate that in sentence comprehension, the speakers of English relied almost exclusively on word order, whereas Italians focused predominantly on lexical and semantic animacy, marked by inflections.

Methodologies for teaching the active and passive voice in English as L2 usually do not focus on noun animacy and the attendant semantic constructs, such as agentivity (the capacity of the entity expressed by the subject noun to perform the action expressed by the verb) and patienthood (the effect of the action on the entity, expressed by the object noun). In *John kicked the ball*, for example, *John* is the agent of the action *kicked*, and *the ball* is the patient. On the other hand, in *The ball kicked John*, *the ball* cannot be the agent of the action because it is an inanimate (and nonsentient) noun. Although the noun capacity for agency seems to play an important role in grammaticality (or ungrammaticality) of active or passive structures in English, in L2 teaching, presenting the syntactic features and stylistic implications of the active and passive voice uses is often considered sufficient. In fact, in their substantial volume, Quirk, Greenbaum, Leech, and Svartvik (1985) devote two brief mentions to the agentivity and patienthood of animate and inanimate nouns, and Alexander (1988) and Wardhaugh (1995) do not include these lexical notions in their works on the teaching of grammar. In general, little research has addressed the effect of noun animacy on L2 learning and use of L2 passive constructions.

In linguistics, however, many researchers have reported that lexical and semantic features of nouns cannot be studied in isolation from their syntactic functions and pragmatic uses (DeLancey, 1990; Silverstein, 1987). For example, in *The hammer hit the nail, the hammer* is the instrument rather than an agent (Levin & Rappaport Hovav, 1991). Functions of nouns can restrict or expand the number and the type of their lexical features. Bock and Kroch (1989) comment that such notional categories as subjecthood and the animacy of nouns may be affected by the syntactic and lexical features of active and passive phrases in which they occur. They note that lexical features of nouns and, for instance, their capacity for subjecthood, cannot be examined in isolation from the "grammatical vocabulary" and language systems that "manipulate the features of that vocabulary" (p. 173).

Although the findings presented in this chapter are preliminary and require further investigation before definitive conclusions can be made, the overarching goal of the study is to increase teachers' awareness of linguistic features that are prominent in many languages other than English and that may crucially affect the learners' ability to process and use passive voice constructions in English. This investigation compares native speaker (NS) and NNS subjective evaluations of lexical animacy of nouns and noun phrases. The impact of these evaluations on NS and NNS grammaticality judgments of L1 and L2 passive constructions is also examined. Because in many languages other than English, lexical animacy of nouns is closely tied to notions of agentivity (and subjecthood) and verb transitivity, these attendant semantic and lexical characteristics of sentence constituents are also discussed. Suggestions and activities for teaching English passive structures in context are also provided.

Animacy, Nouns, and Entities

In the next two sections, a brief review of some of the relevant literature is not meant to serve as a basis for instruction but rather suggests the complexity of the lexical and semantic issues NNSs may encounter when learning to understand and use the passive voice in English. This overview lays the groundwork for the study and the teaching strategies that can be derived from it.

Because lexical animacy of nouns is a universal lexical and semantic characteristic, practically all studies of language typologies examine its influence on grammar and syntactic features of various languages. For example, Croft (1990) points out that typologically, the hierarchy of animacy establishes the "values" (p. 115) of noun categories with a "cascading" set of features. He states that animacy values of both animate and inanimate nouns often play a crucial role in the syntactic structure of a sentence and the "grammatical behavior" (p. 117) of nouns, such as human, nonhuman animate, and inanimate common nouns. However, he also observes that it is not possible to establish with certainty animacy values of inanimate nouns and pronouns relative to human common nouns. In his view, lexical animacy appears to be a fluid category that may vary, depending on the syntactic and phrasal features of nouns.

Armstrong, Gleitman, and Gleitman's (1983) study demonstrated that identifying semantic features of noun categories appears to be difficult (if at all possible) because the concepts that represent category-specific semantic features are often graded and may be only loosely associated with a particular entity. They specify that even prototypical features of common nouns, such as *bird*, *vehicle*, or names of fruits and terms of kinship, may defy precise characterization. In fact, they proposed a dual (rather than a unified) structure of semantic concepts for prototypical categories for nouns and (meta)physical categorization of objects. As has been mentioned, similar constraints may apply to the conceptual and gradient features of noun animacy in phrases and a metaphysical characterization of entities and changes in their objective properties. In their detailed examination of lexical animacy in several languages, Straus and Brightman (1982) also found that objective properties of entities, such as size, temperature, physical and behavioral environments, color, and other states, are variable and have a great deal of impact on the perceived lexical animacy of nouns that denote these entities. For example, in several languages, *a tree* remains animate until it is cut into firewood or sticks, which are inanimate. Straus and Brightman note that cooking, harvesting, breaking, and tearing change the state of entities and therefore the animacy of nouns that refer to them.

In his seminal work on the English systems of nouns, Talmy (1988) stipulates that to varying degrees, languages can ascribe intrinsic force properties to physical entities that are not sentient, such as *wind, a dam,* and *a ball.* He points out that in many languages other than English, nonsentient entities that are subjects of active verbs are merely seen as agents of the action described by the verb and that another entity that caused the action is usually implicit, for example, *The ball rolled* (moved by the wind or a person). However, in English, the entity that causes the action is not always implied, and the subject of an active verb is psychologically assigned a conceptual "entityhood" (p. 94), as is common in scientific and technical written discourse, for example, *The molecule folds in a way that protects the site.* Talmy specifies that in such sentences, events are "recognized as if in isolation" from their actual causal forces and are seen as autonomous abstractions.

Animacy, Agency, Verb Transitivity, and Other Relatives

In language studies, examinations of the animacy of subject nouns and their capacity for agentivity (and subjecthood), have been accompanied by those of syntactic and semantic features of verbs and nouns as direct objects. In particular, verb transitivity (the capacity to take or not to take direct objects) has been identified as an important factor that affects the syntactic structure of sentences. Hopper and Thompson (1980), who outlined the prototypical features of transitivity, stipulate that, among other considerations, transitivity pivots on such parameters as the subject noun capacity for agentivity (e.g., human or gradiently animate), the action capacity of verb meanings, volitionality of the subject noun, and lexical characteristics of direct objects. Taken together, these and other features of nouns and verbs can make sentences "more or less transitive" (p. 253).

In his analyses of diverse language systems, DeLancey (1985, p. 3) advances the Hopper and Thompson framework of agentivity and verb action features to show that semantic features of subjects, such as sentience and volition, determine whether transitive or intransitive clauses are considered grammatical in particular languages. He also notes that the degree of volitionality or "control" that the subject as the agent "can impute over the object as the patient" determines the syntactic structure of the sentence. In English, for example, *I broke the window* does not reflect considerations of "volitionality," and it may not matter whether the window was broken accidentally or intentionally. On the other hand, in other languages, the degree of "responsibility" (p. 4) for the action determines the gradient features of noun agentivity and whether the subject can be also considered the agent. In his subsequent work, DeLancey (1990) also argues that in many languages, the cognitive model and the conceptualization of event structures underlies the semantics of grammatical forms (e.g., subject/agent and object/patient) in "everyday reality" (p. 292) and "our commonsense understanding of the structure of events" (p. 314), for instance, what entities can (or cannot) perform particular actions (and play the role of sentence subjects) and how these actions can affect the patients (objects). For example, for a speaker of Japanese, in *Mary is suffered from a cold, the cold* (illness) is the agent, and *Mary* is the patient; thus, because *Mary* does not perform the action but is rather affected by it, the sentence verb should take a passive form.

Another consideration to keep in mind is that, in English, inanimate subjects of active verbs can be "oblique" (Levin & Rappaport Hovav, 1991, p. 133), when the agent is not overtly expressed (e.g., *Water filled the ditch* or *The sink emptied*). Grammatical subjects that are not direct agents can often characterize instruments, locations, containers, or materials. Also, for example, in *The lights dimmed*, the verb *dim* denotes the lexicalized "come to be in a state" (p. 134), where the agent is not expressed. The authors point out, however, that in general, verbs may systematically acquire lexicalized meanings and syntactic features (such as variable transitivity) and represent "an important part of the lexical knowledge of a speaker of English" (p. 138).

Although the relationship between linguistic features of languages and their cognitive implications is not well understood, typological studies provide some insights into the functions of nouns and verbs within syntactic systems. Silverstein (1987) points out that noun animacy alone is not sufficient to determine a noun's capacity for subjecthood. It represents only one factor in the hierarchy of features that account for the capacity of a noun to function as an agent (subject) and patient (object), and can be combined with other semantic and lexical features, such as sentience and volitionality. For example, nouns that can be categorized as human or possessing human-like characteristics can be subjects (but not necessarily agents) of volitional verbs associated with accomplishment and achievement (e.g., *I/the team won (the game)*), but almost all animate nouns can be found as agents of verbs referring to involuntary experiences or events (e.g., *he died/yawned/blinked* or *the dog/cat/bird hears the sounds*).

Although noun animacy may be a linguistic universal (Croft, 1990; DeLancey, 1990), Lucy (1992) stipulates that speakers of diverse languages use it in distinct ways and with different implications for the systems of cognition and thought. He goes on to say that this can present a problem for the comparisons of languages and their specific features. In his view, the limitations of the current typological studies of languages lie in the fact that little is known about the cognitive salience of linguistic features for cultural groups of speakers.

The specific purpose of this study is to compare NSs' and NNSs' (speakers of Chinese, Japanese, Korean, and Spanish) perceptions of lexical animacy of English nouns and noun phrases and to assess the influence of these perceptions on the learners' grammaticality judgments of active and passive constructions. Suggestions for teaching the meanings and uses of the English passive to speakers of languages with developed systems of noun animacy are presented.

THE STUDY OF LEXICAL ANIMACY: EXPERIMENTS 1 AND 2

The study discussed in this chapter was based on two experiments dealing with the lexical animacy of nouns and noun phrases. Because many studies have identified lexical animacy as a gradient feature (Croft, 1990; Hopper & Thomson, 1980; Lucy, 1996), NSs and NNSs were asked to rank the perceived lexical animacy of nouns or noun phrases on a Likert scale ranging from 1 to 10, from inanimate to animate. Following the rankings of nouns (Experiment 1) and noun phrases (Experiment 2), in both experiments participants were asked to establish the grammaticality of active or passive sentences that included some of these nouns and noun phrases as sentence subjects.

Experiment 1

Participants.   A total of 179 NSs and NNSs participated in Experiment 1. Of this number, 30 were NSs of English from Midwestern states (Ohio, Indiana, Illinois, and Michigan), 55 were speakers of Chinese, 40 speakers of Korean, 31 speakers of Japanese, and 23 speakers of Spanish. All NNSs had been admitted to a large U.S. university and were deemed sufficiently proficient in English to pursue studies toward their degrees. The TOEFL (Test of English as a Foreign Language) scores of the NNSs ranged from 527 to 623, with an average of 593. The NNSs had resided in the United States for periods of time from 7 months to 6.9 years, with an average of 2.8 years; their ages ranged from 20 to 36 years (a mean of 28.6).

The Instrument and Data Analysis.   According to Master's (1991) observations, speakers of Japanese and other Asian languages may experience particular difficulty with sentences with inanimate subjects and active verbs, commonly found in academic texts. For this reason, some of the nouns included those frequently encountered in introductory textbooks as subjects of active verbs, for example, *experiment, idea, information, method, observation, process, research, theory* (as in, for example, *The experiment/information/observation/demonstrates/shows/proves/validates that...*). Additional nouns were also included from textbooks on biology (*blood, cell, cell membrane, dog, fish, human, molecule, protein*), environmental sciences (*air, daylight, earth, rain, thunder, wind*), and psychology (*love, anger, fear, pain*). To ensure that the lexical items in the instrument were familiar to most NNSs, lists of common "everyday" nouns (DeLancey, 1990) were elicited from five ESL instructors, and an additional set of nouns were selected and included in the instrument (e.g., *apple, automobile, city, computer, country, discussion, house, flower, language, music, television, tree leaf, university, water, word*). The nouns were presented to NS and NNS participants in random order.

After the data were collected, they were compiled to obtain average rankings for each noun by L1 group, that is, group rankings given by the NSs and by the speakers of Chinese, Korean, Japanese, and Spanish. For the purposes of analyses, these were divided into the nine thematic sets: Live Creatures, Plants, Organic Elements, Natural Phenomena, Basic Elements, Sensations and Emotions, Speech and Language, Knowledge and Research, and Man-Made Objects. Cronbach's alpha was selected as a conservative measure of reliability for items on an unweighted scale and was calculated for average rankings in each set of items to obtain internal consistency measurements. The reliability coefficients across all items for all participants in Experiment 1 ranged from .90 to .98.

To determine associations between the average rankings of animacy by L1 groups, rank-difference coefficients between each pair of L1-based groups were obtained for each of the nine sets of nouns and, thus, nine correlation matrices were computed. However, because this study is primarily concerned with similarities and differences in the perceived lexical animacy of NSs and NNSs, the correlation coefficients between NS and NNS values for each noun were extracted and are selectively presented in Table 12.1.

TABLE 12.1
Extracted Rank Correlation Coefficients for Nouns between NSs and NNSs,
by Group

	Thematic Sets of Nouns								
	Live Creatures	Organic Plants	Natural Elements	Basic Phenomena	Sensations Elements	Speech/ Emotions	Knowledge/ Language	Man-made Research	Objects
	NSs	NSs	NSs	NSs	NSs	NSs	NSs	NSs	NSs
Chinese	.74*	.72	.92*	.77	.58	.54	.84*	.90*	.72*
Korean	.73*	.98*	.96*	.75	.99*	.42	.88*	.87*	.77*
Japanese	.81*	.96*	.97*	.95*	.85	.91*	.86	.28	.87*
Spanish	.80*	.93*	.87*	.82	.70	.56	.84	.93*	.90*

*$p \leq .05$ 2-tailed $p \leq .05$.

Results and Discussion. Table 12.1 presents extracted correlation coefficients between the ranks by NSs and NNSs, by group. It appears that the majority of ranks assigned to the noun sets by members of various L1 groups were significantly similar, regardless of their L1s. Specifically, the NSs' and NNSs' judgments of lexical animacy were similar to those of NNSs' in the sets dealing with Live Creatures, Organic Elements, and Man-Made Objects. In the Knowledge and Research set, the rankings of all participants, apart from those of the Japanese participants, were also similar to a large extent (among three of the four NNS groups). In general, in all sets of nouns, of the 36 correlation coefficients between NSs and other L1 groups, 23, or slightly fewer than two thirds, were significant.

In general terms, NS values correlated significantly with those of Chinese and Spanish speakers in five each of the nine sets, those of Japanese in six sets, and those of Koreans in seven sets. The rankings by Koreans correlated highly with those of NSs, except in the Natural Phenomena and Sensations and Emotions sets. Thus, it appears that for individual nouns in these sets, NS and NNS perceptions of animacy were more similar than dissimilar; and there was no evidence of dramatically different evaluations. The implications of this similarity of judgment are discussed in the results of Experiments 3 and 4 later in this chapter.

Experiment 2

Participants. As in Experiment 1, the instrument was administered to 149 NSs and NNSs. Of this number, 30 were native speakers of English from Midwestern states. The NNSs included 34 speakers of Chinese, 36 speakers of Korean, 26 speakers of Japanese, and 23 speakers of Spanish, who were deemed sufficiently proficient in L2 to be enrolled in degree programs in a large U.S. university. As with Experiment 1, the random samples of NNSs included advanced students with TOEFL scores ranging from 533 to 623 (an average of 597). They had resided in the United States for periods of time between 6 months and 6.1 years (a mean of 2.7 years); their ages ranged from a minimum of 19 to a maximum of 33 years (an average of 26.2 years).

Results and Data Analysis.   The noun phrases presented in the instrument in Experiment 2 referred to the same or similar entities as in Experiment 1, with different syntactic or objective properties and/or changed states to determine whether these variations resulted in divergent rankings of animacy. The instrument in Experiment 2 followed the same format as that in Experiment 1, and a similar set of instructions was provided to the participants. The key difference between the two forms was that in Experiment 2, participants were asked to assign rankings to noun phrases instead of nouns, for example, *water in the lake* and *a tree leaf on the ground.*

Many of the nouns in the instrument in Experiment 1 were included in paired noun phrases in Experiment 2. Some were modified by adjectives, for example, *a large city/a small city, an interesting book/a boring book, written language/spoken language, a stormy ocean/a calm ocean, bright light/dim light, teaching method/learning method, an angry conversation/a friendly conversation,* and *hot water/cold water.* Additional nouns were modified by locative and spatial prepositional phrases, such as *an apple on a plate/an apple on a tree, a leaf on a tree/a leaf on the ground, language in speech/language in writing, an idea in speech/an idea in writing, an automobile in the parking lot/an automobile on the highway, water in a tap/water in a lake, a flower in the garden/a flower in a vase.*

As in Experiment 1, the pairs of noun phrases were divided into nine thematic sets: People, Plants, Speech and Language, Natural Objects and Phenomena, Structures, Ideas and Concepts, Liquids, Texts, and Man-Made Objects. The data were compiled to obtain average rankings by L1 groups, and Cronbach's alpha was calculated to establish internal consistency across items in each set. As in Experiment 1, rank-difference coefficients between pairs of L1-based groups were computed for nine correlation matrices, and the extracted correlations between the average ranks of NSs and each of the L1 groups are shown in Table 12.2.

Overall, NNSs seemed to perceive the lexical animacy of abstract concepts and inanimate concrete noun phrases to be slightly higher than NSs did, regardless of their L1s. As with the nouns in Experiment 1, the participants' ranks of paired noun phrases were consistent across items in each set, and the Cronbach α coefficients of reliability were relatively high, that is, between .88 and .99.

In general terms, NS and NNS rank correlations of noun phrases were only moderately different (see Table 12.2). For example, for the sets Plants,

TABLE 12.2
Extracted Rank Correlation Coefficients for Noun Phrases between NSs and
NNSs, by Group

	People	Plants	Speech/ Language	Natural Objects/ Phenomena	Structures	Ideas/ Concepts	Texts	Liquids	Man-made Objects
	NSs	NS	NSs	NSs	NSs	NSs	NSs	NSs	NSs
Chinese	.71	.98*	.36	.83*	.87*	.40	.62	.61	.53*
Korean	.94	.97*	.57	.80*	.68	.76	.58	.92*	.76*
Japanese	.67	.99*	.27	.89*	.95*	.45	.63*	.94*	.68*
Spanish	.87	.91*	.15	.74*	.47	.64	.61	.78*	.69*

$*p \leq 05$ 2-tailed $p \leq .05$.

Natural Objects and Phenomena, Man-Made Objects, and Liquids, the rankings assigned to the noun phrases by NSs were similar to those assigned to them by NNSs in all groups.

For all noun phrases in Table 12.2, however, 18 correlation coefficients between the ranks given by NSs and other L1 groups were significantly similar, whereas another 18 were not. Among the L1 groups, the NS rankings correlated most frequently with those of Japanese in six of the nine sets, and four each with those of speakers of Chinese, Korean, and Spanish. Compared with the number of significant correlation coefficients between NS and NNS animacy values in Table 12.1 (23 of 36), it seems that the change in objective properties of entities and semantic features of nouns in paired noun phrases resulted in a decreased number of similarly ranked noun phrases in Table 12.2 (18 of 36). According to Straus and Brightman (1982), in many languages other than English, changes in the physical characteristics of entities, such as size, temperature, location, motion, purpose, and other states, alter the perceived animacy of the nouns to which these entities refer; for exmaple, cold water may be seen as less animate than hot water. In addition, Siewierska (1984) explains that in many languages, attributive (of the book) and locative (near the river and in the market) prepositional phrases have a great deal of influence on the agentive capacity of nouns and can alter the transitivity of a sentence in which they function as subject/agents or objects/patients. It appears that attributive adjectives and prepositional phrases had an important impact on the perceived lexical animacy of nouns. Because in L2 learning and use nouns are almost always encountered in contexts at least as small as modifiers or phrases, it appears that presence of contextual modifiers may have created a wider gap between NSs' and NNSs' perceptions of a noun capacity for subjecthood in active constructions in English.

Teaching Suggestions: The Concept of Lexical Animacy in English.

(1) It is usually with surprise that learners discover that lexical animacy has no impact on the grammatical structure of English sentences. For example, the teacher can push open the classroom door and allow it to swing back to close. Is it grammatical to say in the learners' first language, "The door is closing" or "The door closed"? Are these grammatical sentences in English? Why is it that such structures are (or are not) grammatical in the learners' first language? On the other hand, in English, sentient and nonsentient nouns can be subjects of active verbs, for example, the *tree leaf is falling/shaking/flying, the water is running/flowing/dripping/leaking,* or *the clouds are gathering/moving/traveling.* What is the difference between "the door" that cannot close on its own and "the water/the river" that can move without any visible or noticeable force that causes it to do so? Is animacy a variable feature? In English grammar, it does not necessarily have to be variable, and inanimate nouns can be used as subjects of active verbs that can take "oblique" nouns (e.g., *the coffee spilled* or *the hose is leaking)* as subjects (see the discussion of Levin, 1993, and Levin & Rappaport Hovav, 1991, earlier in this chapter).

(2) For listening practice, examples of nonsentient nouns that serve as subjects of active verbs can be found in many informercials in the United States, United Kingdom, and other English-speaking countries, particularly those that describe cooking appliances and utensils and other types of mechanical and electric devices. Another good source of text-based examples of structures with nonsentient subjects and active verbs are excerpts from (junior) encyclopedias that explain how machines and devices operate (e.g., regular and cell telephones, a computer, an automobile, a typewriter, staplers, radio, or TV). These can be analyzed and discussed with students to promote their noticing of such structures in English. For example, students' attention can be brought to the common uses of nonsentient nouns as subjects of active verbs, as in *The knife cuts the apple like butter; the cake/turkey goes in the oven (and bakes) for an hour; the cleaner can remove any stain, the drill/grill/saw works in any weather conditions, the sunscreen protects your skin; the juice/grease/fluid/water gathers/collects/sits/accumulates at the bottom of the pan;* and *the TV/radio/phone sounds wonderful.*

(3) Activities associated with the teaching of nonsentient nouns as subjects of animate verbs can be numerous and serve to increase learners' exposure to contextualized language use. In fact, the learner "noticing" that nonsentient nouns can be subjects of active verbs in English does not need to be associated with the teaching of the passive voice but can take place during the early steps in language learning when active voice structures are accessible to them. The activities can be simple and practical, and they usually become very enjoyable for students at the beginning and intermediate levels of proficiency and can be used in ESL and/or EFL settings.

In pairs or small groups, students can perform "scientific experiments" and present their descriptions of procedures to others (e.g., a small juice maker can be used to make juice, fruit and vegetables can be grated, and the physical process of juice-making/grating/cutting described). Also, making paper, dough, vegetable, flower, and colored paper designs or posters/montages also become enjoyable classroom activities that promote learners' noticing of structures with nonsentient nouns and animate verbs.

(4) Students can be assigned to create their own oral or written descriptions of how machines, appliances, and devices work, or of rules of board, card, or chess games. This type of writing can be timed to coincide with composition work dealing with process/enumerative descriptions that students often work with at beginning and/or intermediate levels of proficiency. Some of the ideas for written descriptions can include a pay phone, roller blades, a Walkman, a washing machine, a bicycle, a camera, a bus route, a trip to a city or a city center, a museum exposition, or even a fountain. When working on these assignments, students can be asked to pay particular attention to the use of nonsentient subjects with active verbs.

GRAMMATICALITY JUDGMENTS
OF PASSIVE CONSTRUCTIONS

In many languages, the notion of noun animacy and its capacity for agentivity may be closely associated with the active and passive voice and other syntactic features. Unlike English, in Chinese, for example, the concept of noun animacy often determines the types of syntactic constituents that may occur, such as direct objects and directional phrases (Huang, 1994; Li & Thompson, 1981). Similarly, in Korean, in addition to the syntactic markers on the noun and the verb, the lexical animacy of the subject noun determines the order in which events are presented (Kim, 1990). The Korean scale of lexical animacy is relatively rigid and places human common nouns above animate common nouns and inanimate common nouns, respectively (Palmer, 1994).

The structure, meaning, and use of the passive voice in Japanese is recognizably complex. The active voice is found in structures with sentient subjects, and, according to Shibatani (1990), the Japanese passive can be used with both transitive and intransitive verbs. The feature that distinguishes the meaning of passive in English and Chinese, Korean, and Japanese is that in the latter three languages passive constructions necessarily entail a meaning that the entity denoted by the subject affects the entity denoted by the object (Shibatani, 1990).

Two types of passive constructions exist in Spanish, those with *be* verbs and those with reflexives. Although Spanish has a developed system of noun animacy marked by gender and number inflections, animacy does not seem to have a great deal of impact on the type of nouns that can function as subjects in active and passive constructions (Posner, 1996). However, the distinction between animate and inanimate objects is overtly marked by the preposition *a*, which is used to mark animate direct objects (usually employed to mark indirect objects), whereas inanimate objects are not marked.

The additional purpose of Experiments 3 and 4 was to examine whether NSs and advanced NNSs, speakers of Chinese, Japanese, Korean, and Spanish, have similar grammaticality judgments of English active and passive verbs in paired and single sentences. This portion of the study was designed to determine whether the perceptual values of the lexical animacy of English nouns and noun phrases, addressed in the first part of the study, have an effect on NS and NNS judgments of grammaticality.

The Instrument and Data Analysis

The instruments in Experiments 3 and 4 included 24 and 16 sentences, respectively, that NSs and NNSs were asked to evaluate for grammaticality. In Experiment 3, the majority of sentences included animate and inanimate nouns. The instructions for both instruments were identical:

> In this Part, sentences are presented to you. Please mark (check or circle) all sentences in which you think the verb(s) is (are) used *grammatically correctly*.

Experiment 3

In Experiment 3, the sentences were used in 12 minimal pairs with the active or passive voice in mixed order within each pair (see Table 12.3). Three sentences (1–3) included nouns without modifiers, another four contained adjective modifiers of nouns (4–7), the next three (8–10) included adjectives and postpositional prepositional phrases, and the last two sentences (11 and 12) contained compound noun modifiers. The verb phrases in paired active/passive sentences were identical in every way except the voice distinctions. All included subjects, transitive verbs, and explicit direct objects (in both correct and incorrect forms). To focus the NNSs' attention on transitivity and verb passivization, all main verbs (predicates) in incorrect passive sentences were altered only by the addition of the auxiliary *BE* and a change from the base form of the main verb to the past participle. Such syntactic features and morphological and inflectional markers as tense, modality, number, and person were identical in both active and passive sentences in each pair. The verb form in only one (active) sentence in each pair was correct because the presence and the order of subjects and direct objects remained identical in each pair. For example:

TABLE 12.3
NS and NNS Grammaticality Judgments in Paired Sentences by Group

	Number Selected[a]									
Sentence	NSs (n = 30)	CH (n = 55)	p	JP (n = 40)	p	KR (n = 31)	p	SP (n = 23)	p
Nouns without modifiers									
1 (a) *An elephant can be heard sounds that humans cannot.	0	1	ns	2	ns	0	ns	0	ns
(b) An elephant can hear sounds that humans cannot.	30	54	ns	38	ns	31	ns	23	ns
2 (a) *In business meetings, discussions are allowed participants to present their views.	0	25	≤.00	19	≤.00	9	≤.00	5	≤.01
(b) In business meetings, discussions allow participants to present their views.	30	30	≤.00	21	≤.00	22	≤.00	18	≤.01
3 (a) *Soil is contained minerals essential for the cultivation of crops.	0	11	≤.01	12	≤.00	9	≤.00	0	ns
(b) Soil contains minerals essential for the cultivation of crops.	30	44	≤.01	28	≤.00	22	≤.00	23	ns
Nouns with adjective modifiers									
4 (a) Highly trained dogs can guide their blind owners on busy sidewalks and street crossings.	30	55	ns	37	ns	31	ns	23	ns
(b) *Highly trained dogs can be guided by their blind owners on busy sidewalks and street crossings.	0	0	ns	3	ns	0	ns	0	ns
5 (a) Typically, small cities surround larger ones to provide the local population additional housing areas.	30	45	≤.01	29	≤.00	23	≤.00	23	ns
(b) *Typically, small cities are surrounded larger ones to provide local population additional housing areas.	0	10	≤.01	11	≤.00	8	≤.00	0	ns
6 (a) Classical music enjoys a great deal of popularity among people of all ages.	30	41	≤.00	28	≤00	19	≤.00	17	≤.00
(b) *Classical music is enjoyed a great deal of popularity among people of all ages.	0	14	≤.00	12	≤.00	12	≤.00	6	≤.00

(continued)

TABLE 12.3

(continued)

Sentence	NSs (n = 30)	CH (n = 55)	p	JP (n = 40)	p	KR (n = 31)	p	SP (n = 23)	p
				Number Selected[a]					
7 (a) The interesting textbook develops the students' ability to consider important issues.	30	25	≤.00	34	≤.03	19	≤.00	22	ns
(b) *The interesting textbook is developed by the students' ability to consider important issues.	0	30	≤.00	6	≤.03	12	≤.00	1	ns
Nouns with adjective modifiers and postpositional prepositional phrases									
8 (a) *A new method of teaching biology is shown an improvement in student grades.	0	9	<.02	13	<.00	7	<.01	1	ns
(b) A new method of teaching biology shows an improvement in student grades.	30	46	≤.02	27	≤.00	24	≤.01	22	ns
9 (a) *Special molecules in flowers are attracted insects that gather pollen.	0	14	≤.00	6	≤.03	5	≤.03	1	ns
(b) Special molecules in flowers attract insects that gather pollen.	30	41	≤.00	34	≤.03	26	≤.03	22	ns
10 (a) Basic knowledge of mathematics frequently includes elementary algebra.	30	44	≤.01	28	≤.00	19	≤.00	20	ns
(b) *Basic knowledge of mathematics is frequently included in elementary algebra.	0	11	≤.01	12	≤.00	12	≤.00	3	ns
Nouns with noun modifiers									
11 (a) *A flu virus can be demonstrated by its resistance to medication.	0	18	≤.00	11	≤.00	8	≤.00	3	ns
(b) A flu virus can demonstrate its resistance to medication.	30	37	≤.00	29	≤.00	23	≤.00	20	ns
12 (a) Rain water affects farming activities in most regions.	30	43	≤.01	30	≤.00	23	≤.00	22	ns
(b) *Rain water are affect farming activities in most regions.	0	12	≤.01	10	≤.00	8	≤.00	1	ns

Note. All comparisons are relative to NSs; ns = not significant, 2-tailed $p ≤ .05$.
[a]CH = Chinese; JP = Japanese; KR = Korean; SP = Spanish.

*A new method of teaching biology **is shown** an improvement in student grades.*

*A new method of teaching biology **shows** an improvement in student grades.*

The participants whose grammaticality judgments were obtained for Experiment 3 were those described above for Experiment 1.

Grammaticality Judgments in Paired Sentences.   The data in Table 12.3 show counts of NSs and NNSs who selected the verb phrase in a particular sentence as grammatically correct. The number of NSs' and NNSs' selections of verbs was compared in each sentence. Fisher's exact test was employed to establish similarities and differences for each pair of NS and NNS counts because some of the cell sizes were too small for a chi-square test to be appropriate.

The grammaticality judgments of all NNSs, except Spanish speakers, differed significantly from those of NSs for a majority of the 12 paired sentences. Of the 12 pairs, only 2 included animate subjects—1, *an elephant* and 4, *dogs.* These pairs were the only ones in which the judgments of almost all NNSs were similar to those of NSs. These nouns also received particularly high animacy rankings and were perceived to be indisputably animate by practically all participants. However, overall, the animacy rankings of participants in all L1 groups did not differ dramatically from those of NSs for both nouns (Table 12.1) and noun phrases (Table 12.2). In fact, two thirds to a half of the rank correlations for nouns and noun phrases were significantly similar to those of NSs. For example, the nouns *cities* (5) and *music* (6) were classified as Man-Made Objects (Tables 12.1 and 12.2), and the animacy rankings of NNSs in all groups correlated significantly with those of NSs. Similarly, *molecule* (9) and *virus* (11) were placed in the category of Organic Elements, in which the animacy rankings were also similar to those of NSs.

Nonetheless, the grammaticality judgments of Chinese, Japanese, and Koreans were distinct from those of NSs in all paired sentences in Table 12.3, and hence, it seems that perceived animacy or inanimacy of nouns did not make a great deal of difference in the participants' grammaticality judgments of active or passive constructions in English. In addition, it appears that whether sentences included modified or unmodified nouns as subjects also did not affect participants' grammaticality judgments. However, the sentience of the entity to which subject nouns referred did make a difference in the grammaticality judgments of NNSs, that is, the two sentences in which their judgments were significantly similar to those of NSs included sentient subjects.

The meaning of passive constructions in Chinese, Japanese, and Korean often refers to an action performed by the inanimate subject of an active verb, and the subject entity is expected to affect to the object entity. Hence, the sentence subject also serves as the agent of the action and the object as the patient (Li & Thompson, 1981; Palmer, 1994). In his detailed study of Japanese passive constructions, Shibatani (1990) notes that they convey the meaning that "the subject is somehow affected" (p. 332). Palmer (1994) also explains that, in Korean, the subject of the active verb must also be the agent and the passive subject must be "in general, animate and conscious," for example, "The child was given medicine by the mother" (p. 30). Palmer (1994) comments that in languages that distinguish between the subject and agent functions of nouns, "animacy and potentiality of agency seem to be almost the same thing," but with inanimate nouns, the hierarchy of agentivity comes into play. The gradient agentivity requires that, for example, in sentences with two inanimate nouns where one is the subject and the other is the object, the entity higher on the hierarchy be the agent (and thus the subject) and the lower be the patient (and, therefore, the object). For example, speakers of Japanese or Korean would consider the sentence *The car needs gas* to be grammatical because *the car* has a higher animacy value than *gas*. On the other hand, *the article discusses the government* would not be seen as correct if on the hierarchy of animacy, the subject noun *the article* is lower than the patient *the government*, and in this case, for speakers of Japanese or Korean, a passive construction would be more appropriate, for example, *The government is discussed in/by the article.*

On the other hand, in Chinese, active and passive constructions cannot always be easily distinguished, unless they are overtly marked by means of particles. Li and Thompson (1981) point out that in Chinese, the passive particle *bei* represents one of the few constructions in which the patient noun phrase is advanced to the position of the sentence subject. They emphasize that *bei* constructions are predominantly used to show that the subject of the sentence affects the object and that the agent of the action can be inferred or stated directly, as in *The balloon was blown away by the wind* (p. 505). However, Norman (1988, p. 165) observes that because grammatical voice is absent in Chinese, active-passive sentence relationships cannot always be determined, for instance, "*The fish has eaten*" or "*The fish has been eaten*" cannot be easily distinguished. In light of this information, it may be that some of the Chinese participants simply were not able to clearly identify the syntactic and/or the semantic differences between the paired sentences and occasionally made erroneous guesses when they had to make a choice.

As in many Indo-European languages, Spanish has a developed inflectional system that includes masculine and feminine gender markers of nouns, determiners, and adjectives. Posner (1996, p. 55) explains that gender markings in all languages imply that "referents are animate beings." However, she notes that although in Spanish the notion of lexical animacy is well established and prominent, it may be difficult to discern its functional role. The grammatical functions of subjects/agents and objects/patients are also marked for nominative (subject) and accusative (object) cases. Furthermore, Spanish is sensitive to human/nonhuman object distinctions, marked by particles. In this study, NSs and Spanish speakers demonstrated similar grammaticality judgments of paired sentences in Table 12.3, with the exceptions of Sentences 2 and 6. In Sentence 2, the pseudo-modal *allow* + direct object (+ infinitive) is used in a syntactic structure that effectively reverses the order of the semantic patient *(discussions)* and agent *(participants)* and is markedly different from the common subject + transitive verb + direct object Spanish constructions (Lozano, 1993). In addition, the Spanish verb *gozar de (enjoy)* (Sentence 6) is typically classified as direct intransitive with the experiencer as subject, that is, the entity that "experiences" the emotional reaction denoted by the verb (e.g., **I enjoy of his support)* (Whitley, 1995, p. 573). On the other hand, the English equivalent *enjoy* is often considered to be transitive and requires a direct object without a preposition.

All the English sentences in Table 12.3 included transitive verbs and contained direct objects. In many languages, verb transitivity and the presence of the object represents an important factor in the grammaticality of active or passive constructions. For example, Palmer (1994) indicates that in Spanish, as in English, the presence of a direct object clearly marks the verb as active and transitive, but in Japanese, transitive verbs require animate subjects, and a sentence such as *The apple was eaten by John* is ungrammatical. According to Palmer, in Korean the subject usually has a higher potentiality for agency than the object, that is, the subject noun performs the verb action that affects the object noun. In Chinese, the presence of the object determines the agentive character of the subject whose "behavior is directed toward the direct object" (Li & Thompson, 1981, p. 157), and a vast majority of verbs can be either transitive or intransitive. In this study, in all L1s, however, the presence of the direct object provides a likely indicator that the verb is used in the active voice, and thus, the direct objects in the sentences in Table 12.3 may have served as similar markers of active verbs.

Grammaticality Judgments in Single Sentences: Experiment 4

One of the main differences between the sentences in Experiments 3 and 4 is that, unlike those in Experiment 3, the sentences in Experiment 4 were not paired or contrasted, for example:

> *The magazine presents an interesting story about the city.*
>
> *The highway connects Michigan and Ohio.*

Another important change between the sentences in Experiment 4, compared to those in Experiment 3, is that the sentences included various syntactic and semantic features of subject nouns and verbs not included in Experiment 3. For example, none of the sentences in Experiment 4 (see Table 12.4) included animate and/or sentient subjects. All sentences in Experiment 3 (see Table 12.3) included transitive verbs and direct objects. In Experiment 4 (Table 12.4), half of the verbs were transitive *(show, present, connect, influence, make, provide, cause,* and *affect),* and the other half were intransitive *(fall, travel, break, come, shine, spill, roll,* and *move).* All sentences included in Experiment 4 were grammatically correct.

The participants who were asked to judge the grammaticality of single sentences in Experiment 4 were the same as described earlier for Experiment 2. Again, the counts of NSs' and NNSs' choices of grammatical verb structures were compared for each sentence, and Fisher's exact test was employed for each pair of NS and NNS counts.

It appears that such lexical and syntactic features of verbs as transitivity and the presence of direct objects made a substantial difference in NNSs' grammaticality judgments. Specifically, of the 16 sentences, in only 9 did Spanish speakers display grammaticality judgments similar to those of NSs. Participants in other L1 groups judged the grammatically of all sentences in Table 12.4 significantly differently from NSs. As in the sentences in Experiment 1, the noun animacy did not appear to make a substantial difference in the judgment of the Chinese, Japanese, and Korean speakers. For example, the nouns *photograph, highway, pencil,* and *pen* in Sentences 1, 3, 5, and 9, respectively, were included among those classified as Man-Made Objects (Table 12.1), the NNS animacy rankings of which correlated significantly among all language groups, including NSs. Similarly, the noun phrases *bright light* and *a big stone* in Sentences 13 and 15, respectively, were included among Natural Objects/Phenomena (Table 12.2) that were ranked significantly similarly by NSs and NNSs alike. On the other hand, *written language* in Sentence 4 and *an angry conversation* in Sentence 7 were attributed to the Speech/Language set that did not exhibit significant correlations of animacy ranks in NS and NNS evaluations. In addition, because none of the sentences included sentient subjects, significant proportions of participants in Chinese, Korean, Japanese, and Spanish groups believed the grammatical sentences in Table 12.4 to be ungrammatical. As has been discussed, in Japanese and Korean, passive verbs are used in sentences where the subject is usually required to be sentient or occupy a higher position in the hierarchy of animacy than the object does. Also, as has been noted, Chinese does not always provide clear-cut distinctions between active and passive constructions.

TABLE 12.4
NS and NNS Grammaticality Judgments in Single Sentences by Group

Sentence	NSs (n = 30)	CH (n = 34)	p	JP (n = 26)	p	KR (n = 36)	p	SP (n = 23)	p
Nouns without modifiers; transitive verbs									
1. The photograph shows my teachers and classmates.	30	22	≤.00	18	≤.00	19	≤.00	21	ns
2. The magazine presents an interesting story about the city.	30	24	≤.01	20	≤.02	24	≤.00	21	ns
3. The highway connects Michigan and Ohio.	30	28	≤.02	17	≤.00	23	≤.00	20	ns
Nouns with adjective modifiers; transitive verbs									
4. Written language usually influences people more than speech.	30	25	≤.01	19	≤.00	26	≤.00	21	ns
5. A sharp pencil makes thin lines on paper.	30	24	≤.01	20	≤.02	29	≤.01	21	ns
6. English teaching provides many job opportunities.	30	21	≤.00	20	≤.02	24	≤.00	20	ns
7. An angry conversation often causes additional problems.	30	28	≤.02	20	≤.02	23	≤.00	22	ns
8. Teaching methods frequently affect classroom interactions.	30	25	≤.01	21	≤.01	28	≤.02	22	ns
Nouns without modifiers; intransitive verbs									
9. The pen fell on the floor.	30	25	≤.01	15	≤.00	14	≤.00	12	≤.00
10. Clouds can travel at very low altitudes.	30	19	≤.00	15	≤.00	13	≤.00	18	≤.01
11. The glass in the window broke.	30	14	≤.00	11	≤.00	11	≤.00	5	≤.00
12. The water in the tap comes from the Ohio River.	30	28	≤.02	21	≤.01	28	≤.02	19	≤.03
Nouns with adjective/noun modifiers; intransitive verbs									
13. Bright light shines into the room at sunset.	30	25	≤.01	21	≤.01	21	≤.00	18	≤.01
14. The hot coffee spilled over the edge of the cup.	30	17	≤.00	16	≤.00	11	≤.00	16	≤.00
15. A big stone is rolling down the hill.	30	23	≤.01	21	≤.01	26	≤.00	20	ns
16. The tree leaf on the ground is moving in the wind.	30	23	≤.01	20	≤.02	18	≤.00	14	≤.00

Note. All comparisons are relative to NSs; ns = not significant, 2-tailed $p ≤ .05$.
[a] CH = Chinese; JP = Japanese; KR = Korean; SP = Spanish.

On the other hand, it appears that verb transitivity did affect the grammatically judgments of Spanish speakers. It further appears that Spanish speakers had particular difficulty with intransitive verbs in Sentences 9–14 and 16. Keeping in mind that in Spanish intransitive verbs are treated differently than in English when reflexives and experiencer subjects can be employed, it is not particularly surprising that Spanish speakers had trouble with intransitive verbs in English. In Sentence 15, *A big stone is rolling down the hill*, verb transitivity seems to be somewhat ambiguous because adverbials, such as *around, away, back, over, up, down, in*, and *to* often affect transitive verbs and make them pseudo-intransitive (as in *give back, move over, show up, shut down, climb up/over*, and *make up*).

Noun animacy appears to be a semantic feature of nouns that exists in many languages (Croft, 1990; DeLancey, 1985, 1990; Silverstein, 1976, 1984). It represents a gradient lexical characteristic that varies depending on the syntactic and semantic features of nouns and verbs and depends on the objective properties of the entity to which a particular noun or noun phrase refers. Furthermore, the perceived lexical animacy of nouns in many cases appears to correlate significantly between groups of speakers of diverse languages. However, establishing the lexical animacy of subject nouns in sentences does not seem to be sufficient to determine how and when NS and NNS consider active and passive constructions grammatical. The results of this study indicate that specifically subject noun sentience (and thus potentiality for agency and subjecthood) and verb transitivity marked by the presence of direct objects play important roles in the NNSs' ability to identify the grammaticality of L2 active and passive constructions. Although noun animacy represents a salient semantic feature in many languages, verb transitivity and the attendant presence of the direct object entail additional syntactic considerations that are not readily accessible to even proficient NNSs.

Teaching Suggestions: The Concept of Transitivity and Transitive Verbs in English

Because verb transitivity is a universal phenomenon (Croft, 1990), most L2 learners are familiar with it intuitively. For this reason, it is not difficult to explain how it works in English, and only a few good examples are required *(Is it okay to say in English "I found/ bought/sold/gave/took" without a noun? The verbs that are/sound/feel incorrect when used in sentences without direct objects are called transitive)*. Although practically all ESL grammar textbooks describe how to derive passive sentences from their active counter parts (e.g., *John ate the apple*, vs. *The apple was eaten by John*), few actually note that such passive derivations require the active sentence to include a transitive verb and a direct object. This is why, for instance, the sentence **I am suffered from a terrible cold* (as in Example 1) is ungrammatical, that is, *suffer* is for the most part an intransitive verb in English.[1]

(1) The activities mentioned in Teaching Suggestions: The Concept of Lexical Animacy in English can be also used to show that distinctions between active or passive voice uses are often stylistic and are common in academic texts (and writing) (Talmy, 1988). The "scientific experiments" or the work with small appliances and utensils can be transformed into writing projects, poster sessions, or class science fairs.

(2) (a) Students at the high-intermediate and advanced levels of proficiency can analyze excerpts from introductory textbooks in various disciplines, such as sociology, psychology, and/or economics, to determine the frequencies of active or passive constructions and the contexts in which they are employed, while paying particular attention to transitive and intransitive verbs.[2] These can become very useful and interesting discovery tasks that prepare academically bound students for their work in the future.

(b) The work with introductory academic texts can also become an opportunity for paraphrase and citation practice when students need to restate the ideas or examples found in sources of information. Such assignments can also be carried out in pairs or small groups.

(3) Also in pairs or small groups, students can receive short lists of common verbs (5 to 15); (appropriate for their proficiency level) from the teacher or other groups, determine whether a particular verb is transitive or intransitive, and "prove" their conclusions with "data" from their examples of its transitive or intransitive uses in contexts. Groups can also compete for speed and accuracy in such assignments, and an in-class discussion of groups' "findings" can become a very enjoyable practice with an added benefit of increasing the students lexical repertoire.

(4) If the transitive or intransitive verbs chosen are to be somewhat contextually cohesive (e.g., *read, write, speak, tell, talk, learn, study, improve, practice* or *shine, rain, blow, pour, change, remain, increase, decrease),* pairs or small groups can be assigned to construct short narratives or reports with these verbs in context and present them to other groups. Many of the

---

[1]In some fixed expressions, such as *suffer the consequences* or *suffer the advice of fools,* or literary allusions (*suffer the slings and arrows of outrageous fortune*), *suffer* can be used as a transitive verb.

[2]In their book on grammar teaching, Celce-Murcia and Larsen-Freeman (1999) offer another view of active voice constructions with inanimate subjects and discuss them as "middle voice," for example, *The store opens in five minutes.*

short stories, news reports, or narratives created in such contexts can be humorous and entertaining (e.g., *It was a dark and stormy night. The wind was blowing/howling, the rain was pouring/streaming/coming down like Niagara Falls, and the lightening lit up the sky. But we were sitting in the library and diligently doing our homework on verbs*).

CONCLUSIONS AND IMPLICATIONS FOR TEACHING THE ENGLISH PASSIVE VOICE

Although this study's findings are based on a relatively small number of sentences, some preliminary conclusions can be made. For instance, the lexical and semantic features of sentence constituents not common in English but salient in other languages seem to have an impact on the NNS grammaticality judgments, for instance, sentient-nonsentient distinctions of nouns that serve as sentence subjects, and the function of nouns as agents or patients in the subject or object position. The features of sentience, and agentivity and patienthood, influential in the NNS L1s but less developed in English, may be transferred from L1 to L2 and may affect NNSs' L2 learning. As Bates et al. (1982) determined earlier, NNSs usually employ L1 sentence-processing strategies when dealing with L2 constructions. In this study, speakers of Japanese and Korean may also have relied on L1 conceptual sentient agent and nonsentient patient distinctions. L2 grammar instruction for NNSs may need to emphasize that the meanings of passive constructions in English do not involve considerations of agentivity and patienthood.

It appears that lexical features of individual nouns and noun phrases, such as animacy and sentience, have an impact on NNS perceptions of their potentiality for agentivity (and subjecthood) and patienthood (in object positions), but the amount of correlation between NS and NNS animacy values declines when nouns are placed in contexts and syntactic environments even as small as adjective and/or prepositional phrases. Although the NS and NNS perceptions of noun animacy showed a relatively high number of positive correlations, their grammaticality judgments of passive sentences were significantly different in most cases. Thus, the lexical animacy of nouns seems to have a diminished effect on the NNSs' ability to determine the grammaticality of active or passive constructions in English.

They point out that the "middle voice" usually occurs with change-of-sate verbs, such as verbs or cooking or physical movement, when the use of the active voice does not imply an agent.

Contrasting active and passive sentences seems to provide NNSs a point of reference and means of comparing the syntactic functions of nouns and noun phrases and may improve their grammaticality judgments. Agentivity and patienthood of nouns in passive constructions and verb transitivity in such languages as Chinese, Japanese, and Korean seems to have a negative effect on grammaticality judgments of speakers of these languages in English. On the other hand, Spanish speakers may have difficulty with intransitive verbs in English. One implication of this finding is that the forms, functions, and meanings of English passive constructions need to be addressed in detail in L2 instruction.

It also appears that for NNSs the presence of the direct object may serve as an overt marker and imply the active voice of the verb. However, speakers of Chinese may have a particular disadvantage when dealing with English passive constructions because their L1 does not have a syntactically derived passive voice.

Another important finding to be noted is that NNSs who have attained relatively high L2 proficiency as established by their TOEFL scores do not appear to have grammaticality judgments similar to those of NSs even after several years of L2 learning. Despite their exposure to L2 for substantial lengths of time, NNSs' constructs associated with semantic animacy, agentivity, and patienthood appear to be markedly different from those of NSs. It may be that for NNSs, the convergence of these semantic and syntactic features of nouns, combined with L2 verb transitivity, often present in their L1s but absent in L2, make the meanings and uses of active and passive in English so complex that meanings and uses of the passive voice are not readily accessible to them without focused and thorough instruction.

The teaching of the L2 active and passive voice may need to address such fundamental syntactic features of English as the functions of verbs as predicates (and possibly, syntactic properties of various verb classes; (Levin & Rappaport Hovav, 1991), and direct objects. In the teaching of L2 grammar, the most prevalent methodology is to address the syntactic and semantic properties of subjects and verbs in English (Alexander, 1988; Quirk et al., 1985; Wardhaugh, 1995) with the assumption that given sufficient L2 training and exposure, NNSs are thus enabled to construct appropriate models of English grammar and syntactic systems. It may be, however, that even proficient L2 learners of English may be at a considerable disadvantage when the syntactic and semantic features of their L1s find few manifestations in L2 because common L2-based approaches to teaching L2 grammar do not address them in any way. L2 pedagogy may need to take a broader view of language as reflecting diverse complex cognitive systems with varied means of expressing common functions of nouns and verbs in sentences. In addition to focusing on the systems that the English language includes, L2 pedagogy needs to refer to linguistic constructs that it does not.

ACKNOWLEDGMENTS

My sincere appreciation to Marianne Celce-Murcia (University of California, Los Angeles), Kit Carpenter (Greenfield Community College, Greenfield, Mass.), and Mary Geary (Seattle University) for their helpful comments and patience with this chapter.

REFERENCES

Alexander, L. (1988). *Longman English grammar*. London: Longman.

Armstrong, S., Gleitman, L., & Gleitman, H. (1983). What some concepts might not be. *Cognition, 13*, 263–308.

Bates, E., MacWhinney, B., McNew, S., Davescovi, A., & Smith, S. (1982). Functional constraints on sentence processing: A cross-linguistic study. *Cognition, 11*, 245–299.

Bock, K., & Kroch, A. (1989). The isolability of syntactic processing. In G. Carlson & M. Tanenhaus (Eds.), *Linguistic structure in language processing* (pp. 157–196). London: Kluwer.

Celce-Murcia, M., & Larsen-Freeman, D. (1999). *The grammar book*. Boston: Heinle & Heinle.

Croft, W. (1990). *Typology and universals*. Cambridge, UK: Cambridge University Press.

DeLancey, S. (1985). Agentivity and syntax. *Chicago Linguistic Society, 21*, 1–12.

DeLancey, S. (1990). Ergativity and the cognitive model of event structure in Lhasa Tibetan. *Cognitive Linguistics, 1*, 289–321.

Hopper, P., & Thompson, S. (1980). Transitivity in grammar and discourse. *Language, 56*, 251–299.

Huang, Y. (1994). *The syntax and pragmatics of anaphora: A study with special reference to Chinese*. Cambridge, UK: Cambridge University Press.

Kim, H. (1990). Continuity of action and topic in discourse. In H. Hoji (Ed.), *Japanese and Korean linguistics* (pp. 76–96). Palo Alto, CA: Center for Study of Language and Information.

Levin, B. (1993). *English verb classes and alternations*. Chicago: University of Chicago Press.

Levin, B., & Rappaport Hovav, M. (1991). Wiping the slate clean: A lexical semantic exploration. In B. Levin & S. Pinker (Eds.), *Lexical and conceptual semantics* (pp. 123–151). Cambridge, MA: Blackwell.

Li, C., & Thompson, S. (1981). *Mandarin Chinese*. Berkeley: University of California Press.

Lozano, A. (1993). Graphic sequences of Spanish nominals and reflexives. *Hispania, 76*, 627–633.

Lucy, J. (1992). *Language diversity and thought*. Cambridge, UK: Cambridge University Press.

Lucy, J. (1996). The scope of linguistic relativity: An analysis and review of empirical research. In J. Gumperz & S. Levinson (Eds.), *Rethinking linguistic relativity* (pp. 37–69). Cambridge, UK: Cambridge University Press.

Master, P. (1991). Active verbs with inanimate subjects in scientific prose. *English for Specific Purposes, 10*, 15–33.

Norman, J. (1988). *Chinese*. Cambridge, UK: Cambridge University Press.

Palmer, F. R. (1994). *Grammatical roles and relations.* Cambridge, UK: Cambridge University Press.

Pfaff, C. W. (1987). Functional approaches to interlanguage. In C. W. Pfaff (Ed.), *First and second language acquisition processes* (pp. 81–102). Cambridge, MA: Newbury House.

Posner, R. (1996). *The Romance languages.* Cambridge, UK: Cambridge University Press.

Quirk, R., Greenbaum, S., Leech, G., & Svartvik, J. (1985). *A comprehensive grammar of the English language.* London: Longman.

Shibatani, M. (1990). *The languages of Japan.* Cambridge, UK: Cambridge University Press.

Siewierska, A. (1984). *The passive: A comparative linguistic analysis.* London: Croom Helm.

Silverstein, M. (1987). Cognitive implications of a referential hierarchy. In M. Hickmann (Ed.), *Social and functional approaches to language and thought* (pp. 125–164). Orlando: Academic Press.

Steer, J., & Carlisi, K. (1998). *The advanced grammar book.* Boston: Heinle & Heinle.

Straus, A., & Brightman, R. (1982). The implacable raspberry. *Papers in Linguistics, 15,* 97–137.

Talmy, L. (1988). Force dynamics in language and cognition. *Cognitive Science, 2,* 49–100.

Wardhaugh, R. (1995). *Understanding English grammar.* Oxford: Blackwell.

Whitley, M. (1995). *Gustar* and other psych verbs: A problem in transitivity. *Hispania, 78,* 573–585.

Author Index

Two indexes are provided: an author index and a subject index. All page numbers appearing in italic type refer to page references in the bibliographic references of each chapter.

Subject Index

Two indexes are provided: an author index and a subject index. All page numbers appearing in italic type refer to page references in the bibliographic references of each chapter.

113174

418.0071
H6633 LINCOLN CHRISTIAN COLLEGE AND SEMINARY

3 4711 00177 3748